THE INTERESTING NARRATIVE OF

THE LIFE OF
OLAUDAH EQUIANO,

OR GUSTAVUS VASSA, THE AFRICAN.
WRITTEN BY HIMSELF

THE INTERESTING NARRATIVE OF

THE LIFE OF
OLAUDAH EQUIANO,

OR GUSTAVUS VASSA, THE AFRICAN.
WRITTEN BY HIMSELF

Olaudah Equiano

edited by Angelo Costanzo

broadview literary texts

Canadian Cataloguing in Publication Data

Equiano, Olaudah, b. 1745
     The interesting narrative of the life of Olaudah Equiano, or Gustavus Vassa,
the African
(Broadview literary texts)
Includes bibliographical references.
ISBN 1-55111-262-0

1. Equiano, Olaudah, b. 1745.   2. Slaves—Great Britain—Biography.
3. Slaves—United States—Biography.   I. Costanzo, Angelo, 1934- .
II. Title. III. Series.

HT869.E6A3 2001   305.5'67'092   C00-932852-1

Broadview Press Ltd., is an independent, international publishing house, incorporated in 1985.

North America:
P.O. Box 1243, Peterborough, Ontario, Canada K9J 7H5
3576 California Road, Orchard Park, NY 14127
TEL: (705) 743-8990; FAX: (705) 743-8353;
E-MAIL: customerservice@broadviewpress.com

United Kingdom:
Turpin Distribution Services Ltd.,
Blackhorse Rd., Letchworth, Hertfordshire SG6 1HN
TEL: (1462) 672555; FAX (1462) 480947; E-MAIL: turpin@rsc.org

Australia:
St. Clair Press, P.O. Box 287, Rozelle, NSW 2039
TEL: (02) 818-1942; FAX: (02) 418-1923

www.broadviewpress.com

Broadview Press gratefully acknowledges the financial support of the Book
Publishing Industry Development Program, Ministry of Canadian Heritage,
Government of Canada.

Broadview Press is grateful to Professor Eugene Benson for advice on
editorial matters for the Broadview Literary Texts series and to Professor
L.W. Conolly for editorial advice on this volume.

Text design and composition by George Kirkpatrick

PRINTED IN CANADA

Contents

Preface

My fascination with Olaudah Equiano's great and important autobiography has existed for over thirty years; ever since his story was brought to a modern audience's attention in the 1960s by Paul Edwards, of the University of Edinburgh, Scotland, and also by Arna Bontemps, the African-American poet of the Harlem Renaissance. It was Bontemps, in the introduction to his book *Great Slave Narratives* (1969), who first gave credit to Equiano for inventing the new genre of literature that became known as the slave narrative, a personal work that played a significant role in the nineteenth-century abolitionist movement in the United States. Equiano's narrative was still in print during that era, but after the American Civil War his name and text were almost forgotten. The rediscovery of Equiano's literary achievement was made by Edwards during the late 1960s. Digging deeply into the origins and merits of *The Interesting Life of Olaudah Equiano*, Edwards produced extensive information and delivered startling insights into Equiano's life and narrative work.

It is to those two great scholars, Edwards and Bontemps, that I wish to dedicate this new edition of Equiano's 1789 spiritual autobiography and slave narrative. Coming to grips with all the truth that Equiano presents in his personal story has been a project of mine for many years, but one that continues to be a very rewarding and exciting endeavor. When reading Equiano's narrative, we are led to consider the vital issues and truths that circulated widely among the abolitionist fighters of the eighteenth century. Thus, I have included in this Broadview Edition excerpts from the works of the leading writers of the first abolitionist movement in the West. Many of these antislavery books, essays, and pamphlets were familiar to Equiano, some of which he refers to in his narrative.

I extend my thanks to all those persons who have helped me increase my interest over the years as I have pursued my work on Equiano. Among these are William L. Andrews, of the University of North Carolina-Chapel Hill; Henry Louis Gates, Jr., of Harvard University; Vincent Freimarck, of SUNY-Binghamton; Vincent Carretta, of the University of Maryland; Carla Mulford, of Penn State University; Wilfred D. Samuels, of the University of Utah; and Steve Martin and Arthur Torrington, of The Equiano Society in London. I also wish to thank the research staff members who assisted me at the British Library in London and at the Shippensburg University Library in Pennsylvania. A special measure of gratitude goes to my wife Dolores who sacrificed many hours of her time to proofread my manuscript and to offer editorial suggestions.

Introduction

The Slave Narrative

The autobiographical mode of writing is gaining much consideration as a literary genre that continues to shape many prose works. In particular, spiritual autobiography has been especially influential ever since the North African Saint Augustine composed his *Confessions* during the fifth century A.D. Augustine dwelt upon the serious examination of his inner self and established a popular pattern of spiritual writing. It is a literary form that consists of a three-part structure depicting a person's enslavement to sin, harrowing conversion experience, and subsequent state of spiritual rebirth. Augustine's method of spiritual expression has been used or adapted by many authors, including John Bunyan whose *Grace Abounding to the Chief of Sinners* appeared in 1666.

In the eighteenth century, when the abolitionist movement in both England and America called on former slaves to write or orally dictate their experiences in slavery, the narratives that resulted appeared in this popular form of spiritual autobiography. This literary choice guaranteed that the story of an ex-slave's passage from physical bondage, to escape, and finally to freedom would be tied-in with the account of that person's religious life. Despite their white editors' propaganda and devotional aims, the black narrators expressed in intelligent and graphic ways the terrible conditions endured by enslaved men and women. Many times these former slaves accomplished their goals by using indirect means or even subterfuge to reveal the truth; and, remarkably, each one of them exerted a strong speaking presence in a written or dictated account that demonstrated the autobiographer's high degree of command and control over the entire composition process.

Olaudah Equiano, or Gustavus Vassa as he was known throughout his life, was a former slave who became extremely active in the abolitionist cause. In 1789 he also became the first person to write a major autobiography that combined the form of the spiritual conversion autobiography with that of the three progressive stages usually experienced by a former slave. Each stage of Equiano's narrative has its own tone, style, and voice. In the first section Equiano describes his bondage and presents evidence of the injustice of his state of victimization. Then in the second part he chronicles his desires to gain an education, to receive the benefits of his own business pursuits, and to win his freedom. At this time in his life the young slave is seen as confused and depressed. He is full of doubts and anxieties about ever becoming a free person. In the third and final segment of his narrative, Equiano depicts himself as a free person playing the role of a confident and courageous individual who fights for justice. Freedom has given him the opportunity to develop both his personal character and his spiritual condition. All the events and character portrayals are presented in a vivid and exciting manner that fascinates and instructs the reader, while the narrative also reveals the enormous talent of an African ex-slave's mastery of the English language.

Equiano's work ushered in a new genre of writing that became known as the slave narrative, a genre that has influenced countless numbers of other diverse works, both fiction and nonfiction. In the early and mid-nineteenth century, hundreds of American slave narratives were published for purposes of convincing the public that slavery should be abolished. Chief among these accounts was the *Narrative of the Life of Frederick Douglass, an American Slave. Written by Himself* (1845). Douglass used the same pattern and many of the elements of Equiano's work, as did many of the other slave writers of the period, such as William Wells Brown in his *Narrative* (1847) and Harriet A. Jacobs in her *Incidents in the Life of a Slave Girl* (1861). In her famous abolitionist book, *Uncle Tom's Cabin* (1852), Harriet Beecher Stowe, a white writer, used the slave narrative's three-part structure and each section's different tone and style to present a fictionalized, but representative, account of slavery. Uncle Tom's hard journey from harsh captivity to Christian belief and spiritual freedom does not include physical liberty; but although he is brutally killed, the kindly slave snatches the moral victory. Thus his life story delivers a strong indictment of those persons in white society who support slavery.

The slave narrative continued to exert its power throughout the nineteenth and twentieth centuries. Its form and style can be observed in the works of many authors. The best examples are Booker T. Washington's *Up From Slavery* (1901), W.E.B. DuBois's *The Souls of Black Folk* (1903), Richard Wright's *Native Son* (1940), Ralph Ellison's *Invisible Man* (1952), Malcolm X's *The Autobiography of Malcolm X* (1965), and Toni Morrison's *Beloved* (1987).

Equiano, the Kidnapped African

When Olaudah Equiano published his two-volume autobiographical narrative in London in March 1789, the debate on whether or not to abolish the lucrative slave trade was heating up in the British Parliament. The controversy was spreading throughout the British Isles and was joining itself to the same struggle occurring in the United States. At this time, Equiano was allied with the major black and white abolitionist crusaders, many of whom wrote tracts, essays, and letters denouncing the slave trade. Because of his numerous efforts on behalf of the black poor in Britain and also because of his constant letter-writing on antislavery subjects, Equiano was already known, especially from the early 1780s, as a public figure, a leader in the fight to end slavery. However, upon the publication of his work, Equiano's role in the first abolitionist movement in the West became increasingly significant. His book was widely subscribed to, circulated, and read; and it thrust Equiano into the centre of the national debate on slavery.

Writing from the perspective of a mature and respected African-British freeman in the late 1780s, Equiano reflected on and searched for meaning in the early events of his life. Around the year 1755 he had been kidnapped near his home in the interior region of West Africa, where modern-day Nigeria is situated. He then served as a slave to several African families until he was sold to European slavetraders on the Atlantic coast.

Soon the youth was transported across the ocean on the horrible Middle Passage route that marked the second part of Great Britain's triangular sea commerce. This lucrative trade was carried on all through the eighteenth century. Trading vessels laden with weapons and cotton products sailed from British ports to buy slaves in Africa. The kidnapped Africans were then taken across the Atlantic and sold to estate owners in the Americas in exchange for rum and sugar. The ships then sailed again with full cargoes back to England.

After witnessing terrible scenes aboard the slave ship (described in his autobiography), Equiano arrived on the Caribbean island of Barbados. The frightened slave was almost immediately sent to Virginia in North America, where he soon was purchased by a British naval captain, Michael Henry Pascal. Captain Pascal placed the young slave aboard his vessel, and thus introduced Equiano to a life of service at sea. Pascal also changed his new slave's name to Gustavus Vassa, prophetically after the name of a sixteenth-century Swedish freedom fighter.

By his own account, Equiano claimed that his capture in Africa occurred when he was about eleven years of age. For the next ten or eleven years, the youth lived in bondage. Owned by several masters, he laboured aboard American and British merchant and military vessels sailing the Atlantic. His voyages took him to the islands of the British Caribbean and to the coastal areas of Europe, especially along the Mediterranean Sea. In addition, while serving aboard several warships during the Seven Years' War (1756-1763), the young slave witnessed and took part in several crucial contests waged along the French coast. He also did service during bloody battles fought in French Canada for the capture of Louisbourg, a town situated at the entrance to the St. Lawrence River.

On 10 July 1766, Equiano finally purchased his freedom from Robert King, his master at that time. King was a Philadelphia Quaker merchant doing business in the West Indies. Although the Quakers were strongly opposed to slavery, a number of them continued to hold slaves. King signed the formal manumission paper in the evening; and on the next day, July 11, Equiano had it legally registered. Although he was now a free person, Equiano continued to sail on commercial vessels, and at times served aboard ships outfitted for scientific expeditions, including a 1773 Arctic expedition with Captain Constantine John Phipps. And in 1775-76 Equiano was involved in establishing a plantation colony in Central America, one of his responsibilities, ironically, being the purchase and supervision of slaves. In his autobiography Equiano emphasizes that he always treated the slaves "with care and affections, and did every thing I could to comfort the poor creatures, and render their condition easy." However, there is no question but that Equiano, the impassioned antislavery advocate, compromised his principles in this episode of his life. It is also troubling that there are other signs of his ambivalent attitude towards slavery in the autobiography – his defence of slavery in Africa, for example, and his advice to slave owners on how to increase the work productivity of their slaves.

During his early years as a slave, Equiano learned how to read and write and he also received instruction in the Christian religion from his fellow sailors who took a liking to him. He always made certain to attend the schools conducted on shipboard for the members of the crew. Moreover, whenever he landed in England, before and after his status as a free person, Equiano encountered many kind men and women who contributed to his education. The Guerin sisters, who were related to Captain Pascal, figured prominently among those who assisted him, furthering his literary and religious education. Equiano was converted to Anglican Christianity and baptized while still a slave in 1759, in St. Margaret's Church, next to Westminster Abbey in London.

It is difficult to determine how sincere Equiano was about his conversion and baptism. The youth might have been acting under the assumption that baptism conveyed freedom upon a slave. This was a heated issue on which people were divided in the eighteenth century. In his narrative Equiano devotes a great deal of space to describing his search for a particular faith, and he dwells at some length on his anxiety-ridden conversion experience. It may well be that he never regarded his original baptism as a deeply-felt spiritual event, but rather as an attempt by a young slave to conform to the expectations of white men and women. And, of course, Equiano's baptism might have been more connected to his quest for freedom than to his desire to become a Christian. He remained, however, a life-long Christian, ultimately, however, of Methodist rather than Anglican persuasion.

The misery, cruelty, and humiliation that Equiano suffered and witnessed as a slave only strengthened his determination to fight against slavery and the slave trade as a free man, particularly after he settled in London in 1777.

In England, Equiano campaigned actively and prominently with abolitionist groups, including the Sons of Africa, which he helped organize in 1787. It was also in 1787 that Equiano was dismissed from his position as Commissary for Stores for the Sierra Leone project, a British government initiative to relocate freed slaves to Sierra Leone. There were estimated to be between 10,000 and 20,000 black people living in England at the time, mostly male and mostly unemployed or working in low-paying jobs, many of whom immigrated into the country having served in the British army in the American Revolutionary War. Equiano accused his superiors in the project of corruption and incompetence. Prior to the publication of his 1789 *Interesting Narrative*, Equiano had also written and submitted a petition to Queen Charlotte, wife of King George III, urging the replacement of the slave trade with a trade in manufactured goods.

In his private life, Equiano married Susanna Cullen, a white woman, in Cambridgeshire in 1792. Their children, Ann Maria and Johanna, were born in 1793 and 1795. Susanna died in 1796, and the following year, on 31 March 1797, Equiano died, a decade before the abolition of the slave trade in England and America, an outcome for which Equiano – along with friends and colleagues such as William Wilberforce and John Wesley – deserves considerable credit.

Equiano's Autobiography

At the beginning of his autobiography Equiano argues that Africa and the Africans should not be excluded from the historical account of the achievements of the human race. He recalls his early experiences in his African homeland and combines them with information he has picked up in his extensive readings into the history and culture of African societies, including eighteenth-century primitivistic literature, which promoted the concept of Noble Savages living in close harmony with nature prior to corruption by modern Western society. Equiano shows how socially advanced Africa was before the Europeans contaminated that continent, and he then makes a point of depicting his own childhood years happily spent in an Edenic Africa. Although he is kidnapped and becomes a slave in his homeland, he is treated relatively well by the Africans he serves. Later in his narrative Equiano argues that African slavery is far less harsh than in the West, and that the Africans who sell their countrymen into Western slavery have been corrupted by Europeans. The climax of this section occurs when the young Equiano himself is sold and taken to the coast where he views the slave ship that is ready to deliver him to a life of bondage. He writes: "the first object which saluted my eyes when I arrived on the coast was the sea, and a slave ship, which was then riding at anchor, and waiting for its cargo." Then, giving a reverse impression of the Western view of Africans, Equiano writes that when he is placed aboard the slave ship he becomes extremely frightened by his belief that the horrible and ugly-looking white sailors are cannibals who are preparing to eat him. They toss him up and around to acertain his soundness and then whip him severely when he refuses to take food. Soon, Equiano's long journey into slavery in the West begins as he is transported across the Middle Passage to British America.

In this part of his narrative, Equiano concentrates on the personal account of himself as a slave encountering both wonders and terrors in the Western World. At this point his aim is to give the reader a feeling derived from the travel literature of the day, such as one can find, for example, in Daniel Defoe's *Robinson Crusoe* (1719). This work imparts a sense of awe generated by Defoe's powerful descriptions of the marvels found in strange lands. Equiano achieves this same feeling of magical wonder as he relates his experiences in Western culture, but at the same time he also demonstrates his abilities to accommodate the new society and to raise his stature within its system. He does this by role-playing and self-promotion.

Equiano builds himself up as a versatile and talented character who works hard in his entrepreneurial pursuits and willingly assumes various heroic roles, especially during several naval battles. He also makes clear that he has the ability and bravery to take charge in times of crisis, such as when he acts as a ship's captain, performs as a parson at a burial, and fights to receive fair treatment in his business efforts. As he describes his courageous acts, Equiano boasts about the manner in which he conducts each one of these roles, many of which occur after and because of his freedom, acquired by means of hard work and thrifty ways.

When Equiano obtains his manumission on the Caribbean island of Montserrat in 1766, the third stage of his life begins. Now he faces the difficult task of being a free man in a world of slavery. He has witnessed the uncertain status of other freed black men and women in Britain and America who have suffered discrimination or even have been forced back into slavery. Thus, the year after he buys his freedom, Equiano decides that eventually he will take up residence in London – the seat of the British Empire – where, ironically, ex-slaves are allowed some degree of liberty. Perhaps it also passes his mind that in London he can pursue his religious and abolitionist goals in a more direct and forceful way.

Choosing to live in England, Equiano now seriously sets his sights on the spiritual life. He describes in the tenth chapter of the narrative how he undergoes an intense and anxiety-ridden conversion experience culminating in his mystical vision of Jesus Christ on the Cross. This occurs on 6 October 1774, when his ship is docked in the harbour at Cadiz, Spain. After his spiritual conversion, Equiano is ready to commence his program of religious and moral advancement. He studies the tenets and practices of several church groups, and eventually decides to join the members of the Methodist faith, possibly because their leader John Wesley (1703-91) is opposed to slavery. Finally, to highlight and celebrate his conversion, Equiano inserts at the end of the tenth chapter a lengthy poem about his Christian beliefs.

Although he comes to regard Christianity as the true faith, Equiano never condemns the religion of his African homeland.

He makes several references to similarities, especially to the idea of providential design, between African and Christian religious tenets; and he also notes parallels between Hebrew and African customs and precepts. What he seems to be suggesting is that both the African and Hebrew religions are valid and significant forerunners of Christianity's later system of belief. Thus, while choosing the Christian faith as his own, Equiano never accepts the view of white persons that the African religion is a superstitious one.

After his conversion, Equiano is able to draw strength from this new spiritual source. He serves as a missionary to the Indians in Central America, attempts to relocate impoverished British blacks to Sierra Leone, and writes antislavery letters and petitions to British leaders. It is clear now that his physical and spiritual freedom has empowered Equiano to become a more confident and committed person.

In writing his autobiography, Equiano relied on his powers of recall, probably aided by the written journal he kept from time to time during his expeditions. He also dug into his wide reading of the major abolitionist essays and books. The first eleven chapters of *The Interesting Narrative* contain the record of Equiano's experiences up to 1777. From that year to the time he published his work in 1789, he lived in England; but at several times he signed for service on ships voyaging to America. This is the period in his life when he became active in the abolitionist movement and joined the black antislavery group, the Sons of Africa. During this time, Equiano submitted numerous letters on racial matters to the editors of London newspapers, a few of which he inserts into the body of his narrative, including the antislavery petition to Britain's Queen Charlotte.

All these activities he describes in the twelfth and last chapter of his book, but here Equiano reports that there have been fewer incidents in his life since 1777. He says, "I therefore hasten to the conclusion of a narrative, which I fear the reader may think already sufficiently tedious." Actually, the story that has been related up to this point has been anything but tedious, and perhaps here Equiano is once again resorting to the customary humility he thinks his audience expects. The truth is that the personal story related up to the twelfth chapter is an interesting and fascinating depiction of people and events. It is an account filled with the images of a vivid and energetic young man travelling across the globe to far-flung lands and learning how to survive in a new, strange world. When he settles in London, however, he finds himself in one place living a relatively staid and somewhat unexciting life; and although he continues to pursue abolitionist aims, his days of vigorous exploits and daring adventures are mostly over.

Thus, because of the way Equiano views his life in London, his narrative's final chapter becomes a hodgepodge collection of various loose ends that he has brought together. Several contemporary reviewers of his work criticized this flat, uninteresting section of the autobiography, in which Equiano sometimes digresses from his story with letters, testimonials, and petitions. He also dwells here at length on his troubles in the Sierra Leone project. Equiano too hastily covers the last fourteen years of his life omitting, contrary to what he writes, many interesting events of his later years. Perhaps he does so, in part, because he is hurrying to finish his slave narrative so that he can publish it in time for the crucial abolitionist debate in Parliament.

Equiano's narrative has many different aims. Writing during the Enlightenment Period when human reason was prized and egalitarian principles were proclaimed, Equiano strove to place himself on an equal footing with the best thinkers of his time. This was a difficult goal to achieve in light of the opinion of the day, which saw even the abolitionists holding firmly onto ideas of black racial inferiority. Equiano also had to give credence to his life story by building up his character and demonstrating his extraordinary accomplishments.

Thus, in various parts of his narrative he indulges in considerable boasting. Boasting is a method of ego-building that can be traced to African oral traditions and to black American folk tales and literature. In these traditions heroic figures appear as biblical characters or mythic tricksters, such as when an autobiographer identifies with Moses or Jesus Christ or when a storyteller depicts the mischievous figure of the Signifying Monkey fable or the clever Rabbit of the Tar Baby account. The trickster tales demonstrate how an oppressed character can achieve superiority over an opponent by means of indirect and devious techniques involving the use of ambiguous language and deceitful actions. As expected, these stories became very popular within the slave communities of British America.

Equiano's boasting takes the form of heroic and clever role-playing. After he obtains his freedom, the former slave portrays himself in courageous situations. He is seen commanding a storm-tossed ship at sea, confronting dangerous Indians in Central America, attempting to free ex-slaves who have been recaptured in England, and finally taking on the moral responsibilities of an abolitionist leader.

Equiano also emphasizes the special circumstances and talents that have contributed to his strength of character. Near the beginning of his account, he mentions that he has always regarded himself as a *"particular favourite of Heaven."* And he also stresses the prophetic quality of his name: "I was named *Olaudah*, which, in our language, signifies vicissitude or fortunate, also, one favoured, and having a loud voice and well spoken." Here, Equiano credits special providential care for his constant deliverance during enslavement when he is placed in harm's way, and he believes that much of his protection comes from his adherence to God's law. By way of contrast, Equiano presents several examples of people who commit evil and sinful acts, especially the foul-mouthed sailors who blaspheme against God. Most of these people end up suffering great afflictions and experiencing horrible deaths.

After he purchases his freedom, Equiano's displays of boasting increase. He proudly demonstrates his maritime skill when he saves the ship formerly under the command of his good friend Captain Farmer, who had taken ill and died. Later, Equiano also highlights an incident that shows his capacity to handle an unusual request. When he is asked to officiate as a parson at a black child's burial, he delivers a fine performance to everyone's satisfaction. As he proceeds in narrating his adventures, Equiano becomes more and more didactic in his pronouncements on daily living and religious matters, preaching directly to the reader. However, at times Equiano wisely resorts to self-deflating irony to tone down his excessive ego-building. Sometimes he is duped by others, such as when he and Captain Farmer foolishly believe they are going to inherit a dying silversmith's money, and he also admits to his own stupid and foolhardy actions. He relates how he endangers his life by riding a runaway horse and how he almost burns himself to death when he is careless with a candle.

The most humiliating incident is the encounter he has in England with Captain Pascal, from whom Equiano had parted on bitter terms some years before. When the surprised Pascal asks him how he "came back" to England, Equiano sarcastically answers, "In a ship." To which the annoyed captain dryly replies, "I suppose you did not walk back to London on the water." Of course, the biblical reference to Jesus Christ walking upon the water is a slap against Equiano's sense of self-importance. In relating the exact words of this tense exchange, Equiano does not try to cover up the disquieting trait that his former master detects in him. Here again, Equiano deprecates himself in order to scale down the peaks of self-regard that rise up in his narrative.

After the 1789 two-volume edition of *The Interesting Narrative*, there were eight subsequent editions, most in one volume. These editions variously contained alterations in paragraph breaks and corrections of misprints. More importantly, because his work was viciously attacked in racist circles and his narrative was said to be a fabricated story written in a rough and unpolished style, Equiano felt obliged to include in later editions various authenticating pieces. These consisted of documents written by reputable political, religious, and social leaders attesting to the veracity of Equiano's story. Also inserted were letters that Equiano wrote for his readers or that he had sent to his colleagues in the antislavery crusade. One such letter refutes the accusation that Equiano was not born in Africa at all, but on the Danish Caribbean island of Santa Cruz (now St. Croix). This falsehood especially irked him because he claimed it hurt the sales of his book.

Equiano also included in the later editions several pieces of information and self-promotion describing his visits to major cities in England, Wales, Scotland, and Ireland, in which places he advertised his book and sold copies to the members of receptive audiences. In addition, he appended favourable assessments and letters written about his work, but, understandably perhaps, not the few racist or mixed reviews that were printed in newspapers. After his marriage in 1792, he even included his and Susanna Cullen's wedding notice.

Although these additional items provide interesting and important historical and biographical information, they do not measurably increase the original effect of Equiano's narrative. The documents do, however, reveal the side of Equiano that is self-promotional and strongly driven when it comes to assuring his book's success; and they also show his intense eagerness to be believed as he defends himself and his cause.

It is no wonder then that Equiano's narrative resulted in the financial success he hoped for. The profits he earned from his book, together with a moneylending business he carried on, enabled him to become a wealthy man in his later years.

The Abolitionist Movement

When he settled in England in 1777, Equiano devoted his efforts to the abolitionist crusade to end the slave trade. Five years earlier Lord Chief Justice William Mansfield (1705-93) had declared in the case of a runaway black man from Massachusetts, James Somerset, that slaves living in England were to be considered free persons. Although there was some ambiguity about Mansfield's ruling, the decision spurred the efforts of those who attacked the system of slavery. Also heightening the opposition were the evident contradictions revealed by Mansfield's decision that proclaimed the freedom of a small number of slaves living in England, but kept in bondage tens of thousands of Africans in colonial outposts whose slave labour greatly contributed to the wealth of the British Empire.

Encouraged by the Mansfield ruling, the following years saw the publication of great numbers of antislavery tracts, essays, poems, treatises, leaflets, and pamphlets. After the American War for Independence, which had popularized Enlightenment principles of freedom and equality, the clamour for an end to slavery or at least for the abolition of the slave trade, increased in Great Britain. The volume of abolitionist literature, along with antislavery sermons, plays, and speeches quickly grew, especially in the years preceding 1788, when the bill to abolish the slave trade was introduced in Parliament.

Soon after arriving in London, Equiano allied himself with other African-British leaders, alongside such prominent white antislavery reformers as Granville Sharp (1735-1813), James Ramsay (1733-89), Thomas Clarkson (1760-1846), and William Wilberforce (1759-1833). Several of these abolitionists extended the movement's efforts across the Atlantic by keeping in touch with their counterparts in America. Granville Sharp was especially active in corresponding with Philadelphia Quaker Anthony Benezet (1713-84), and also with the prominent American patriots, Benjamin Franklin (1706-90), Benjamin Rush (1745-1813), and John Jay (1745-1829).

In the mid-1780s, Equiano also became an active participant in the Sons of Africa. This group of black abolitionists included the protest author Quobna Ottobah Cugoano (1757-91), who published in 1787 his antislavery tract *Thoughts and Sentiments on the Evil and Wicked Traffic of the Slavery and Commerce of the Human Species*. The Sons of Africa members wrote antislavery letters and petitions, and they also kept themselves in touch with the leading white British opponents of the slave trade, especially Sharp, Clarkson, and Wilberforce.

Sharp had been a leading player in the Somerset case, and his work on behalf of many other black persons had endeared him to the African-British community. Understandably then, it was to Sharp that Equiano turned in seeking help to bring to justice the persons who committed murderous acts in 1781 aboard the slave ship Zong. Equiano's plea for assistance set in motion the process that resulted in the widely publicized trial of those involved in the events aboard the Zong, when 132 sickly captives had been thrown overboard so the owners could make an insurance claim on the monetary value of the discarded slaves. The case was tried in 1783, but to the disappointment of Sharp, Equiano, and many others, the court never charged with murder those persons responsible for the crimes aboard the Zong.

In the 1770s and 1780s, many well-known poets and prose writers expressed humanitarian concerns about the slave trade. In America, Franklin, Thomas Jefferson (1743-1826) – himself a slave owner – and St. John de Crèvecoeur (1735-1813) wrote against the slave trade, while in England poets Hannah More (1745-1833) and William Cowper (1731-1800) composed widely-circulated verses condemning slavery. More, an evangelical Anglican, wrote "Slavery, a Poem" at the behest of the Abolition Committee. The 1788 verse-narrative ends with a vision to be realized with the successful passage of the bill in Parliament to abolish the slave trade:

> What page of human annals can record
> A deed so bright as human rights restor'd?
> O may that god-like deed, that shining page,
> Redeem our fame, and consecrate our age!
> And let this glory mark our favour'd shore,
> To curb False Freedom and the True restore.

Another popular antislavery poem, *The Dying Negro*, had been published in 1773 by Thomas Day (1748-89) and John Bicknell. Equiano quotes from it in his autobiography.

Many prose writers also expressed their views on slavery. Edmund Burke (1729-97) urged the improvement of living conditions for slaves, but did not support their immediate freedom because he regarded them as sensation-seeking and mentally inferior persons. However, in his later years, he did support the abolition of the slave trade. Mary Wollstonecraft (1759-97) directly attacked Burke's conservative and limited view of human nature in her *A Vindication of the Rights of Men* (1790), and she also expressed her antislavery ideas in book reviews, one of which was a mixed, but generally favourable piece on Equiano's 1789 narrative.

More and Wollstonecraft were joined by other white women writers of the time. The educator Anna Laetitia Barbauld (1743-1825) and the working-class poet Ann Yearsley (1752-1806) wrote very popular antislavery works, as did the leading radical writer Helen Maria Williams (c. 1762-1827). Other women supported the boycotting of sugar harvested by slaves in the West Indies; still others circulated petitions against slavery and subscribed to abolitionist publications and joined antislavery societies throughout Great Britain. Women, however, were not always readily accepted in many of the mostly male-dominated organizations; and when they were, they had to abide by the division of antislavery labours decreed by male members. The belief was that men would concentrate on rational and legal arguments to combat slavery, while women would be left to dwell on "sentimental" scenes of family separation and sexual abuse.

American and British abolitionists were united in their efforts to achieve the end of the slave trade, but not all agreed that black persons were on an equal level with white persons. While some antislavery proponents viewed blacks as exemplifying the natural and innocent qualities of the Noble Savage figure, there were others who agreed with the slavery advocates that blacks were insensible brutes. To those abolitionists who held this latter opinion, the most notable being Edmund Burke, black men and women were believed to possess inferior reasoning powers and to dwell mostly in the realm of uncontrolled emotion. For these and other reasons, there were those white abolitionists who desired an end to the slave trade but were against racial intermarriage and the assimilation of blacks into Western societies.

Adding fuel to the negative views of blacks was the frequent reporting in the second half of the eighteenth century of slave insurrections taking place in the British American and West Indian colonies. Abolitionist supporters countered such alarming news by blaming the institution of slavery itself, arguing that its demise would ensure the safety of the white populations. However, when American black loyalists started arriving in England after the end of the War for Independence, several white abolitionist leaders offered serious proposals for segregation or even for sending blacks back to Africa. Granville Sharp was one of the foremost advocates of transplanting the African British poor to Sierra Leone. Many free blacks themselves, even those born in British America and in England, thought that resettling in Africa would be just and beneficial, especially since all blacks encountered hostility and discrimination in Western societies. Equiano himself believed in black resettlement during the time he served as commissary of supplies for the British government's project to outfit an expedition for transporting the British blacks to Sierra Leone.

Another feature of the abolitionist crusade was the enormous hurdle created by the commercial nature of the whole practice of slavery, which had enriched the British merchant class and had significantly contributed to the general wealth of Great Britain. Many mercantile and government leaders argued that the end of the slave trade would cause irreparable harm to the economic health of the British Empire. To protect the business interests of those involved in the slave industry, powerful lobbying groups of planters and merchants exerted pressure on British politicians.

Equiano was well-acquainted with the commercial question of the slave trade. He and other abolitionists knew that the major obstacle to eliminating slavery was the profit motive. He was familiar with the proposals of economic historian Malachy Postlethwayt (1707-67), Quaker writer Anthony Benezet, and antislavery advocates Ramsay and Clarkson. Postlethwayt, writing in 1757, branded slavery as immoral, but his position was that the reality of the lucrative benefits of the slave trade had to be dealt with if slavery was ever to come to an end. Postlethwayt argued, therefore, that the slave trade in Africa should gradually be replaced with a just-as-profitable trade in manufactured goods with the peoples of the vast continent of Africa. British influence would "civilize" the inhabitants so that they would dress and live in the Western manner, and this beneficial cultural change would create a consumer demand for superior British tools, articles of clothing, and other Western products. Above all else, the new trade would enhance the prosperity of Britain while removing the empire's dependence on the evil taint of African slavery. In the meantime, he argued, the whole business of the slave trade should be overseen by a joint-stock colonialist enterprise such as the well-known East India Company.

Anthony Benezet, who had been born in France and educated in London, but now lived as a Quaker in Philadelphia, supported Postlethwayt's solution for stopping the slave trade in works such as *A Caution and Warning to Great Britain and her Colonies* (1766) and *Some Historical Account of Guinea* (1771), a subsequent edition of which (1788) drew on Postlethwayt's idea and was read by Equiano.

But even if there was some agreement among abolitionists about the viability of the commercial proposal, there remained a fundamental disagreement about whether or not slavery should be abolished immediately. Many of the white crusaders who sought the end of the slave trade were hesitant about actually abolishing slavery itself. Because they were not convinced of the equal capacities of black persons, the whites fought for a gradual approach that would include proper education and religious training to prepare the slaves for freedom. The black abolitionists, on the other hand, wanted the immediate end of slavery, although at times they adopted the strategy of working to end the slave trade now and slavery later. While they were not against ameliorating the existing conditions of the slaves, abolitionist writers, including Equiano, were well aware that freedom itself would be required before black men and women could develop themselves as full-fledged members of Western society. No matter how much training the slaves received, the lack of freedom would always prove to be a hindrance to their advancement.

Black Autobiographical Works

The first active slavery opponents were the Quakers, known officially as the Society of Friends. They were in the forefront of organizing abolitionist societies and initiating antislavery petitions in Great Britain and North America. Evangelical religious groups also joined the campaign. The British clergyman George Whitefield (1714-70), whose preaching was heard by Equiano, stirred up intense spiritual fervour in America, especially during the era in the late 1730s and early 1740s that became known as the Great Awakening. Joining the evangelicals were the newly-formed denominations of Methodists, Baptists, and Unitarians whose members actively laboured to improve living conditions among the downtrodden and to secure spiritual and bodily freedom for all enslaved men and women.

As a result of the Enlightenment (led by the thinking of British philosophers John Locke, 1632-1704, and David Hume, 1711-76, and French political philosopher Montesquieu, 1689-1755) and the reform religious movements, the works of most of the antislavery writers contained both rational and moral arguments frequently supported by sentiments and feelings stirred up with graphic images of the terrors endured by slaves. Some of the abolitionist writings also consisted of fact-finding accounts conducted by authors who wished to seek out accurate information for use against the slave trade. Thomas Clarkson spent months investigating the trade's shipping practices in the English port cities of Bristol and Liverpool, where he conducted interviews with seamen and former slaves. He was able to amass a large body of evidence, including hand-drawn illustrations of crowded slave ships and instruments of torture, that he used to bolster the abolitionist debates in Parliament.

However, other than an outsider's investigation of slave-trading practices, such as Clarkson's, most of the rational and humanitarian efforts by the abolitionist leaders were based upon the written and oral testimony produced by the antislavery societies. An important practice of these groups was the seeking out of ex-slaves who could describe the actual conditions and feelings of a life of bondage. The accounts – either dictated or written by slave storytellers – were also used to prove that black men and women were capable of some level of spiritual and mental achievement and thus should be regarded and treated as full members of the human family. Consequently, blacks played a major role in the written contributions supporting the abolitionist movement during the 1780s and 1790s in England and America. Their narratives were published mostly in England, but also circulated among the antislavery forces in America.

Although the earliest black authors cannot be strictly considered antislavery narrators, they must be credited for bravely opening the way and setting the personal and humanitarian tone for the black abolitionist writers who emerged in the mid to late 1780s.

As early as 1760, a Boston slave gave the first-known slave account, *A Narrative of the Uncommon Sufferings and Surprizing Deliverance of Briton Hammon, a Negro Man*. The only available information on Hammon's life is in the chronicle of his thirteen-year captivity under hostile Indians in Florida and then under the Spaniards in Cuba. He was ultimately saved by the British who took him to London where he was glad to meet by accident his American master. Another slave work was published around the year 1772, this one in the form of the popular genre of spiritual autobiography. *A Narrative of the Most Remarkable Particulars in the Life of James Albert Ukawsaw Gronniosaw, an African Prince, as Related by Himself* came out in both England and America and was reprinted many times during the latter part of the eighteenth century. Gronniosaw (c. 1710–c. 1772) was captured in Africa when he was a child and taken to the American South. Upon his master's death, he gained his freedom and soon moved to England where he and his family were aided by the Methodists, whose founder John Wesley expressed his opposition to slavery in *Thoughts upon Slavery* (1774).

In 1782 appeared *The Letters of the Late Ignatius Sancho, an African*. Sancho (1729–80) had been a slave who worked as a servant in a royal household and who later in life started a grocery business in London. His letters reveal the day-to-day existence of black men and women living in England and also contain cautious comments on the plight of the slaves.

A few years before the height of the abolitionist crusade, the English Methodists associated with the Countess of Huntingdon's religious circle known as the Connexion began to sponsor the accounts of blacks living in England. The works of Gronniosaw and the Boston slave poet Phillis Wheatley (1753–84) were supported by the Huntingdon Connexion. In 1773, Wheatley accompanied her master's family to London, where her first volume of verse, *Poems on Various Subjects, Religious and Moral*, was published and soon thereafter became a popular book.

Another such effort by the Methodist group resulted in the appearance of the 1785 autobiography, *A Narrative of the Life of*

John Marrant; of N.Y. in North America with Account of the Conversion of the King of the Cherokees and His Daughter. John Marrant (1755–91) was a freeborn black man who had undergone Indian captivity in the American South and had served aboard British ships during the American Revolutionary War. After the war, Marrant lived in England where he was trained by the Methodists for missionary duty in the Canadian province of Nova Scotia. His personal account became an extremely popular Indian captivity story, and it stayed in print in England and America well into the nineteenth century.

While Gronniosaw and Marrant had indirectly dealt with slavery, Cugoano and Equiano attacked the institution head-on. Cugoano's vitriolic *Thoughts and Sentiments* (1787) contains no supporting testimony by white authorities and was not enthusiastically received. Although he inserted some autobiographical information in the shortened version of his book in 1791, there remained little direct personal experience in the work. Nonetheless, *Thoughts and Sentiments* is a strong polemical narrative characterized by feeling, intelligence, and knowledge.

Similar characteristics appear in Equiano's autobiography, but it is the unique blend of travel writing, spiritual autobiography, and polemic that sets his narrative apart from the works of his predecessors.

Denied full acceptance into white society, black writers of necessity became bicultural, but also sought to restore their African identities. Thus Equiano revived his African name, John Stewart (or Stuart) signed himself Ottobah Cugoano, and James Albert named himself Ukawsaw Gronniosaw. Such name changes represented not just a restoration of integrity and identity, but also signalled black writers' determination to bring into Western consciousness a truer sense of the African's condition in both Africa and the New World.

Equiano's Birthplace

Suspicions about the authenticity of Equiano's autobiography surfaced a few years after its publication in 1789. Newspaper reports appeared that claimed Equiano was born not in Africa, but on the Caribbean island of St. Croix. Equiano quickly denied the accusations; and in the fifth edition of *The Interesting Narrative* in 1792, he inserted letters from respected persons who supported his refutation of the newspaper accounts (see Appendix A). In the latter half of the twentieth century, the Nigerian writer S. E. Ogude suggested that Equiano's autobiography consisted of a mixture of fictional and actual events. He noted, as well as did several other critics, the heavy borrowings of factual content from antislavery authors Anthony Benezet and Thomas Clarkson. Ogude and other reviewers also pointed out the narrative's stylistic similarities to the works of eighteenth-century travel writers Daniel Defoe and Jonathan Swift. At the same time, however, the scholars Paul Edwards and Catherine Obianju Acholonu wrote essays containing evidence of Equiano's African origins and background.

Recently, Vincent Carretta, who has conducted extensive research on historical records relating to Equiano's narrative, has made a challenge to Equiano's claim of an African birth. In an essay, "Olaudah Equiano or Gustavus Vassa? New Light on an Eighteenth-Century Question of Identity," Carretta cites documents giving Equiano's birthplace as South Carolina, and he also comes up with evidence that places the young slave aboard Captain Pascal's ship several years earlier than stated in *The Interesting Narrative*. The suggestions are that Equiano was much younger than the 11 years of age he claimed to be when kidnapped in Africa, and that he made himself older in the narrative in order to add credence to the African part of his story; Carretta suggests Equiano may have relied on "oral history and reading" rather than on personal experience for his African account.

Presently, a great deal of attention is being directed to Equiano's work, and it is hoped that further study will decide the issues concerning Equiano's birth and the veracity of his African account. Regardless, *The Interesting Narrative* continues to be acknowledged as a work of far-reaching literary and historical importance—a status it has retained since the former slave wrote and published it over two hundred years ago.

Olaudah Equiano: A Brief Chronology

1688 Quakers in Pennsylvania colony officially protest slavery.

1745c. Olaudah Equiano is born into the Ibo nation in an interior region of West Africa (present-day Nigeria).

1753 c. Equiano is kidnapped in Africa and sold into slavery.

1754 John Woolman, American Quaker, writes *Some Considerations on the Keeping of Negroes.*

1756 Seven Years' War commences between Great Britain and France over colonial control of North America, where the conflict known as the French and Indian War began two years earlier.

1757 Malachy Postlethwayt publishes *Britain's Commercial Interest Explained and Improved,* a discussion of the economic impact of the slave trade and its possible replacement.

1757 Philosopher Edmund Burke's *An Account of the European Settlements in America* deals with the issue of slavery.

1758-59 Equiano participates in fierce military naval engagements against the French in Canada and off the shores of Western Europe.

1759 Equiano (now named Gustavus Vassa) is baptized as a Christian in London at St. Margaret's Church, Westminster.

1762 Philadelphia Quaker Anthony Benezet publishes antislavery work, *A Short Account of that Part of Africa, Inhabited by the Negroes.*

1766 On July 10, Equiano purchases his freedom from Robert King on the West Indian island of Montserrat. The legal manumission paper is registered on the following day, July 11.

1766 Benezet's *A Caution and Warning to Great Britain and her Colonies* appears in Philadelphia and in the following year in London.

1769 Antislavery advocate Granville Sharp publishes *A*

Representation of the Injustice and Dangerous Tendency of Tolerating Slavery; or of Admitting the Least Claim of Private Property in the Persons of Men, in England.

1771 *Some Historical Account of Guinea* is published by Benezet. It contains an extract from Sharp's treatise on slavery.

1772 Ukawsaw Gronniosaw, former American slave, publishes in England his spiritual life story: *A Narrative of the Most Remarkable Particulars in the Life of James Albert Ukawsaw Gronniosaw, an African Prince, as Related by Himself.*

1772 Lord Chief Justice William Mansfield deciding the case of runaway James Somerset rules that slaves living in Great Britain are to be considered free persons.

1773 Boston slave poet Phillis Wheatley's *Poems on Various Subjects, Religious and Moral* published in England.

1773 Equiano goes with Captain Constantine John Phipps on a scientific expedition to the Arctic region to seek a northeast passage to India.

1774 Equiano attempts and fails to free John Annis, a fugitive black kidnapped in London and sent back to his death in the West Indies.

1774 Methodist founder John Wesley publishes *Thoughts upon Slavery.*

1774 On October 6, in Cadiz, Spain, Equiano reaches the climax of his spiritual conversion when he experiences a mystical vision of the crucified Jesus Christ. Eventually, Equiano joins the Methodist faith.

1775 Quakers establish the antislavery society in the American colonial city of Philadelphia. Benjamin Franklin eventually becomes the organization's president.

1775-76 Dr. Charles Irving and Equiano are in Central America to set up a plantation colony. Equiano is in charge of purchasing slaves and supervising their work.

1776 The Declaration of Independence signed in Philadelphia ushering in the American Revolution. Attack on the British slave trade is removed from Thomas Jefferson's declaration draft.

1776 *The Just Limitation of Slavery* published by Granville Sharp.

1777 Slavery is abolished in Vermont in North America.

1777 Equiano settles in London.

1780 Pennsylvania allows for gradual end of slavery.

1780 Bloody Gordon Riots break out on June 6 in London over issue of Catholic rights. Some former slaves join large white Protestant working-class mob in storming Newgate prison. Several black rebels are hanged.

1782 *The Letters of the Late Ignatius Sancho, an African* is published in London.

1782-83 Quakers in London and Philadelphia join forces to fight slave trade.

1783 English Quakers present antislavery petition to Parliament.

1783 The Zong case tried after complaints presented by Olaudah Equiano and Granville Sharp reveal that more than 132 Africans suffering ill health on the Zong slave vessel were thrown overboard in 1781 for the purpose of collecting insurance funds.

1784 *An Essay on the Treatment and Conversion of African Slaves in the Sugar Colonies* is published in London by Rev. James Ramsay, a former slave owner in the Caribbean.

1784-86 Equiano visits New York and Philadelphia while once again serving aboard ships.

1785 Proslavery merchant James Tobin publishes *Cursory Remarks upon the Reverend Mr. Ramsay's Essay.*

1785 John Marrant, a free black person from the American South, writes his spiritual autobiography, *A Narrative of the Life of John Marrant*, relating his adventures among the Indians in the southern American wilderness. The Countess of Huntingdon's Methodist group called the Connexion aids him in printing his work in England.

1786 In London, Rev. Thomas Clarkson publishes *An Essay on the Slavery and Commerce of the Human Species, Particularly the African*. He visits British ports to collect factual evidence about the slave trade.

1786 Committee for the Relief of the Black Poor is created to aid unemployed black Britons.

1786 Equiano is appointed Commissary for Stores for the British government's project to relocate poor blacks to Sierra Leone.

1787 Equiano dismissed from his commissary post after complaining of mismanagement and immorality by officers in charge of the naval expedition to Sierra Leone.

1787 Quobna Ottobah Cugoano (John Stewart or Stuart) publishes *Thoughts and Sentiments on the Evil and Wicked Traffic of the Slavery and Commerce of the Human Species*.

1787 A group comprised mostly of Quakers forms the Society for Effecting the Abolition of the Slave Trade. Members include William Wilberforce, Granville Sharp, and Thomas Clarkson. Sharp is appointed chairman. Josiah Wedgwood , noted ceramic craftsman, designs the society's antislavery cameo depicting a kneeling slave asking, "Am I Not a Man and a Brother?" The official seal soon becomes a fashion item. It appears inlaid in gold on the lids of snuffboxes and is used to ornament ladies bracelets and hair pins.

1787 Equiano and others organize The Sons of Africa, with Cugoano as one of the members. The Sons of Africa frequently write letters explaining their abolitionist views to readers of major British newspapers.

1788 Equiano petitions Britain's Queen Charlotte concerning the end of the slave trade. He proposes replacing the human commerce with a trade in manufactured products.

1788 Parliament is petitioned again to abolish the slave trade. The Privy Council Committee for Trade and

Plantations is set up to investigate and invite evidence from involved persons.

1788 Rev. John Newton, former slave ship captain, writes *Thoughts upon the African Slave Trade* describing the brutality of slavery.

1788 Sir William Dolben leads legislative fight for passage of The Slave Limitation Act restricting the overcrowding of captured Africans aboard slave ships.

1788 In France, an antislavery group founds the *Amis des Noirs*. French leader Henri Grégoire (1750-1831) champions egalitarian rights for black men and women.

1789 Wilberforce leads Parliamentary debate on the slave trade. Privy Council hears evidence from Clarkson, who conducts on-the-spot investigations at the major slave ports of Bristol and Liverpool. The Privy Council also listens to former slave captain and now clergyman John Newton, who regrets the years he spent transporting slaves across the Middle Passage.

1789 Equiano publishes *The Interesting Narrative of the Life of Olaudah Equiano, or Gustavus Vassa, the African. Written by Himself*. His autobiography is subscribed to by leading personalities in Great Britain. He sends copies of his work to Members of Parliament and begins advertising his book and speaking about it on lecture tours in England, Scotland, Wales and Ireland.

1789 An attack on the Bastille prison in Paris sparks the French Revolution.

1791 On his deathbed, Methodist leader John Wesley reads Equiano's narrative.

1791 On April 19, Wilberforce's motion to abolish the slave trade is defeated in Parliament by a vote of 163 to 88.

1792 London Corresponding Society is formed by reformist Thomas Hardy to promote democratic progress. Hardy's friend, Equiano, becomes a member.

1792 April wedding of Susanna Cullen and Olaudah

Equiano takes place at Soham Church in Cambridgeshire. Ann Maria is born in 1793, and Johanna in 1795. Their mother Susanna dies in 1796, and in the following year both Equiano and Ann Maria die.

1792 British House of Lords defeats bill to abolish the slave trade.

1793 Eli Whitney invents the cotton gin which increases production and thus requires a larger slave workforce on the plantations of the American South.

1794 Ninth British edition of Equiano's autobiography is published. It becomes the last one to appear during his lifetime.

1797 Olaudah Equiano, Gustavus Vassa, dies on March 31.

1807 Slave trade is abolished in both the United States and Great Britain. However, a clandestine commerce continues to exist.

1814 Leeds British edition of Equiano's narrative is published with Wedgwood's antislavery medallion appearing on the title page. Wedgwood's plaque becomes the trademark of the abolitionist movement in the United States.

1816 Johanna Vassa at 21 years of age inherits a huge sum of money from her father's estate.

1829 Abridged version of Equiano's slave narrative autobiography is printed in New York.

1838 Slavery ends in the British Empire after a four-year apprenticeship period.

1845 Narrative of the Life of Frederick Douglass, an American Slave. Written by Himself is printed and becomes the most esteemed of the hundreds of ex-slave autobiographies published by abolitionist societies in the two decades before the American Civil War.

1863 President Abraham Lincoln signs Emancipation Proclamation freeing slaves during the Civil War in the United States. However, slaves in the Confederate South remain in bondage until the conflict ends in 1865.

A Note on the Text

I have chosen the original 1789 edition of Olaudah Equiano's *The Interesting Narrative* because it was this edition that first struck and shocked readers at the time of the legal battle to end the slave trade. Published at the start of the first great abolitionist movement, Equiano's narrative played a major part in stirring up the antislavery sentiments in the British Parliament. The 1789 edition appeared with a list of well-noted subscribers and a dedicatory letter "To the Lords Spiritual and Temporal, and the Commons of the Parliament of Great Britain," which indicated Equiano's wish to influence Parliamentary discussions. Within a few months of its publication, there was no doubt that Equiano's stark and truthful autobiography had its author's desired effect on the national debate. Moreover, besides the impact the slave narrative work had on government circles, Equiano's work greatly assisted the efforts of many other abolitionist leaders in England and America.

Another reason I have chosen the original 1789 edition lies in my belief that the number of revisions to the text made by Equiano during his lifetime did not increase the effectiveness of his narrative. The changes consisted mostly of paragraph divisions and the reworking or addition of several phrases and paragraphs. Because he had come under attack by racist critics who claimed his narrative was fraudulent or probably the work of other abolitionist writers, Equiano also added to the later editions contemporary letters of testimony and favorable reviews of his book. While these pieces are interesting from an historical perspective, and perhaps understandable from a marketing point of view, most of the apparatus Equiano attached does not enhance the integrity of the 1789 edition. In fact, the inclusion of promotional paragraphs and letters designed to advertise his book conflicts with the general, although not always followed, tone of personal and spiritual humility in Equiano's text.

The 1789 text is here presented almost exactly as it was originally published, including Equiano's inconsistent spelling.

Only minor changes involving modernization and obvious printing errors have been made. Equiano's footnotes are kept and some explanatory notes are given. Also included are several of the pieces of updated biographical information, including his marriage to Susanna Cullen in 1792, that Equiano inserted in later editions. The testimonial letters and book reviews that Equiano added to later editions of his narrative are given in Appendix A.

After his death, editions of Equiano's autobiography were published that contained varieties of documents. Antislavery introductions, testimonial letters, and Neoclassical verse by the Boston slave poet Phillis Wheatley were placed before and after the narrative text. An abridged version appeared in 1829, and several full editions came out during the nineteenth-century abolitionist movement in the United States. A more recent abridgement was printed in 1967 by Paul Edwards, who "rediscovered" Equiano's *The Interesting Narrative* in the latter half of the 1960s.

In 1969, Edwards wrote a fine introduction to a facsimile publication of the 1789 two-volume narrative edition. Enormous credit must be given to Edwards for reviving scholarly interest in Equiano. In the last few years, several reprints of Equiano's later texts have appeared, some with excellent essays by noted scholars. Vincent Carretta's edition and study of *The Interesting Narrative* (1995) is a valuable source for those readers seeking accurate explanatory material on many of the references, allusions, and historical events that exist in Equiano's work.

THE

INTERESTING NARRATIVE

OF

THE LIFE

OF

OLAUDAH EQUIANO,

OR

GUSTAVUS VASSA,

THE AFRICAN.

WRITTEN BY HIMSELF.

VOL I.

Behold, God is my salvation; I will trust and not be afraid, for the Lord Jehovah is my strength and my song; he also is become my salvation.
And in that day shall ye say, Praise the Lord, call upon his name, declare his doings among the people. Isaiah xii. 2, 4.

LONDON:

Printed for and sold by the AUTHOR, No. 10, Union-Street, Middlesex Hospital;

Sold also by Mr. Johnson, St. Paul's Church-Yard; Mr. Murray, Fleet-Street; Messrs. Robson and Clark, Bond-Street; Mr. Davis, opposite Gray's Inn, Holborn; Messrs. Shepperson and Reynolds, and Mr. Jackson, Oxford-Street; Mr. Lackington, Chiswell-Street; Mr. Mathews, Strand; Mr. Murray, Prince's-Street, Soho; Mess. Taylor and Co. South Arch, Royal Exchange; Mr. Button, Newington-Causeway; Mr. Parsons, Paternoster-Row; and may be had of all the Booksellers in Town and Country.

[Entered at Stationer's Hall.]

Olaudah Equiano or Gustavus Vassa, the African.

TO THE LORDS SPIRITUAL AND TEMPORAL, AND THE COMMONS OF THE PARLIAMENT OF GREAT BRITAIN.

My Lords and Gentlemen,

PERMIT me, with the greatest deference and respect, to lay at your feet the following genuine Narrative; the chief design of which is to excite in your august assemblies a sense of compassion for the miseries which the Slave-Trade has entailed on my unfortunate countrymen. By the horrors of that trade was I first torn away from all the tender connexions that were naturally dear to my heart; but these, through the mysterious ways of Providence, I ought to regard as infinitely more than compensated by the introduction I have thence obtained to the knowledge of the Christian religion, and of a nation which, by its liberal sentiments, its humanity, the glorious freedom of its government, and its proficiency in arts and sciences, has exalted the dignity of human nature.

I am sensible I ought to entreat your pardon for addressing to you a work so wholly devoid of literary merit; but, as the production of an unlettered African, who is actuated by the hope of becoming an instrument towards the relief of his suffering countrymen, I trust that *such a man*, pleading in *such a cause*, will be acquitted of boldness and presumption.

May the God of heaven inspire your hearts with peculiar benevolence on that important day when the question of Abolition is to be discussed, when thousands, in consequence of your Determination, are to look for Happiness or Misery!

I am,

MY LORDS AND GENTLEMEN,

Your most obedient,

And devoted humble Servant,

OLAUDAH EQUIANO,

OR

GUSTAVUS VASSA.

Union-Street, Mary-le-bone,

March 24, 1789[1]

---

1 After his address to the British Parliament, Equiano placed a "List of Subscribers" that named 311 persons, including 37 women, who had supported the funding of his book by ordering copies in advance of publication. Among the prominent sponsors were members of royalty, including the Prince of Wales and the Duke of York. Also listed were numerous clergymen, abolitionists, writers, and political leaders, such as Thomas Clarkson, Granville Sharp, John Wesley, James Ramsay, Ottobah Cugoano, and Hannah More.

CONTENTS OF VOLUME I.

THE LIFE, &C.

CHAPTER I.

*The author's account of his country, and their manners and customs —
Administration of justice — Embrenche — Marriage ceremony, and public entertainments — Mode of living — Dress — Manufactures Buildings
— Commerce — Agriculture — War and religion — Superstition of the
natives — Funeral ceremonies of the priests or magicians — Curious
mode of discovering poison — Some hints concerning the origin of the
author's countrymen, with the opinions of different writers on that
subject.*

I BELIEVE it is difficult for those who publish their own memoirs to escape the imputation of vanity; nor is this the only
disadvantage under which they labour: it is also their misfortune, that what is uncommon is rarely, if ever, believed, and
what is obvious we are apt to turn from with disgust, and to
charge the writer with impertinence. People generally think
those memoirs only worthy to be read or remembered which
abound in great or striking events, those, in short, which in a
high degree excite either admiration or pity: all others they
consign to contempt and oblivion. It is therefore, I confess, not
a little hazardous in a private and obscure individual, and a
stranger too, thus to solicit the indulgent attention of the public; especially when I own I offer here the history of neither a
saint, a hero, nor a tyrant. I believe there are few events in my
life, which have not happened to many: it is true the incidents
of it are numerous; and, did I consider myself an European, I
might say my sufferings were great: but when I compare my lot
with that of most of my countrymen, I regard myself as a *particular favourite of Heaven*, and acknowledge the mercies of Providence in every occurrence of my life. If then the following
narrative does not appear sufficiently interesting to engage general attention, let my motive be some excuse for its publication.
I am not so foolishly vain as to expect from it either immortal-

ity or literary reputation. If it affords any satisfaction to my numerous friends, at whose request it has been written, or in the smallest degree promotes the interests of humanity, the ends for which it was undertaken will be fully attained, and every wish of my heart gratified. Let it therefore be remembered, that, in wishing to avoid censure, I do not aspire to praise.

That part of Africa, known by the name of Guinea, to which the trade for slaves is carried on, extends along the coast above 3400 miles, from the Senegal to Angola, and includes a variety of kingdoms. Of these the most considerable is the kingdom of Benin, both as to extent and wealth, the richness and cultivation of the soil, the power of its king, and the number and warlike disposition of the inhabitants. It is situated nearly under the line, and extends along the coast about 170 miles, but runs back into the interior part of Africa to a distance hitherto I believe unexplored by any traveller; and seems only terminated at length by the empire of Abyssinia, near 1500 miles from its beginning. This kingdom is divided into many provinces or districts: in one of the most remote and fertile of which , called Eboe, I was born, in the year 1745, in a charming fruitful vale, named Essaka. The distance of this province from the capital of Benin and the sea coast must be very considerable; for I had never heard of white men or Europeans, nor of the sea: and our subjection to the king of Benin was little more than nominal; for every transaction of the government, as far as my slender observation extended, was conducted by the chiefs or elders of the place. The manners and government of a people who have little commerce with other countries are generally very simple; and the history of what passes in one family or village may serve as a specimen of a nation. My father was one of those elders or chiefs I have spoken of, and was styled Embrenche; a term, as I remember, importing the highest distinction, and signifying in our language a *mark* of grandeur. This mark is conferred on the person entitled to it, by cutting the skin across at the top of the forehead, and drawing it down to the eyebrows; and while it is in this situation applying a warm hand, and rubbing it until it shrinks up into a thick *weal* across the lower part of the forehead. Most of the judges and senators were thus marked; my father had long borne it: I had seen it conferred on one of my brothers, and I was also *destined* to receive it by my parents. Those Embrenche, or chief men, decided disputes and punished crimes; for which purpose they always assembled together. The proceedings were generally short; and in most cases the law of retaliation prevailed. I remember a man was brought before my father, and the other judges, for kidnapping a boy; and, although he was the son of a chief or senator, he was condemned to make recompense by a man or woman slave. Adultery, however, was sometimes punished with slavery or death; a punishment which I believe is inflicted on it throughout most of the nations of Africa:[1] so sacred among them is the honour of the marriage bed, and so jealous are they of the fidelity of their wives. Of this I recollect an instance: – a woman was convicted before the judges of adultery, and delivered over, as the custom was, to her husband to be punished. Accordingly he determined to put her to death: but it being found, just before her execution, that she had an infant at her breast; and no woman being prevailed on to perform the part of a nurse, she was spared on account of the child. The men, however, do not preserve the same constancy to their wives, which they expect from them; for they indulge in a plurality, though seldom in more than two. Their mode of marriage is thus: – both parties are usually betrothed when young by their parents, (though I have known the males to betroth themselves). On this occasion a feast is prepared, and the bride and bridegroom stand up in the midst of all their friends, who are assembled for the purpose, while he declares she is thenceforth to be looked upon as his wife, and that no other person is to pay any addresses to her. This is also immediately proclaimed in the vicinity, on which the bride retires from the assembly. Some time after she is brought home to her husband, and then another feast is made, to which the relations of both parties are invited: her parents then deliver her to the bridegroom, accompanied with a number of blessings, and at the same time they tie round her waist a cotton string of the

---

1   [Equiano's note] See Benezet's "Account of Guinea" throughout.

thickness of a goose-quill, which none but married women are permitted to wear: she is now considered as completely his wife; and at this time the dowry is given to the new married pair, which generally consists of portions of land, slaves, and cattle, household goods, and implements of husbandry. These are offered by the friends of both parties; besides which the parents of the bridegroom present gifts to those of the bride, whose property she is looked upon before marriage; but after it she is esteemed the sole property of her husband. The ceremony being now ended the festival begins, which is celebrated with bonfires, and loud acclamations of joy, accompanied with music and dancing.

We are almost a nation of dancers, musicians, and poets. Thus every great event, such as a triumphant return from battle, or other cause of public rejoicing is celebrated in public dances, which are accompanied with songs and music suited to the occasion. The assembly is separated into four divisions, which dance either apart or in succession, and each with a character peculiar to itself. The first division contains the married men, who in their dances frequently exhibit feats of arms, and the representation of a battle. To these succeed the married women, who dance in the second division. The young men occupy the third; and the maidens the fourth. Each represents some interesting scene of real life, such as a great achievement, domestic employment, a pathetic story, or some rural sport; and as the subject is generally founded on some recent event, it is therefore ever new. This gives our dances a spirit and variety which I have scarcely seen elsewhere.[1] We have many musical instruments, particularly drums of different kinds, a piece of music which resembles a guitar, and another much like a stickado.[2] These last are chiefly used by betrothed virgins, who play on them on all grand festivals.

As our manners are simple, our luxuries are few. The dress of both sexes is nearly the same. It generally consists of a long piece of calico, or muslin, wrapped loosely round the body,

---

1   [Equiano's note] When I was in Smyrna I have frequently seen the Greeks dance after this manner.
2   Stickado: a musical instrument similar to a xylophone.

somewhat in the form of a highland plaid. This is usually dyed blue, which is our favourite colour. It is extracted from a berry, and is brighter and richer than any I have seen in Europe. Besides this, our women of distinction wear golden ornaments; which they dispose with some profusion on their arms and legs. When our women are not employed with the men in tillage, their usual occupation is spinning and weaving cotton, which they afterwards dye, and make it into garments. They also manufacture earthen vessels, of which we have many kinds. Among the rest tobacco pipes, made after the same fashion, and used in the same manner, as those in Turkey.[1]

Our manner of living is entirely plain; for as yet the natives are unacquainted with those refinements in cookery which debauch the taste: bullocks, goats, and poultry, supply the greatest part of their food. These constitute likewise the principal wealth of the country, and the chief articles of its commerce. The flesh is usually stewed in a pan; to make it savoury we sometimes use also pepper, and other spices, and we have salt made of wood ashes. Our vegetables are mostly plantains, eadas, yams, beans, and Indian corn. The head of the family usually eats alone; his wives and slaves have also their separate tables. Before we taste food we always wash our hands: indeed our cleanliness on all occasions is extreme; but on this it is an indispensable ceremony. After washing, libation is made, by pouring out a small portion of the drink, in a certain place, for the spirits of departed relations, which the natives suppose to preside over their conduct, and guard them from evil. They are totally unacquainted with strong or spirituous liquours; and their principal beverage is palm wine. This is gotten from a tree of that name by tapping it at the top, and fastening a large gourd to it; and sometimes one tree will yield three or four gallons in a night. When just drawn it is of a most delicious sweetness; but in a few days it acquires a tartish and more spirituous flavour: though I never saw any one intoxicated by it. The same tree also produces nuts and oil. Our principal luxury

---

1   [Equiano's note] The bowl is earthen, curiously figured, to which a long reed is fixed as a tube. This tube is sometimes so long as to be borne by one, and frequently out of grandeur by two boys.

is in perfumes; one sort of these is an odoriferous wood of delicious fragrance: the other a kind of earth; a small portion of
which thrown into the fire diffuses a most powerful odour.[1] We
beat this wood into powder, and mix it with palm oil; with
which both men and women perfume themselves.

In our buildings we study convenience rather than ornament. Each master of a family has a large square piece of
ground, surrounded with a moat or fence, or enclosed with a
wall made of red earth tempered; which, when dry, is as hard as
brick. Within this are his houses to accommodate his family
and slaves; which, if numerous, frequently present the appearance of a village. In the middle stands the principal building,
appropriated to the sole use of the master, and consisting of two
apartments; in one of which he sits in the day with his family,
the other is left apart for the reception of his friends. He has
besides these a distinct apartment in which he sleeps, together
with his male children. On each side are the apartments of his
wives, who have also their separate day and night houses. The
habitations of the slaves and their families are distributed
throughout the rest of the enclosure. These houses never
exceed one story in height: they are always built of wood, or
stakes driven into the ground, crossed with wattles, and neatly
plastered within, and without. The roof is thatched with reeds.
Our dayhouses are left open at the sides; but those in which we
sleep are always covered, and plastered in the inside, with a
composition mixed with cow-dung, to keep off the different
insects, which annoy us during the night. The walls and floors
also of these are generally covered with mats. Our beds consist
of a platform, raised three or four feet from the ground, on
which are laid skins, and different parts of a spungy tree called
plaintain. Our covering is calico or muslin, the same as our
dress. The usual seats are a few logs of wood; but we have
benches, which are generally perfumed, to accommodate
strangers: these compose the greater part of our household furniture. Houses so constructed and furnished require but little

---

1   [Equiano's note] When I was in Smyrna I saw the same kind of earth, and brought
    some of it with me to England; it resembles musk in strength, but is more delicious
    in scent, and is not unlike the smell of a rose.

skill to erect them. Every man is a sufficient architect for the purpose. The whole neighbourhood afford their unanimous assistance in building them and in return receive, and expect no other recompense than a feast.

As we live in a country where nature is prodigal of her favours, our wants are few and easily supplied; of course we have few manufactures. They consist for the most part of calicoes, earthen ware, ornaments, and instruments of war and husbandry. But these make no part of our commerce, the principal articles of which, as I have observed, are provisions. In such a state money is of little use; however we have some small pieces of coin, if I may call them such. They are made something like an anchor; but I do not remember either their value or denomination. We have also markets, at which I have been frequently with my mother. These are sometimes visited by stout mahogany-coloured men from the south west of us: we call them Oye-Eboe, which term signifies red men living at a distance. They generally bring us fire-arms, gunpowder, hats, beads, and dried fish. The last we esteemed a great rarity, as our waters were only brooks and springs. These articles they barter with us for odoriferous woods and earth, and our salt of wood ashes. They always carry slaves through our land; but the strictest account is exacted of their manner of procuring them before they are suffered to pass. Sometimes indeed we sold slaves to them, but they were only prisoners of war, or such among us as had been convicted of kidnapping, or adultery, and some other crimes, which we esteemed heinous. This practice of kidnapping induces me to think, that, notwithstanding all our strictness, their principal business among us was to trepan[1] our people. I remember too they carried great sacks along with them, which not long after I had an opportunity of fatally seeing applied to that infamous purpose.

Our land is uncommonly rich and fruitful, and produces all kinds of vegetables in great abundance. We have plenty of Indian corn, and vast quantities of cotton and tobacco. Our pine apples grow without culture; they are about the size of the

---

1 Trepan: trick, deceive.

largest sugar-loaf, and finely flavoured. We have also spices of different kinds, particularly pepper; and a variety of delicious fruits which I have never seen in Europe; together with gums of various kinds, and honey in abundance. All our industry is exerted to improve those blessings of nature. Agriculture is our chief employment; and every one, even the children and women, are engaged in it. Thus we are all habituated to labour from our earliest years. Every one contributes something to the common stock; and as we are unacquainted with idleness, we have no beggars. The benefits of such a mode of living are obvious. The West India planters prefer the slaves of Benin or Eboe to those of any other part of Guinea, for their hardiness, intelligence, integrity, and zeal. Those benefits are felt by us in the general healthiness of the people, and in their vigour and activity; I might have added too in their comeliness. Deformity is indeed unknown amongst us, I mean that of shape. Numbers of the natives of Eboe now in London might be brought in support of this assertion: for, in regard to complexion, ideas of beauty are wholly relative. I remember while in Africa to have seen three negro children, who were tawny, and another quite white, who were universally regarded by myself, and the natives in general, as far as related to their complexions, as deformed. Our women too were in my eyes at least uncommonly graceful, alert, and modest to a degree of bashfulness; nor do I remember to have ever heard of an instance of incontinence amongst them before marriage. They are also remarkably cheerful. Indeed cheerfulness and affability are two of the leading characteristics of our nation.

Our tillage is exercised in a large plain or common, some hours walk from our dwellings, and all the neighbours resort thither in a body. They use no beasts of husbandry; and their only instruments are hoes, axes, shovels, and beaks, or pointed iron to dig with. Sometimes we are visited by locusts, which come in large clouds, so as to darken the air, and destroy our harvest. This however happens rarely, but when it does, a famine is produced by it. I remember an instance or two wherein this happened. This common is often the theatre of war; and therefore when our people go out to till their land, they not only go in a body, but generally take their arms with them for fear of a surprise; and when they apprehend an invasion they guard the avenue to their dwellings, by driving sticks into the ground, which are so sharp at one end as to pierce the foot, and are generally dipt in poison. From what I can recollect of these battles, they appear to have been irruptions of one little state or district on the other, to obtain prisoners or booty. Perhaps they were incited to this by those traders who brought the European goods I mentioned amongst us. Such a mode of obtaining slaves in Africa is common; and I believe more are procured this way, and by kidnapping, than any other.[1] When a trader wants slaves, he applies to a chief for them, and tempts him with his wares. It is not extraordinary, if on this occasion he yields to the temptation with as little firmness, and accepts the price of his fellow creatures liberty with as little reluctance as the enlightened merchant. Accordingly he falls on his neighbours, and a desperate battle ensues. If he prevails and takes prisoners, he gratifies his avarice by selling them; but, if his party be vanquished, and he falls into the hands of the enemy, he is put to death: for, as he has been known to foment their quarrels, it is thought dangerous to let him survive, and no ransom can save him, though all other prisoners may be redeemed. We have fire-arms, bows and arrows, broad two-edged swords and javelins: we have shields also which cover a man from head to foot. All are taught the use of these weapons; even our women are warriors, and march boldly out to fight along with the men. Our whole district is a kind of militia: on a certain signal given, such as the firing of a gun at night, they all rise in arms and rush upon their enemy. It is perhaps something remarkable, that when our people march to the field a red flag or banner is borne before them. I was once a witness to a battle in our common. We had been all at work in it one day as usual, when our people were suddenly attacked. I climbed a tree at some distance, from which I beheld the fight. There were many women as well as men on both sides; among others my mother was there, and armed with a broad sword. After fight-

---

1   [Equiano's note] See Benezet's "Account of Africa" throughout.

ing for a considerable time with great fury, and after many had been killed our people obtained the victory, and took their enemy's Chief prisoner. He was carried off in great triumph, and, though he offered a large ransom for his life, he was put to death. A virgin of note among our enemies had been slain in the battle, and her arm was exposed in our market-place, where our trophies were always exhibited. The spoils were divided according to the merit of the warriors. Those prisoners which were not sold or redeemed we kept as slaves: but how different was their condition from that of the slaves in the West Indies! With us they do no more work than other members of the community, even their masters; their food, clothing and lodging were nearly the same as theirs, (except that they were not permitted to eat with those who were free-born); and there was scarce any other difference between them, than a superior degree of importance which the head of a family possesses in our state, and that authority which, as such, he exercises over every part of his household. Some of these slaves have even slaves under them as their own property, and for their own use.

As to religion, the natives believe that there is one Creator of all things, and that he lives in the sun, and is girted round with a belt that he may never eat or drink; but, according to some, he smokes a pipe, which is our own favourite luxury. They believe he governs events, especially our deaths or captivity; but, as for the doctrine of eternity, I do not remember to have ever heard of it: some however believe in the transmigration of souls in a certain degree. Those spirits, which are not transmigrated, such as our dear friends or relations, they believe always attend them, and guard them from the bad spirits or their foes. For this reason they always before eating, as I have observed, put some small portion of the meat, and pour some of their drink, on the ground for them; and they often make oblations of the blood of beasts or fowls at their graves. I was very fond of my mother, and almost constantly with her. Wl en she went to make these oblations at her mother's tomb, which was a kind of small solitary thatched house, I sometimes attended her. There she made her libations, and spent most of the night in cries and lamentations. I have been often extremely terrified on these occasions. The loneliness of the place, the darkness of the night, and the ceremony of libation, naturally awful and gloomy, were heightened by my mother's lamentations; and these, concurring with the cries of doleful birds, by which these places were frequented, gave an inexpressible terror to the scene.

We compute the year from the day on which the sun crosses the line, and on its setting that evening there is a general shout throughout the land; at least I can speak from my own knowledge throughout our vicinity. The people at the same time make a great noise with rattles, not unlike the basket rattles used by children here, though much larger, and hold up their hands to heaven for a blessing. It is then the greatest offerings are made; and those children whom our wise men foretell will be fortunate are then presented to different people. I remember many used to come to see me, and I was carried about to others for that purpose. They have many offerings, particularly at full moons; generally two at harvest before the fruits are taken out of the ground: and when any young animals are killed, sometimes they offer up part of them as a sacrifice. These offerings, when made by one of the heads of a family, serve for the whole. I remember we often had them at my father's and my uncle's, and their families have been present. Some of our offerings are eaten with bitter herbs. We had a saying among us to any one of a cross temper, "That if they were to be eaten, they should be eaten with bitter herbs."

We practised circumcision like the Jews, and made offerings and feasts on that occasion in the same manner as they did. Like them also, our children were named from some event, some circumstance, or fancied foreboding at the time of their birth. I was named *Olaudah*, which, in our language, signifies vicissitude or fortunate, also, one favoured, and having a loud voice and well spoken. I remember we never polluted the name of the object of our adoration; on the contrary, it was always mentioned with the greatest reverence; and we were totally unacquainted with swearing, and all those terms of abuse and reproach which find their way so readily and copiously into the languages of more civilized people. The only expressions of that kind I remember were "May you rot, or may you swell, or may a beast take you."

I have before remarked that the natives of this part of Africa are extremely cleanly. This necessary habit of decency was with us a part of religion, and therefore we had many purifications and washings; indeed almost as many, and used on the same occasions, if my recollection does not fail me, as the Jews. Those that touched the dead at any time were obliged to wash and purify themselves before they could enter a dwelling-house. Every woman too, at certain times, was forbidden to come into a dwelling-house, or touch any person, or any thing we ate. I was so fond of my mother I could not keep from her, or avoid touching her at some of those periods, in consequence of which I was obliged to be kept out with her, in a little house made for that purpose, till offering was made, and then we were purified.

Though we had no places of public worship, we had priests and magicians, or wise men. I do not remember whether they had different offices, or whether they were united in the same persons, but they were held in great reverence by the people. They calculated our time, and foretold events, as their name imported, for we called them Ah-affoe-way-cah, which signifies calculators or yearly men, our year being called Ah-affoe. They wore their beards, and when they died they were succeeded by their sons. Most of their implements and things of value were interred along with them. Pipes and tobacco were also put into the grave with the corpse, which was always perfumed and ornamented, and animals were offered in sacrifice to them. None accompanied their funerals but those of the same profession or tribe. These buried them after sunset, and always returned from the grave by a different way from that which they went.

These magicians were also our doctors or physicians. They practised bleeding by cupping; and were very successful in healing wounds and expelling poisons. They had likewise some extraordinary method of discovering jealousy, theft, and poisoning; the success of which no doubt they derived from their unbounded influence over the credulity and superstition of the people. I do not remember what those methods were, except that as to poisoning: I recollect an instance or two, which I hope it will not be deemed impertinent here to insert, as it may serve as a kind of specimen of the rest, and is still used by the negroes in the West Indies. A virgin had been poisoned, but it was not known by whom: the doctors ordered the corpse to be taken up by some persons, and carried to the grave. As soon as the bearers had raised it on their shoulders, they seemed seized with some[1] sudden impulse, and ran to and fro unable to stop themselves. At last, after having passed through a number of thorns and prickly bushes unhurt, the corpse fell from them close to a house, and defaced it in the fall; and, the owner being taken up, he immediately confessed the poisoning.[2] The natives are extremely cautious about poison. When they buy any eatable the seller kisses it all round before the buyer, to shew him it is not poisoned; and the same is done when any meat or drink is presented, particularly to a stranger. We have serpents of different kinds, some of which are esteemed ominous when they appear in our houses, and these we never molest. I remember two of those ominous snakes, each of which was as thick as the calf of a man's leg, and in colour resembling a dolphin in the water, crept at different times into my mother's night-house, where I always lay with her, and coiled themselves into folds, and each time they crowed like a cock. I was desired by some of our wise men to

---

1 [Equiano's note] See also Leut. Matthew's Voyage, p. 123.
2 [Equiano's note] An instance of this kind happened at Montserrat in the West Indies in the year 1763. I then belonged to the Charming Sally, Capt. Doran. – The chief mate, Mr. Mansfield, and some of the crew being one day on shore, were present at the burying of a poisoned negro girl. Though they had often heard of the circumstance of the running in such cases, and had even seen it, they imagined it to be a trick of the corpse-bearers. The mate therefore desired two of the sailors to take up the coffin, and carry it to the grave. The sailors, who were all of the same opinion, readily obeyed; but they had scarcely raised it to their shoulders, before they began to run furiously about, quite unable to direct themselves, till, at last, without intention, they came to the hut of him who had poisoned the girl. The coffin then immediately fell from their shoulders against the hut, and damaged part of the wall. The owner of the hut was taken into custody on this, and confessed the poisoning. – I give this story as it was related by the mate and crew on their return to the ship. The credit which is due to it I leave with the reader.

touch these, that I might be interested in the good omens, which I did, for they were quite harmless, and would tamely suffer themselves to be handled; and then they were put into a large open earthen pan, and set on one side of the highway. Some of our snakes, however, were poisonous: one of them crossed the road one day when I was standing on it, and passed between my feet without offering to touch me, to the great surprise of many who saw it; and these incidents were accounted by the wise men, and therefore by my mother and the rest of the people, as remarkable omens in my favour.

Such is the imperfect sketch my memory has furnished me with of the manners and customs of a people among whom I first drew my breath. And here I cannot forbear suggesting what has long struck me very forcibly, namely, the strong analogy which even by this sketch, imperfect as it is, appears to prevail in the manners and customs of my countrymen and those of the Jews, before they reached the Land of Promise, and particularly the patriarchs while they were yet in that pastoral state which is described in Genesis – an analogy, which alone would induce me to think that the one people had sprung from the other. Indeed this is the opinion of Dr. Gill,[1] who, in his commentary on Genesis, very ably deduces the pedigree of the Africans from Afer and Afra, the descendants of Abraham by Keturah his wife and concubine (for both these titles are applied to her). It is also conformable to the sentiments of Dr. John Clarke, formerly Dean of Sarum, in his Truth of the Christian Religion:[2] both these authors concur in ascribing to us this original. The reasonings of these gentlemen are still further confirmed by the scripture chronology; and if any further corroboration were required, this resemblance in so many respects is a strong evidence in support of the opinion. Like the Israelites in their primitive state, our government was conducted by our chiefs or judges, our wise men and elders; and the

---

1 John Gill (1697-1771) was the Baptist author of *An Exposition of the Old Testament, in which Are Recorded the Original of Mankind, of the Several Nations of the World, and of the Jewish Nation in Particular....* (London, 1788).
2 John Clarke (1682-1757) had translated a seventeenth-century religious work by Hugo Grotius, *The Truth of the Christian Religion* (London, 1786).

head of a family with us enjoyed a similar authority over his household with that which is ascribed to Abraham and the other patriarchs. The law of retaliation obtained almost universally with us as with them: and even their religion appeared to have shed upon us a ray of its glory, though broken and spent in its passage, or eclipsed by the cloud with which time, tradition, and ignorance might have enveloped it; for we had our circumcision (a rule I believe peculiar to that people:) we had also our sacrifices and burnt-offerings, our washings and purifications, on the same occasions as they had.

As to the difference of colour between the Eboan Africans and the modern Jews, I shall not presume to account for it. It is a subject which has engaged the pens of men of both genius and learning, and is far above my strength. The most able and Reverend Mr. T. Clarkson, however, in his much admired Essay on the Slavery and Commerce of the Human Species, has ascertained the cause, in a manner that at once solves every objection on that account, and, on my mind at least, has produced the fullest conviction. I shall therefore refer to that performance for the theory,[1] contenting myself with extracting a fact as related by Dr. Mitchel.[2] "The Spaniards, who have inhabited America, under the torrid zone, for any time, are become as dark coloured as our native Indians of Virginia; of which *I myself have been a witness.*" There is also another instance[3] of a Portuguese settlement at Mitomba, a river in Sierra Leona; where the inhabitants are bred from a mixture of the first Portuguese discoverers with the natives, and are now become in their complexion, and in the wooly quality of their hair, *perfect negroes*, retaining however a smattering of the Portuguese language.

These instances, and a great many more which might be adduced, while they shew how the complexions of the same persons vary in different climates, it is hoped may tend also to remove the prejudice that some conceive against the natives of Africa on account of their colour. Surely the minds of the

---

1   [Equiano's note] Page 178 to 216.
2   [Equiano's note] Philos. Trans. No. 476, Sect. 4, cited by Mr. Clarkson, p. 205.
3   [Equiano's note] Same page.

Spaniards did not change with their complexions! Are there not causes enough to which the apparent inferiority of an African may be ascribed, without limiting the goodness of God, and supposing he forbore to stamp understanding on certainly his own image, because "carved in ebony." Might it not naturally be ascribed to their situation? When they come among Europeans, they are ignorant of their language, religion, manners, and customs. Are any pains taken to teach them these? Are they treated as men? Does not slavery itself depress the mind, and extinguish all its fire and every noble sentiment? But, above all, what advantages do not a refined people possess over those who are rude and uncultivated. Let the polished and haughty European recollect that his ancestors were once, like the Africans, uncivilized, and even barbarous. Did Nature make *them* inferior to their sons? And should *they too* have been made slaves? Every rational mind answers, No. Let such reflections as these melt the pride of their superiority into sympathy for the wants and miseries of their sable brethren, and compel them to acknowledge, that understanding is not confined to feature or colour. If, when they look round the world, they feel exultation, let it be tempered with benevolence to others, and gratitude to God, "who hath made of one blood all nations of men for to dwell on all the face of the earth;[1] and whose wisdom is not our wisdom, neither are our ways his ways."

---

1   [Equiano's note] Acts, c. xvii. v. 26.

CHAP. II.

The author's birth and parentage – His being kidnapped with his sister
– Their separation – Surprise at meeting again – Are finally separated
– Account of the different places and incidents the author met with till
his arrival on the coast – The effect the sight of a slave ship had on
him – He sails for the West Indies – Horrors of a slave ship – Arrives
at Barbadoes, where the cargo is sold and dispersed.

I HOPE the reader will not think I have trespassed on his
patience in introducing myself to him with some account of
the manners and customs of my country. They had been
implanted in me with great care, and made an impression on
my mind, which time could not erase, and which all the
adversity and variety of fortune I have since experienced
served only to rivet and record; for, whether the love of one's
country be real or imaginary, or a lesson of reason, or an
instinct of nature, I still look back with pleasure on the first
scenes of my life, though that pleasure has been for the most
part mingled with sorrow.

I have already acquainted the reader with the time and place
of my birth. My father, besides many slaves, had a numerous
family, of which seven lived to grow up, including myself and
a sister, who was the only daughter. As I was the youngest of
the sons, I became, of course, the greatest favourite with my
mother, and was always with her; and she used to take particular pains to form my mind. I was trained up from my earliest
years in the art of war; my daily exercise was shooting and
throwing javelins; and my mother adorned me with emblems,
after the manner of our greatest warriors. In this way I grew up
till I was turned the age of eleven, when an end was put to my
happiness in the following manner: – Generally when the
grown people in the neighbourhood were gone far in the fields
to labour, the children assembled together in some of the
neighbours' premises to play; and commonly some of us used
to get up a tree to look out for any assailant, or kidnapper, that
might come upon us; for they sometimes took those opportunities of our parents' absence to attack and carry off as many as

they could seize. One day, as I was watching at the top of a tree in our yard, I saw one of those people come into the yard of our next neighbour but one, to kidnap, there being many stout young people in it. Immediately on this I gave the alarm of the rogue, and he was surrounded by the stoutest of them, who entangled him with cords, so that he could not escape till some of the grown people came and secured him. But alas! ere long it was my fate to be thus attacked, and to be carried off, when none of the grown people were nigh. One day, when all our people were gone out to their works as usual, and only I and my dear sister were left to mind the house, two men and a woman got over our walls, and in a moment seized us both, and, without giving us time to cry out, or make resistance, they stopped our mouths, and ran off with us into the nearest wood. Here they tied our hands, and continued to carry us as far as they could, till night came on, when we reached a small house, where the robbers halted for refreshment, and spent the night. We were then unbound, but were unable to take any food; and, being quite overpowered by fatigue and grief, our only relief was some sleep, which allayed our misfortune for a short time. The next morning we left the house, and continued travelling all the day. For a long time we had kept the woods, but at last we came into a road which I believed I knew. I had now some hopes of being delivered; for we had advanced but a little way before I discovered some people at a distance, on which I began to cry out for their assistance: but my cries had no other effect than to make them tie me faster and stop my mouth, and then they put me into a large sack. They also stopped my sister's mouth, and tied her hands; and in this manner we proceeded till we were out of the sight of these people. When we went to rest the following night they offered us some victuals; but we refused it; and the only comfort we had was in being in one another's arms all that night, and bathing each other with our tears. But alas! we were soon deprived of even the small comfort of weeping together. The next day proved a day of greater sorrow than I had yet experienced; for my sister and I were then separated, while we lay clasped in each other's arms. It was in vain that we besought them not to part us; she was torn from me, and immediately carried away, while I was left in a state of distraction not to be described. I cried and grieved continually; and for several days I did not eat any thing but what they forced into my mouth. At length, after many days travelling, during which I had often changed masters, I got into the hands of a chieftain, in a very pleasant country. This man had two wives and some children, and they all used me extremely well, and did all they could to comfort me; particularly the first wife, who was something like my mother. Although I was a great many days journey from my father's house, yet these people spoke exactly the same language with us. This first master of mine, as I may call him, was a smith, and my principal employ-ment was working his bellows, which were the same kind as I had seen in my vicinity. They were in some respects not unlike the stoves here in gentleman's kitchens; and were covered over with leather; and in the middle of that leather a stick was fixed, and a person stood up, and worked it, in the same manner as is done to pump water out of a cask with a hand pump. I believe it was gold he worked, for it was of a lovely bright yellow colour, and was worn by the women on their wrists and ancles. I was there I suppose about a month, and they at last used to trust me some little distance from the house. This liberty I used in embracing every opportunity to inquire the way to my own home: and I also sometimes, for the same purpose, went with the maidens, in the cool of the evenings, to bring pitchers of water from the springs for the use of the house. I had also remarked where the sun rose in the morning, and set in the evening, as I had travelled along; and I had observed that my father's house was towards the rising of the sun. I therefore determined to seize the first opportunity of making my escape, and to shape my course for that quarter; for I was quite oppressed and weighed down by grief after my mother and friends; and my love of liberty, ever great, was strengthened by the mortifying circumstance of not daring to eat with the free-born children, although I was mostly their companion. While I was projecting my escape, one day an unlucky event happened, which quite disconcerted my plan, and put an end to my hopes. I used to be sometimes employed in assisting an elderly woman slave to cook and take care of the poultry; and one morning, while I was feeding some chickens, I happened to toss a small pebble at one of them, which hit it on the middle and directly killed it. The old slave, having soon after missed the chicken, inquired after it; and on my relating the accident (for I told her the truth, because my mother would never suffer me to tell a lie) she flew into a violent passion, threatened that I should suffer for it; and, my master being out, she immediately went and told her mistress what I had done. This alarmed me very much, and I expected an instant flogging, which to me was uncommonly dreadful; for I had seldom been beaten at home. I therefore resolved to fly; and accordingly I ran into a thicket that was hard by, and hid myself in the bushes. Soon afterwards my mistress and the slave returned, and, not seeing me, they searched all the house, but not finding me, and I not making answer when they called to me, they thought I had run away, and the whole neighbourhood was raised in the pursuit of me. In that part of the country (as in ours) the houses and villages were skirted with woods, or shrubberies, and the bushes were so thick that a man could readily conceal himself in them, so as to elude the strictest search. The neighbours continued the whole day looking for me, and several times many of them came within a few yards of the place where I lay hid. I then gave myself up for lost entirely, and expected every moment, when I heard a rustling among the trees, to be found out, and punished by my master: but they never discovered me, though they were often so near that I even heard their conjectures as they were looking about for me; and I now learned from them, that any attempt to return home would be hopeless. Most of them supposed I had fled towards home; but the distance was so great, and the way so intricate, that they thought I could never reach it, and that I should be lost in the woods. When I heard this I was seized with a violent panic, and abandoned myself to despair. Night too began to approach, and aggravated all my fears. I had before entertained hopes of getting home, and I had determined when it should be dark to make the attempt; but I was now convinced it was fruitless, and I began to consider that, if possibly I could escape all other animals, I could not those of the human kind; and that, not knowing the way, I must perish in the woods. Thus was I like the hunted deer:

—Ev'ry leaf and ev'ry whisp'ring breath
Convey'd a foe, and ev'ry foe a death.[1]

I heard frequent rustlings among the leaves; and being pretty sure they were snakes I expected every instant to be stung by them. This increased my anguish, and the horror of my situation became now quite insupportable. I at length quitted the thicket, very faint and hungry, for I had not eaten or drank any thing all the day; and crept to my master's kitchen, from whence I set out at first, and which was an open shed, and laid myself down in the ashes with an anxious wish for death to relieve me from all my pains. I was scarcely awake in the morning when the old woman slave, who was the first up, came to light the fire, and saw me in the fire place. She was very much surprised to see me, and could scarcely believe her own eyes. She now promised to intercede for me, and went for her master, who soon after came, and, having slightly reprimanded me, ordered me to be taken care of, and not to be ill-treated.

Soon after this my master's only daughter, and child by his first wife, sickened and died, which affected him so much that for some time he was almost frantic, and really would have killed himself, had he not been watched and prevented. However, in a small time afterwards he recovered, and I was again sold. I was now carried to the left of the sun's rising, through many different countries, and a number of large woods. The people I was sold to used to carry me very often, when I was tired, either on their shoulders or on their backs. I saw many convenient well-built sheds along the roads, at proper distances, to accommodate the merchants and travellers, who lay in those buildings along with their wives, who often accompany them; and they always go well armed.

---

1 These slightly altered lines are from *Cooper's Hill* (1642) by John Denham (1615-69), lines 287-88.

From the time I left my own nation I always found somebody that understood me till I came to the sea coast. The languages of different nations did not totally differ, nor were they so copious as those of the Europeans, particularly the English. They were therefore easily learned; and, while I was journeying thus through Africa, I acquired two or three different tongues. In this manner I had been travelling for a considerable time, when one evening, to my great surprise, whom should I see brought to the house where I was but my dear sister! As soon as she saw me she gave a loud shriek, and ran into my arms – I was quite overpowered: neither of us could speak; but, for a considerable time, clung to each other in mutual embraces, unable to do any thing but weep. Our meeting affected all who saw us; and indeed I must acknowledge, in honour of those sable destroyers of human rights, that I never met with any ill treatment, or saw any offered to their slaves, except tying them, when necessary, to keep them from running away. When these people knew we were brother and sister they indulged us together; and the man, to whom I supposed we belonged, lay with us, he in the middle, while she and I held one another by the hands across his breast all night; and thus for a while we forgot our misfortunes in the joy of being together: but even this small comfort was soon to have an end; for scarcely had the fatal morning appeared, when she was again torn from me for ever! I was now more miserable, if possible, than before. The small relief which her presence gave me from pain was gone, and the wretchedness of my situation was redoubled by my anxiety after her fate, and my apprehensions lest her sufferings should be greater than mine, when I could not be with her to alleviate them. Yes, thou dear partner of all my childish sports! thou sharer of my joys and sorrows! happy should I have ever esteemed myself to encounter every misery for you, and to procure your freedom by the sacrifice of my own. Though you were early forced from my arms, your image has been always rivetted in my heart, from which neither *time nor fortune* have been able to remove it; so that, while the thoughts of your sufferings have damped my prosperity, they have mingled with adversity and increased its bitterness. To that Heaven which protects the weak from the strong, I commit the care of your innocence and virtues, if they have not already received their full reward, and if your youth and delicacy have not long since fallen victims to the violence of the African trader, the pestilential stench of a Guinea ship, the seasoning in the European colonies, or the lash and lust of a brutal and unrelenting overseer.

I did not long remain after my sister. I was again sold, and carried through a number of places, till, after travelling a considerable time, I came to a town called Tinmah, in the most beautiful country I had yet seen in Africa. It was extremely rich, and there were many rivulets which flowed through it, and supplied a large pond in the centre of the town, where the people washed. Here I first saw and tasted cocoa-nuts, which I thought superior to any nuts I had ever tasted before; and the trees, which were loaded, were also interspersed amongst the houses, which had commodious shades adjoining, and were in the same manner as ours, the insides being neatly plastered and whitewashed. Here I also saw and tasted for the first time sugar-cane. Their money consisted of little white shells, the size of the finger nail. I was sold here for one hundred and seventy-two of them by a merchant who lived and brought me there. I had been about two or three days at his house, when a wealthy widow, a neighbour of his, came there one evening, and brought with her an only son, a young gentleman about my own age and size. Here they saw me; and, having taken a fancy to me, I was bought of the merchant, and went home with them. Her house and premises were situated close to one of those rivulets I have mentioned, and were the finest I ever saw in Africa: they were very extensive, and she had a number of slaves to attend her. The next day I was washed and perfumed, and when meal-time came I was led into the presence of my mistress, and ate and drank before her with her son. This filled me with astonishment; and I could scarce help expressing my surprise that the young gentleman should suffer me, who was bound, to eat with him who was free; and not only so, but that he would not at any time either eat or drink till I had taken first, because I was the eldest, which was agreeable to our custom. Indeed every thing here, and all their treatment of me, made me forget that I was a slave. The language of these people resembled ours so nearly, that we understood each other perfectly. They had also the very same customs as we. There were likewise slaves daily to attend us, while my young master and I with other boys sported with our darts and bows and arrows, as I had been used to do at home. In this resemblance to my former happy state I passed about two months; and I now began to think I was to be adopted into the family, and was beginning to be reconciled to my situation, and to forget by degrees my misfortunes, when all at once the delusion vanished; for, without the least previous knowledge, one morning early, while my dear master and companion was still asleep, I was wakened out of my reverie to fresh sorrow, and hurried away even amongst the uncircumcised.

Thus, at the very moment I dreamed of the greatest happiness, I found myself most miserable; and it seemed as if fortune wished to give me this taste of joy, only to render the reverse more poignant. The change I now experienced was as painful as it was sudden and unexpected. It was a change indeed from a state of bliss to a scene which is inexpressible by me, as it discovered to me an element I had never before beheld, and till then had no idea of, and wherein such instances of hardship and cruelty continually occurred as I can never reflect on but with horror.

All the nations and people I had hitherto passed through resembled our own in their manners, customs, and language: but I came at length to a country, the inhabitants of which differed from us in all those particulars. I was very much struck with this difference, especially when I came among a people who did not circumcise, and ate without washing their hands. They cooked also in iron pots, and had European cutlasses and cross bows, which were unknown to us, and fought with their fists amongst themselves. Their women were not so modest as ours, for they ate, and drank, and slept, with their men. But, above all, I was amazed to see no sacrifices or offerings among them. In some of those places the people ornamented themselves with scars, and likewise filed their teeth very sharp. They wanted sometimes to ornament me in the same manner, but I would not suffer them; hoping that I might some time be among a people who did not thus disfigure themselves, as I thought they did. At last I came to the banks of a large river, which was covered with canoes, in which the people appeared to live with their household utensils and provisions of all kinds. I was beyond measure astonished at this, as I had never before seen any water larger than a pond or a rivulet: and my surprise was mingled with no small fear when I was put into one of these canoes, and we began to paddle and move along the river. We continued going on thus till night; and when we came to land, and made fires on the banks, each family by themselves, some dragged their canoes on shore, others stayed and cooked in theirs, and laid in them all night. Those on the land had mats, of which they made tents, some in the shape of little houses: in these we slept; and after the morning meal we embarked again and proceeded as before. I was often very much astonished to see some of the women, as well as the men, jump into the water, dive to the bottom, come up again, and swim about. Thus I continued to travel, sometimes by land, sometimes by water, through different countries and various nations, till, at the end of six or seven months after I had been kidnapped, I arrived at the sea coast. It would be tedious and uninteresting to relate all the incidents which befell me during this journey, and which I have not yet forgotten; of the various hands I passed through, and the manners and customs of all the different people among whom I lived: I shall therefore only observe, that in all the places where I was the soil was exceedingly rich; the pomkins, eadas, plantains, yams, &c. &c. were in great abundance, and of incredible size. There were also vast quantities of different gums, though not used for any purpose; and every where a great deal of tobacco. The cotton even grew quite wild; and there was plenty of red-wood. I saw no mechanics whatever in all the way, except such as I have mentioned. The chief employment in all these countries was agriculture, and both the males and females, as with us, were brought up to it, and trained in the arts of war.

The first object which saluted my eyes when I arrived on

the coast was the sea, and a slave ship, which was then riding at anchor, and waiting for its cargo. These filled me with astonishment, which was soon converted into terror when I was carried on board. I was immediately handled and tossed up to see if I were sound by some of the crew; and I was not persuaded that I had gotten into a world of bad spirits, and that they were going to kill me. Their complexions too differing so much from ours, their long hair, and the language they spoke, (which was very different from any I had ever heard) united to confirm me in this belief. Indeed such were the horrors of my views and fears at the moment, that, if ten thousand worlds had been my own, I would have freely parted with them all to have exchanged my condition with that of the meanest slave in my own country. When I looked round the ship too and saw a large furnace of copper boiling, and a multitude of black people of every description chained together, every one of their countenances expressing dejection and sorrow, I no longer doubted of my fate; and, quite overpowered with horror and anguish, I fell motionless on the deck and fainted. When I recovered a little I found some black people about me, who I believed were some of those who brought me on board, and had been receiving their pay; they talked to me in order to cheer me, but all in vain. I asked them if we were not to be eaten by those white men with horrible looks, red faces, and long hair. They told me I was not; and one of the crew brought me a small portion of spirituous liquor in a wine glass; but, being afraid of him, I would not take it out of his hand. One of the blacks therefore took it from him and gave it to me, and I took a little down my palate, which, instead of reviving me, as they thought it would, threw me into the greatest consternation at the strange feeling it produced, having never tasted any such liquor before. Soon after this the blacks who brought me on board went off, and left me abandoned to despair. I now saw myself deprived of all chance of returning to my native country, or even the least glimpse of hope of gaining the shore, which I now considered as friendly; and I even wished for my former slavery in preference to my present situation, which was filled with horrors of every kind, still heightened by my ignorance of what I was to undergo. I was not long suffered to indulge my grief; I was soon put down under the decks, and there I received such a salutation in my nostrils as I had never experienced in my life: so that, with the loathsomeness of the stench, and crying together, I became so sick and low that I was not able to eat, nor had I the least desire to taste any thing. I now wished for the last friend, death, to relieve me; but soon, to my grief, two of the white men offered me eatables; and, on my refusing to eat, one of them held me fast by the hands, and laid me across I think the windlass, and tied my feet, while the other flogged me severely. I had never experienced any thing of this kind before; and although, not being used to the water, I naturally feared that element the first time I saw it, yet nevertheless, could I have got over the nettings, I would have jumped over the side, but I could not; and, besides, the crew used to watch us very closely who were not chained down to the decks, lest we should leap into the water: and I have seen some of these poor African prisoners most severely cut for attempting to do so, and hourly whipped for not eating. This indeed was often the case with myself. In a little time after, amongst the poor chained men, I found some of my own nation, which in a small degree gave ease to my mind. I inquired of these what was to be done with us; they gave me to understand we were to be carried to these white people's country to work for them. I then was a little revived, and thought, if it were no worse than working, my situation was not so desperate: but still I feared I should be put to death, the white people looked and acted, as I thought, in so savage a manner; for I had never seen among any people such instances of brutal cruelty; and this not only shewn towards us blacks, but also to some of the whites themselves. One white man in particular I saw, when we were permitted to be on deck, flogged so unmercifully with a large rope near the foremast, that he died in consequence of it; and they tossed him over the side as they would have done a brute. This made me fear these people the more; and I expected nothing less than to be treated in the same manner. I could not help expressing my fears and apprehensions to some of my countrymen: I asked them if these people had no country, but lived in this hollow place (the ship): they told me they did not, but came from a distant one. "Then," said I, "how comes it in all our country we never heard of them?" They told me because they lived so very far off. I then asked where were their women? had they any like themselves? I was told they had: "and why," said I, "do we not see them?" they answered, because they were left behind. I asked how the vessel could go? they told me they could not tell; but that there were cloths put upon the masts by the help of the ropes I saw, and then the vessel went on; and the white men had some spell or magic they put in the water when they liked in order to stop the vessel. I was exceedingly amazed at this account, and really thought they were spirits. I therefore wished much to be from amongst them, for I expected they would sacrifice me: but my wishes were vain; for we were so quartered that it was impossible for any of us to make our escape. While we stayed on the coast I was mostly on deck; and one day, to my great astonishment, I saw one of these vessels coming in with the sails up. As soon as the whites saw it, they gave a great shout, at which we were amazed; and the more so as the vessel appeared larger by approaching nearer. At last she came to an anchor in my sight, and when the anchor was let go I and my countrymen who saw it were lost in astonishment to observe the vessel stop; and were now convinced it was done by magic. Soon after this the other ship got her boats out, and they came on board of us, and the people of both ships seemed very glad to see each other. Several of the strangers also shook hands with us black people, and made motions with their hands, signifying I suppose we were to go to their country; but we did not understand them. At last, when the ship we were in had got in all her cargo, they made ready with many fearful noises, and we were all put under deck, so that we could not see how they managed the vessel. But this disappointment was the least of my sorrow. The stench of the hold while we were on the coast was so intolerably loathsome, that it was dangerous to remain there for any time, and some of us had been permitted to stay on the deck for the fresh air; but now that the whole ship's cargo were confined together, it became absolutely pestilential. The closeness of the place, and the heat of the climate, added to the number in the ship, which was so crowded that each had scarcely room to turn himself, almost suffocated us. This produced copious perspirations, so that the air soon became unfit for respiration, from a variety of loathsome smells, and brought on a sickness among the slaves, of which many died, thus falling victims to the improvident avarice, as I may call it, of their purchasers. This wretched situation was again aggravated by the galling of the chains, now become insupportable; and the filth of the necessary tubs, into which the children often fell, and were almost suffocated. The shrieks of the women, and the groans of the dying, rendered the whole a scene of horror almost inconceivable. Happily perhaps for myself I was soon reduced so low here that it was thought necessary to keep me almost always on deck; and from my extreme youth I was not put in fetters. In this situation I expected every hour to share the fate of my companions, some of whom were almost daily brought upon deck at the point of death, which I began to hope would soon put an end to my miseries. Often did I think many of the inhabitants of the deep much more happy than myself. I envied them the freedom they enjoyed, and as often wished I could change my condition for theirs. Every circumstance I met with served only to render my state more painful, and heighten my apprehensions, and my opinion of the cruelty of the whites. One day they had taken a number of fishes; and when they had killed and satisfied themselves with as many as they thought fit, to our astonishment who were on the deck, rather than give any of them to us to eat as we expected, they tossed the remaining fish into the sea again, although we begged and prayed for some as well as we could, but in vain; and some of my countrymen, being pressed by hunger, took an opportunity, when they thought no one saw them, of trying to get a little privately; but they were discovered, and the attempt procured them some very severe floggings. One day, when we had a smooth sea and moderate wind, two of my wearied countrymen who were chained together (I was near them at the time), preferring death to such a life of misery, somehow made through the nettings and jumped into the sea: immediately another quite dejected fellow, who, on account of his illness, was suffered to be out of irons, also followed their example; and I believe many more would very soon have done the same if they had not been prevented by the ship's crew, who were instantly alarmed. Those of us that were the most active were in a moment put down under the deck, and there was such a noise and confusion amongst the people of the ship as I never heard before, to stop her, and get the boat out to go after the slaves. However two of the wretches were drowned, but they got the other, and afterwards flogged him unmercifully for thus attempting to prefer death to slavery. In this manner we continued to undergo more hardships than I can now relate, hardships which are inseparable from this accursed trade. Many a time we were near suffocation from the want of fresh air, which we were often without for whole days together. This, and the stench of the necessary tubs, carried off many. During our passage I first saw flying fishes, which surprised me very much: they used frequently to fly across the ship, and many of them fell on the deck. I also now first saw the use of the quadrant; I had often with astonishment seen the mariners make observations with it, and I could not think what it meant. They at last took notice of my surprise; and one of them, willing to increase it, as well as to gratify my curiosity, made me one day look through it. The clouds appeared to me to be land, which disappeared as they passed along. This heightened my wonder; and I was now more persuaded than ever that I was in another world, and that every thing about me was magic. At last we came in sight of the island of Barbadoes, at which the whites on board gave a great shout, and made many signs of joy to us. We did not know what to think of this; but as the vessel drew nearer we plainly saw the harbour, and other ships of different kinds and sizes; and we soon anchored amongst them off Bridge Town. Many merchants and planters now came on board, though it was in the evening. They put us in separate parcels, and examined us attentively. They also made us jump, and pointed to the land, signifying we were to go there. We thought by this we should be eaten by these ugly men, as they appeared to us; and, when soon after we were all put down under the deck again, there was much dread and trembling among us, and nothing but bitter cries to be heard all the night from these apprehensions, insomuch that at last the white people got some old slaves from the land to pacify us. They told us we were not to be eaten, but to work, and were soon to go on land, where we should see many of our country people. This report eased us much; and sure enough, soon after we were landed, there came to us Africans of all languages. We were conducted immediately to the merchant's yard, where we were all pent up together like so many sheep in a fold, without regard to sex or age. As every object was new to me every thing I saw filled me with surprise. What struck me first was that the houses were built with stories, and in every other respect different from those in Africa: but I was still more astonished on seeing people on horseback. I did not know what this could mean; and indeed I thought these people were full of nothing but magical arts. While I was in this astonishment one of my fellow prisoners spoke to a countryman of his about the horses, who said they were the same kind they had in their country. I understood them though they were from a distant part of Africa, and I thought it odd I had not seen any horses there; but afterwards, when I came to converse with different Africans, I found they had many horses amongst them, and much larger than those I then saw. We were not many days in the merchant's custody before we were sold after their usual manner, which is this: — On a signal given, (as the beat of a drum) the buyers rush at once into the yard where the slaves are confined, and make choice of that parcel they like best. The noise and clamour with which this is attended, and the eagerness visible in the countenances of the buyers, serve not a little to increase the apprehensions of the terrified Africans, who may well be supposed to consider them as the ministers of that destruction to which they think themselves devoted. In this manner, without scruple, are relations and friends separated, most of them never to see each other again. I remember in the vessel in which I was brought over, in the men's apartment, there were several brothers, who, in the sale, were sold in different lots; and it was very moving on this occasion to see and hear their cries at parting. O, ye nominal

Christians! might not an African ask you, learned you this from your God, who says unto you, Do unto all men as you would men should do unto you? Is it not enough that we are torn from our country and friends to toil for your luxury and lust of gain? Must every tender feeling be likewise sacrificed to your avarice? Are the dearest friends and relations, now rendered more dear by their separation from their kindred, still to be parted from each other, and thus prevented from cheering the gloom of slavery with the small comfort of being together and mingling their sufferings and sorrows? Why are parents to lose their children, brothers their sisters, or husbands their wives? Surely this is a new refinement in cruelty, which, while it has no advantage to atone for it, thus aggravates distress, and adds fresh horrors even to the wretchedness of slavery.

CHAP. III.

*The author is carried to Virginia — His distress — Surprise at seeing a
picture and a watch — Is bought by Captain Pascal, and sets out for
England — His terror during the voyage — Arrives in England — His
wonder at a fall of snow — Is sent to Guernsey, and in some time goes
on board a ship of war with his master — Some account of the expedition against Louisbourg under the command of Admiral Boscawen, in
1758.*

I NOW totally lost the small remains of comfort I had enjoyed
in conversing with my countrymen; the women too, who used
to wash and take care of me, were all gone different ways, and I
never saw one of them afterwards.

I stayed in this island for a few days; I believe it could not be
above a fortnight; when I and some few more slaves, that were
not saleable amongst the rest, from very much fretting, were
shipped off in a sloop for North America. On the passage we
were better treated than when we were coming from Africa,
and we had plenty of rice and fat pork. We were landed up a
river a good way from the sea, about Virginia county, where we
saw few or none of our native Africans, and not one soul who
could talk to me. I was a few weeks weeding grass, and gathering stones in a plantation; and at last all my companions were
distributed different ways, and only myself was left. I was now
exceedingly miserable, and thought myself worse off than any
of the rest of my companions; for they could talk to each other,
but I had no person to speak to that I could understand. In this
state I was constantly grieving and pining, and wishing for
death rather than any thing else. While I was in this plantation
the gentleman, to whom I suppose the estate belonged, being
unwell, I was one day sent for to his dwelling house to fan him;
when I came into the room where he was I was very much
affrighted at some things I saw, and the more so as I had seen a
black woman slave as I came through the house, who was
cooking the dinner, and the poor creature was cruelly loaded
with various kinds of iron machines; she had one particularly
on her head, which locked her mouth so fast that she could

scarcely speak; and could not eat nor drink. I was much astonished and shocked at this contrivance, which I afterwards learned was called the iron muzzle. Soon after I had a fan put into my hand, to fan the gentleman while he slept; and so I did indeed with great fear. While he was fast asleep I indulged myself a great deal in looking about the room, which to me appeared very fine and curious. The first object that engaged my attention was a watch which hung on the chimney, and was going. I was quite surprised at the noise it made, and was afraid it would tell the gentleman any thing I might do amiss: and when I immediately after observed a picture hanging in the room, which appeared constantly to look at me, I was still more affrighted, having never seen such things as these before. At one time I thought it was something relative to magic; and not seeing it move I thought it might be some way the whites had to keep their great men when they died, and offer them libation as we used to do to our friendly spirits. In this state of anxiety I remained till my master awoke, when I was dismissed out of the room, to my no small satisfaction and relief; for I thought that these people were all made up of wonders. In this place I was called Jacob; but on board the African snow I was called Michael. I had been some time in this miserable, forlorn, and much dejected state, without having any one to talk to, which made my life a burden, when the kind and unknown hand of the Creator (who in very deed leads the blind in a way they know not) now began to appear, to my comfort; for one day the captain of a merchant ship, called the Industrious Bee, came on some business to my master's house. This gentleman, whose name was Michael Henry Pascal, was a lieutenant in the royal navy, but now commanded this trading ship, which was somewhere in the confines of the county many miles off. While he was at my master's house it happened that he saw me, and liked me so well that he made a purchase of me. I think I have often heard him say he gave thirty or forty pounds sterling for me; but I do not now remember which. However, he meant me for a present to some of his friends in England: and I was sent accordingly from the house of my then master, one Mr. Campbell, to the place where the ship lay; I was conducted on horseback by an elderly black man, (a mode of travelling which appeared very odd to me). When I arrived I was carried on board a fine large ship, loaded with tobacco, &c. and just ready to sail for England. I now thought my condition much mended; I had sails to lie on, and plenty of good victuals to eat; and every body on board used me very kindly, quite contrary to what I had seen of any white people before; I therefore began to think that they were not all of the same disposition. A few days after I was on board we sailed for England. I was still at a loss to conjecture my destiny. By this time, however, I could smatter a little imperfect English; and I wanted to know as well as I could where we were going. Some of the people of the ship used to tell me they were going to carry me back to my own country, and this made me very happy. I was quite rejoiced at the sound of going back; and thought if I should get home what wonders I should have to tell. But I was reserved for another fate, and was soon undeceived when we came within sight of the English coast. While I was on board this ship, my captain and master named me *Gustavus Vasa*. I at that time began to understand him a little, and refused to be called so, and told him as well as I could that I would be called Jacob; but he said I should not, and still called me Gustavus; and when I refused to answer to my new name, which at first I did, it gained me many a cuff; so at length I submitted, and was obliged to bear the present name, by which I have been known ever since. The ship had a very long passage; and on that account we had very short allowance of provisions. Towards the last we had only one pound and a half of bread per week, and about the same quantity of meat, and one quart of water a-day. We spoke with only one vessel the whole time we were at sea, and but once we caught a few fishes. In our extremities the captain and people told me in jest they would kill and eat me; but I thought them in earnest, and was depressed beyond measure, expecting every moment to be my last. While I was in this situation one evening they caught, with a good deal of trouble, a large shark, and got it on board. This gladdened my poor heart exceedingly, as I thought it would serve the people to eat instead of their eating me; but very soon, to my astonishment, they cut off a small part of the tail, and tossed the rest over the side. This renewed my consternation; and I did not know what to think of these white people, though I very much feared they would kill and eat me. There was on board the ship a young lad who had never been at sea before, about four or five years older than myself: his name was Richard Baker. He was a native of America, had received an excellent education, and was of a most amiable temper. Soon after I went on board he shewed me a great deal of partiality and attention, and in return I grew extremely fond of him. We at length became inseparable; and, for the space of two years, he was of very great use to me, and was my constant companion and instructor. Although this dear youth had many slaves of his own, yet he and I have gone through many sufferings together on shipboard; and we have many nights lain in each other's bosoms when we were in great distress. Thus such a friendship was cemented between us as we cherished till his death, which, to my very great sorrow, happened in the year 1759, when he was up the Archipelago, on board his majesty's ship the Preston: an event which I have never ceased to regret, as I lost at once a kind interpreter, an agreeable companion, and a faithful friend; who, at the age of fifteen, discovered a mind superior to prejudice; and who was not ashamed to notice, to associate with, and to be the friend and instructor of one who was ignorant, a stranger, of a different complexion, and a slave! My master had lodged in his mother's house in America: he respected him very much, and made him always eat with him in the cabin. He used often to tell him jocularly that he would kill me to eat. Sometimes he would say to me – the black people were not good to eat, and would ask me if we did not eat people in my country. I said, No: then he said he would kill Dick (as he always called him) first, and afterwards me. Though this hearing relieved my mind a little as to myself, I was alarmed for Dick and whenever he was called I used to be very much afraid he was to be killed; and I would peep and watch to see if they were going to kill him: nor was I free from this consternation till we made the land. One night we lost a man overboard; and the cries and noise were so great and confused, in stopping the ship, that I, who did not know what was the matter, began, as usual, to be very much afraid, and to think they were going to make an offering with me, and perform some magic; which I still believed they dealt in. As the waves were very high I thought the Ruler of the seas was angry, and I expected to be offered up to appease him. They filled my mind with agony, and I could not any more that night close my eyes again to rest. However, when daylight appeared I was a little eased in my mind; but still every time I was called I used to think it was to be killed. Some time after this we saw some very large fish, which I afterwards found were called grampusses.[1] They looked to me extremely terrible, and made their appearance just at dusk; and were so near as to blow the water on the ship's deck. I believed them to be the rulers of the sea; and, as the white people did not make any offerings at any time, I thought they were angry with them: and, at last, what confirmed my belief was, the wind just then died away, and a calm ensued, and in consequence of it the ship stopped going. I supposed that the fish had performed this, and I hid myself in the fore part of the ship, through fear of being offered up to appease them, every minute peeping and quaking: but my good friend Dick came shortly towards me, and I took an opportunity to ask him, as well as I could, what these fish were. Not being able to talk much English, I could but just make him understand my question; and not at all, when I asked him if any offerings were to be made to them: however, he told me these fish would swallow any body; which sufficiently alarmed me. Here he was called away by the captain, who was leaning over the quarter-deck railing and looking at the fish; and most of the people were busied in getting a barrel of pitch to light, for them to play with. The captain now called me to him, having learned some of my apprehensions from Dick; and having diverted himself and others for some time with my fears, which appeared ludicrous enough in my crying and trembling, he dismissed me. The barrel of pitch was now lighted and put over the side into the

---

1   Grampusses are a fierce variety of toothed whales.

water: by this time it was just dark, and the fish went after it; and, to my great joy, I saw them no more.

However, all my alarms began to subside when we got sight of land; and at last the ship arrived at Falmouth, after a passage of thirteen weeks. Every heart on board seemed gladdened on our reaching the shore, and none more than mine. The captain immediately went on shore, and sent on board some fresh provisions, which we wanted very much: we made good use of them, and our famine was soon turned into feasting, almost without ending. It was about the beginning of the spring 1757 when I arrived in England, and I was near twelve years of age at that time. I was very much struck with the buildings and the pavement of the streets in Falmouth; and, indeed, any object I saw filled me with new surprise. One morning, when I got upon deck, I saw it covered all over with the snow that fell over-night: as I had never seen any thing of the kind before, I thought it was salt; so I immediately ran down to the mate and desired him, as well as I could, to come and see how somebody in the night had thrown salt all over the deck. He, knowing what it was, desired me to bring some of it down to him: accordingly I took up a handful of it, which I found very cold indeed; and when I brought it to him he desired me to taste it. I did so, and I was surprised beyond measure. I then asked him what it was; he told me it was snow: but I could not in anywise understand him. He asked me if we had no such thing in my country; and I told him, No. I then asked him the use of it, and who made it; he told me a great man in the heavens, called God: but here again I was to all intents and purposes at a loss to understand him; and the more so, when a little after I saw the air filled with it, in a heavy shower, which fell down on the same day. After this I went to church; and having never been at such a place before, I was again amazed at seeing and hearing the service. I asked all I could about it; and they gave me to understand it was worshipping God, who made us and all things. I was still at a great loss, and soon got into an endless field of inquiries, as well as I was able to speak and ask about things. However, my little friend Dick used to be my best interpreter; for I could make free with him, and he always instructed me with pleasure: and from what I could understand by him of this God, and in seeing these white people did not sell one another, as we did, I was much pleased; and in this I thought they were much happier than we Africans. I was astonished at the wisdom of the white people in all things I saw; but was amazed at their not sacrificing, or making any offerings, and eating with unwashed hands, and touching the dead. I likewise could not help remarking the particular slenderness of their women, which I did not at first like; and I thought they were not so modest and shamefaced as the African women.

I had often seen my master and Dick employed in reading; and I had a great curiosity to talk to the books, as I thought they did; and so to learn how all things had a beginning: for that purpose I have often taken up a book, and have talked to it, and then put my ears to it, when alone, in hopes it would answer me; and I have been very much concerned when I found it remained silent.

My master lodged at the house of a gentleman in Falmouth, who had a fine little daughter about six or seven years of age, and she grew prodigiously fond of me; insomuch that we used to eat together, and had servants to wait on us. I was so much caressed by this family that it often reminded me of the treatment I had received from my little noble African master. After I had been here a few days, I was sent on board of the ship; but the child cried so much after me that nothing could pacify her till I was sent for again. It is ludicrous enough, that I began to fear I should be betrothed to this young lady; and when my master asked me if I would stay there with her behind him, as he was going away with the ship, which had taken in the tobacco again, I cried immediately, and said I would not leave him. At last, by stealth, one night I was sent on board the ship again; and in a little time we sailed for Guernsey, where she was in part owned by a merchant, one Nicholas Doberry. As I was now amongst a people who had not their faces scarred, like some of the African nations where I had been, I was very glad I did not let them ornament me in that manner when I was with them. When we arrived at Guernsey, my master placed me to board and lodge with one of his mates, who had a wife and family there; and some months afterwards he went to England, and left me in care of this mate, together with my friend Dick. This mate had a little daughter, aged about five or six years, with whom I used to be much delighted. I had often observed that when her mother washed her face it looked very rosy; but when she washed mine it did not look so: I therefore tried oftentimes myself if I could not by washing make my face of the same colour as my little play-mate (Mary), but it was all in vain; and I now began to be mortified at the difference in our complexions. This woman behaved to me with great kindness and attention; and taught me every thing in the same manner as she did her own child, and indeed in every respect treated me as such. I remained here till the summer of the year 1757; when my master, being appointed first lieutenant of his majesty's ship the Roebuck, sent for Dick and me, and his old mate: on this we all left Guernsey, and set out for England in a sloop bound for London. As we were coming up towards the Nore, where the Roebuck lay, a man of war's boat came alongside to press our people; on which each man ran to hide himself. I was very much frightened at this, though I did not know what it meant, or what to think or do. However I went and hid myself also under a hencoop. Immediately afterwards the press-gang came on board with their swords drawn, and searched all about, pulled the people out by force, and put them into the boat. At last I was found out also: the man that found me held me up by the heels while they all made their sport of me, I roaring and crying out all the time most lustily: but at last the mate, who was my conductor, seeing this, came to my assistance, and did all he could to pacify me; but all to very little purpose, till I had seen the boat go off. Soon afterwards we came to the Nore, where the Roebuck lay; and, to our great joy, my master came on board to us, and brought us to the ship. When I went on board this large ship, I was amazed indeed to see the quantity of men and the guns. However my surprise began to diminish as my knowledge increased; and I ceased to feel those apprehensions and alarms which had taken such strong possession of me when I first came among the Europeans, and for some time after. I began now to pass to an opposite extreme; I was so far from being afraid of any thing new which I saw, that, after I had been some time in this ship, I even began to long for a battle. My griefs too, which in young minds are not perpetual, were now wearing away; and I soon enjoyed myself pretty well, and felt tolerably easy in my present situation. There was a number of boys on board, which still made it more agreeable; for we were always together, and a great part of our time was spent in play. I remained in this ship a considerable time, during which we made several cruises, and visited a variety of places: among others we were twice in Holland, and brought over several persons of distinction from it, whose names I do not now remember. On the passage, one day, for the diversion of those gentlemen, all the boys were called on the quarter-deck, and were paired proportionably, and then made to fight; after which the gentleman gave the combatants from five to nine shillings each. This was the first time I ever fought with a white boy; and I never knew what it was to have a bloody nose before. This made me fight most desperately; I suppose considerably more than an hour: and at last, both of us being weary, we were parted. I had a great deal of this kind of sport afterwards, in which the captain and the ship's company used very much to encourage me. Sometime afterwards the ship went to Leith in Scotland, and from thence to the Orkneys, where I was surprised in seeing scarcely any night: and from thence we sailed with a great fleet, full of soldiers, for England. All this time we had never come to an engagement, though we were frequently cruising off the coast of France: during which we chased many vessels, and took in all seventeen prizes. I had been learning many of the manoeuvres of the ship during our cruise; and I was several times made to fire the guns. One evening, off Havre de Grace, just as it was growing dark, we were standing off shore, and met with a fine large French-built frigate. We got all things immediately ready for fighting; and I now expected I should be gratified in seeing an engagement, which I had so long wished for in vain. But the very moment the word of command was given to fire we heard those on board the other ship cry "Haul down the jib;" and in that instant she hoisted English colours. There was instantly with us an amazing cry of – Avast! or stop firing; and I think one or two guns had been let off, but happily they did no mischief. We had hailed them several times; but they not hearing, we received no answer, which was the cause of our firing. The boat was then sent on board of her, and she proved to be the Ambuscade man of war, to my no small disappointment. We returned to Portsmouth, without having been in any action, just at the trial of Admiral Byng[1] (whom I saw several times during it): and my master having left the ship, and gone to London for promotion, Dick and I were put on board the Savage sloop of war, and we went in her to assist in bringing off the St. George man of war, that had ran ashore somewhere on the coast. After staying a few weeks on board the Savage, Dick and I were sent on shore at Deal, where we remained some short time, till my master sent for us to London, the place I had long desired exceedingly to see. We therefore both with great pleasure got into a waggon, and came to London, where we were received by a Mr. Guerin, a relation of my master. This gentleman had two sisters, very amiable ladies, who took much notice and great care of me. Though I had desired so much to see London, when I arrived in it I was unfortunately unable to gratify my curiosity; for I had at this time the chilblains to such a degree that I could not stand for several months, and I was obliged to be sent to St. George's Hospital. There I grew so ill, that the doctors wanted to cut my left leg off at different times, apprehending a mortification; but I always said I would rather die than suffer it; and happily (I thank God) I recovered without the operation. After being there several weeks, and just as I had recovered, the small-pox broke out on me, so that I was again confined; and I thought myself now particularly unfortunate. However I soon recovered again; and by this time my master having been promoted to be first lieutenant of the Preston man of war of fifty guns, then new at Deptford, Dick and I

---

1   Admiral John Byng (1704-57) was tried for cowardice and negligence after failing to relieve the British garrison on Minorca, which subsequently surrendered to the French. He was convicted and sentenced to death by a firing squad on March 14, 1757.

were sent on board her, and soon after we went to Holland to bring over the late Duke of C[umberland][1] to England. – While I was in this ship an incident happened, which, though trifling, I beg leave to relate, as I could not help taking particular notice of it, and considering it then as a judgment of God. One morning a young man was looking up to the fore-top, and in a wicked tone, common on shipboard, d——d his eyes about something. Just at the moment some small particles of dirt fell into his left eye, and by the evening it was very much inflamed. The next day it grew worse; and within six or seven days he lost it. From this ship my master was appointed a lieutenant on board the Royal George. When he was going he wished me to stay on board the Preston, to learn the French horn; but the ship being ordered for Turkey I could not think of leaving my master, to whom I was very warmly attached; and I told him if he left me behind it would break my heart. This prevailed on him to take me with him; but he left Dick on board the Preston, whom I embraced at parting for the last time. The Royal George was the largest ship I had ever seen; so that when I came on board of her I was surprised at the number of people, men, women, and children, of every denomination; and the largeness of the guns, many of them also of brass, which I had never seen before. Here were also shops or stalls of every kind of goods, and people crying their different commodities about the ship as in a town. To me it appeared a little world, into which I was again cast without a friend, for I had no longer my dear companion Dick. We did not stay long here. My master was not many weeks on board before he got an appointment to be sixth lieutenant of the Namur, which was then at Spithead, fitting up for Vice-admiral Boscawen,[2] who was going with a large fleet on an expedition against Louisburgh.[3] The crew of the Royal George were turned over to her, and the flag of that

---

1   Duke of Cumberland, William Augustus (1721-65) had triumphed over the Jacobite rebels in 1746, but resigned from army service in 1757 after experiencing severe military losses.
2   Vice-Admiral Edward Boscawen (1711-61) was a distinguished naval leader.
3   Louisburg was situated at the entrance to the St. Lawrence River. Its capture was essential for gaining access to the interior parts of Canada and the Great Lakes regions of North America.

gallant admiral was hoisted on board, the blue at the maintop-gallant mast head. There was a very great fleet of men of war of every description assembled together for this expedition, and I was in hopes soon to have an opportunity of being gratified with a sea-fight. All things being now in readiness, this mighty fleet (for there was also Admiral Cornish's fleet in company, destined for the East Indies) at last weighed anchor, and sailed. The two fleets continued in company for several days, and then parted; Admiral Cornish, in the Lenox, having first saluted our admiral in the Namur, which he returned. We then steered for America; but, by contrary winds, we were driven to Teneriffe, where I was struck with its noted peak. Its prodigious height, and its form, resembling a sugar-loaf, filled me with wonder. We remained in sight of this island some days, and then proceeded for America, which we soon made, and got into a very commodious harbour called St. George, in Halifax, where we had fish in great plenty, and all other fresh provisions. We were here joined by different men of war and transport ships with soldiers; after which, our fleet being increased to a prodigious number of ships of all kinds, we sailed for Cape Breton in Nova Scotia. We had the good and gallant General Wolfe[1] on board our ship, whose affability made him highly esteemed and beloved by all the men. He often honoured me, as well as other boys, with marks of his notice; and saved me once a flogging for fighting with a young gentleman. We arrived at Cape Breton in the summer of 1758: and here the soldiers were to be landed, in order to make an attack upon Louisbourgh. My master had some part in superintending the landing; and here I was in a small measure gratified in seeing an encounter between our men and the enemy. The French were posted on the shore to receive us, and disputed our landing for a long time; but at last they were driven from their trenches, and a complete landing was effected. Our troops pursued them as far as the town of Louisbourgh. In this action many were killed on both sides. One thing remarkable I saw this day: – A lieutenant of the

---

1   Colonel James Wolfe (1727-59) became the major general of the attack on the French-Canadian city of Quebec in 1759. His courageous action and death on the battlefield made him an heroic figure to the British.

Princess Amelia, who, as well as any master, superintended the landing, was giving the word of command, and while his mouth was open a musquet ball went through it, and passed out at his cheek. I had that day in my hand the scalp of an indian king, who was killed in the engagement: the scalp had been taken off by an Highlander. I saw this king's ornaments too, which were very curious, and made of feathers.

Our land forces laid siege to the town of Louisbourgh, while the French men of war were blocked up in the harbour by the fleet, the batteries at the same time playing upon them from the land. This they did with such effect, that one day I saw some of the ships set on fire by the shells from the batteries, and I believe two or three of them were quite burnt. At another time, about fifty boats belonging to the English men of war, commanded by Captain George Balfour of the Aetna fire-ship, and another junior captain, Laforey, attacked and boarded the only two remaining French men of war in the harbour. They also set fire to a seventy-gun ship, but a sixty-four, called the Bienfaisant, they brought off. During my stay here I had often an opportunity of being near Captain Balfour, who was pleased to notice me, and liked me so much that he often asked my master to let him have me, but he would not part with me; and no consideration could have induced me to leave him. At last Louisbourgh was taken, and the English men of war came into the harbour before it, to my very great joy; for I had now more liberty of indulging myself, and I went often on shore. When the ships were in the harbour we had the most beautiful procession on the water I ever saw. All the admirals and captains of the men of war, full dressed, and in their barges, well ornamented with pendants, came alongside of the Namur. The vice-admiral then went on shore in his barge, followed by the other officers in order of seniority, to take possession, as I suppose, of the town and fort. Some time after this the French governor and his lady, and other persons of note, came on board our ship to dine. On this occasion our ships were dressed with colours of all kinds, from the topgallant-mast head to the deck; and this, with the firing of guns, formed a most grand and magnificent spectacle.

As soon as every thing here was settled Admiral Boscawen sailed with part of the fleet for England, leaving some ships behind with Rear-admirals Sir Charles Hardy and Durell. It was now winter; and one evening, during our passage home, about dusk, when we were in the channel, or near soundings, and were beginning to look for land, we descried seven sail of large men of war, which stood off shore. Several people on board of our ship said, as the two fleets were (in forty minutes from the first sight) within hail of each other, that they were English men of war; and some of our people even began to name some of the ships. By this time both fleets began to mingle, and our admiral ordered his flag to be hoisted. At that instant the other fleet, which were French, hoisted their ensigns, and gave us a broadside as they passed by. Nothing could create greater surprise and confusion among us than this: the wind was high, the sea rough, and we had our lower and middle deck guns housed in, so that not a single gun on board was ready to be fired at any of the French ships. However, the Royal William and the Somerset being our sternmost ships, became a little prepared, and each gave the French ships a broadside as they passed by. I afterwards heard this was a French squadron, commanded by Mons. Conflans; and certainly had the Frenchmen known our condition, and had a mind to fight us, they might have done us great mischief. But we were not long before we were prepared for an engagement. Immediately many things were tossed overboard; the ships were made ready for fighting as soon as possible; and about ten at night we had bent a new main sail, the old one being split. Being now in readiness for fighting, we wore ship, and stood after the French fleet, who were one or two ships in number more than we. However we gave them chase, and continued pursuing them all night; and at day-light we saw six of them, all large ships of the line, and an English East Indiaman, a prize they had taken. We chased them all day till between three and four o'clock in the evening, when we came up with, and passed within a musquet shot of, one seventy-four gun ship, and the Indiaman also, who now hoisted her colours, but immediately hauled them down again. On this we made a signal for the other ships to take possession of her; and, supposing the man of war would likewise strike, we cheered, but she did not; though if we had fired into her, from being so near, we must have taken her. To my utter surprise the Somerset, who was the next ship a-stern of the Namur, made way likewise; and, thinking they were sure of this French ship, they cheered in the same manner, but still continued to follow us. The French Commodore was about a gun-shot ahead of all, running from us with all speed; and about four o'clock he carried his foretopmast overboard. This caused another loud cheer with us; and a little after the topmast came close by us; but, to our great surprise, instead of coming up with her, we found she went as fast as ever, if not faster. The sea grew now much smoother; and the wind lulling, the seventy-four gun ship we had passed came again by us in the very same direction, and so near, that we heard her people talk as she went by; yet not a shot was fired on either side; and about five or six o'clock, just as it grew dark, she joined her commodore. We chased all night; but the next day they were out of sight, so that we saw no more of them; and we only had the old Indiaman (called Carnarvon I think) for our trouble. After this we stood in for the channel, and soon made the land; and, about the close of the year 1758-9, we got safe to St. Helen's. Here the Namur ran aground; and also another large ship astern of us; but, by starting our water, and tossing many things overboard to lighten her, we got the ships off without any damage. We stayed for a short time at Spithead, and then went into Portsmouth harbour to refit; from whence the admiral went to London; and my master and I soon followed, with a press-gang, as we wanted some hands to complete our complement.

CHAP. IV.

The author is baptized — Narrowly escapes drowning — Goes on an expedition to the Mediterranean — Incidents he met with there — Is witness to an engagement between some English and French ships — A particular account of the celebrated engagement between Admiral Boscawen and Mons. Le Clue, off Cape Logas,[1] in August 1759 — Dreadful explosion of a French ship — The author sails for England — His master appointed to the command of a fire-ship — Meets a negro boy, from whom he experiences much benevolence — Prepares for an expedition against Belle-Isle[2] — A remarkable story of a disaster which befel his ship — Arrives at Belle-Isle — Operations of the landing and siege — The author's danger and distress, with his manner of extricating himself — Surrender of Belle-Isle — Transactions afterwards on the coast of France — Remarkable instance of kidnapping — The author returns to England — Hears a talk of peace, and expects his freedom — His ship sails for Deptford to be paid off, and when he arrives there he is suddenly seized by his master and carried forcibly on board a West India ship and sold.

IT was now between two and three years since I first came to England, a great part of which I had spent at sea; so that I became inured to that service, and began to consider myself as happily situated; for my master treated me always extremely well; and my attachment and gratitude to him were very great. From the various scenes I had beheld on ship-board, I soon grew a stranger to terror of every kind, and was, in that respect at least, almost an Englishman. I have often reflected with surprise that I never felt half the alarm at any of the numerous dangers I have been in, that I was filled with at the first sight of the Europeans, and at every act of theirs, even the most trifling, when I first came amongst them, and for some time afterwards. That fear, however, which was the effect of my ignorance, wore

---

1   Cape Logas: Equiano misspells Cape Lagos situated on the southern end of Portugal. A naval battle was fought at Lagos Bay where Admiral Boscawen defeated the French.

2   Belle-Isle: Belle-Ile located off the French coast in the Bay of Biscay. The siege and surrender of the French garrison on the island took place from April to June, 1761.

away as I began to know them. I could now speak English tolerably well, and I perfectly understood every thing that was said. I not only felt myself quite easy with these new countrymen, but relished their society and manners. I no longer looked upon them as spirits, but as men superior to us; and therefore I had the stronger desire to resemble them; to imbibe their spirit, and imitate their manners; I therefore embraced every occasion of improvement; and every new thing that I observed I treasured up in my memory. I had long wished to be able to read and write; and for this purpose I took every opportunity to gain instruction, but had made as yet very little progress. However, when I went to London with my master, I had soon an opportunity of improving myself, which I gladly embraced. Shortly after my arrival, he sent me to wait upon the Miss Guerins, who had treated me with much kindness when I was there before; and they sent me to school.

While I was attending these ladies their servants told me I could not go to Heaven unless I was baptized. This made me very uneasy; for I had now some faint idea of a future state: accordingly I communicated my anxiety to the eldest Miss Guerin, with whom I was become a favourite, and pressed her to have me baptized; when to my great joy she told me I should. She had formerly asked my master to let me be baptized, but he had refused; however she now insisted on it; and he being under some obligation to her brother complied with her request; so I was baptized in St. Margaret's church, Westminster, in February 1759, by my present name. The clergyman, at the same time, gave me a book, called a Guide to the Indians, written by the Bishop of Sodor and Man.[1] On this occasion Miss Guerin did me the honour to stand as godmother, and afterwards gave me a treat. I used to attend these ladies about the town, in which service I was extremely happy; as I had thus many opportunities of seeing London, which I desired of all things. I was sometimes, however, with my master at his rendezvous-house, which was at the foot of Westminster-bridge. Here I used to enjoy myself in playing about the bridge

---

1   Thomas Wilson (1697-1755) wrote *An Essay towards an Instruction for the Indians* (London, 1740).

stairs, and often in the watermen's wherries,[1] with other boys. On one of these occasions there was another boy with me in a wherry, and we went out into the current of the river: while we were there two more stout boys came to us in another wherry, and, abusing us for taking the boat, desired me to get into the other wherry-boat. Accordingly I went to get out of the wherry I was in; but just as I had got one of my feet into the other boat the boys shoved it off, so that I fell into the Thames; and, not being able to swim, I should unavoidably have been drowned, but for the assistance of some watermen who providentially came to my relief.

The Namur being again got ready for sea, my master, with his gang, was ordered on board; and, to my no small grief, I was obliged to leave my school-master, whom I liked very much, and always attended while I stayed in London, to repair on board with my master. Nor did I leave my kind patronesses, the Miss Guerins, without uneasiness and regret. They often used to teach me to read, and took great pains to instruct me in the principles of religion and the knowledge of God. I therefore parted from those amiable ladies with reluctance; after receiving from them many friendly cautions how to conduct myself, and some valuable presents.

When I came to Spithead, I found we were destined for the Mediterranean, with a large fleet, which was now ready to put to sea. We only waited for the arrival of the admiral, who soon came on board; and about the beginning of the spring 1759, having weighed anchor, and got under way, sailed for the Mediterranean; and in eleven days, from the Land's End, we got to Gibraltar. While we were here I used to be often on shore, and got various fruits in great plenty, and very cheap.

I had frequently told several people, in my excursions on shore, the story of my being kidnapped with my sister, and of our being separated, as I have related before; and I had as often expressed my anxiety for her fate, and my sorrow at having never met her again. One day, when I was on shore, and mentioning these circumstances to some persons, one of them told

---

1   Wherries: long rowboats.

me he knew where my sister was, and, if I would accompany him, he would bring me to her. Improbable as this story was I believed it immediately, and agreed to go with him, while my heart leaped for joy: and, indeed, he conducted me to a black young woman, who was so like my sister, that, at first sight, I really thought it was her: but I was quickly undeceived; and, on talking to her, I found her to be of another nation.

While we lay here the Preston came in from the Levant. As soon as she arrived, my master told me I should now see my old companion, Dick, who had gone in her when she sailed for Turkey. I was much rejoiced at this news, and expected every minute to embrace him; and when the captain came on board of our ship, which he did immediately after, I ran to inquire after my friend; but, with inexpressible sorrow, I learned from the boat's crew that the dear youth was dead! and that they had brought his chest, and all his other things, to my master: these he afterwards gave to me, and I regarded them as a memorial of my friend, whom I loved, and grieved for, as a brother.

While we were at Gibraltar, I saw a soldier hanging by his heels, at one of the moles:[1] I thought this a strange sight, as I had seen a man hanged in London by his neck. At another time I saw the master of a frigate towed to shore on a grating, by several of the men of war's boats, and discharged the fleet, which I understood was a mark of disgrace for cowardice. On board the same ship there was also a sailor hung up at the yard-arm.

After lying at Gibraltar for some time, we sailed up the Mediterranean a considerable way above the Gulf of Lyons; where we were one night overtaken with a terrible gale of wind, much greater than any I had ever yet experienced. The sea ran so high that, though all the guns were well housed, there was a great reason to fear their getting loose, the ship rolled so much; and if they had it must have proved our destruction. After we had cruised here for a short time, we came to Barcelona, a Spanish sea-port, remarkable for its silk manufactures. Here the ships were all to be watered; and my

---

1   [Equiano's note] He had drowned himself in endeavouring to desert. [Moles: long piers.]

master, who spoke different languages, and used often to interpret for the admiral, superintended the watering of ours. For that purpose he and the officers of the other ships, who were on the same service, had tents pitched in the bay; and the Spanish soldiers were stationed along the shore, I suppose to see that no depredations were committed by our men.

I used constantly to attend my master; and I was charmed with this place. All the time we stayed it was like a fair with the natives, who brought us fruits of all kinds, and sold them to us much cheaper than I got them in England. They used also to bring wine down to us in hog and sheep skins, which diverted me very much. The Spanish officers here treated our officers with great politeness and attention; and some of them, in particular, used to come often to my master's tent to visit him; where they would sometimes divert themselves by mounting me on the horses or mules, so that I could not fall, and setting them off at full gallop; my imperfect skill in horsemanship all the while affording them no small entertainment. After the ships were watered, we returned to our old station of cruizing off Toulon, for the purpose of intercepting a fleet of French men of war that lay there. One Sunday, in our cruise, we came off a place where there were two small French frigates lying in shore; and our admiral, thinking to take or destroy them, sent two ships in after them – the Culloden and the Conqueror. They soon came up to the Frenchmen; and I saw a smart fight here, both by sea and land: for the frigates were covered by batteries, and they played upon our ships most furiously, which they as furiously returned, and for a long time a constant firing was kept up on all sides at an amazing rate. At last one frigate sunk; but the people escaped, though not without much difficulty: and a little after some of the people left the other frigate also, which was a mere wreck. However, our ships did not venture to bring her away, they were so much annoyed from the batteries, which raked them both in going and coming: their topmasts were shot away, and they were otherwise so much shattered, that the admiral was obliged to send in many boats to tow them back to the fleet. I afterwards sailed with a man who fought in one of the French batteries during the engagement, and he told me our ships had done considerable mischief that day on shore and in the batteries.

After this we sailed for Gibraltar, and arrived there about August 1759. Here we remained with all our sails unbent, while the fleet was watering and doing other necessary things. While we were in this situation, one day the admiral, with most of the principal officers, and many people of all stations, being on shore, about seven o'clock in the evening we were alarmed by signals from the frigates stationed for that purpose; and in an instant there was a general cry that the French fleet was out, and just passing through the streights. The admiral immediately came on board with some other officers; and it is impossible to describe the noise, hurry and confusion throughout the whole fleet, in bending their sails and slipping their cables; many people and ships' boats were left on shore in the bustle. We had two captains on board of our ship who came away in the hurry and left their ships to follow. We shewed lights from the gun-whale to the main topmast-head; and all our lieutenants were employed amongst the fleet to tell the ships not to wait for their captains, but to put the sails to the yards, slip their cables and follow us; and in this confusion of making ready for fighting we set out for sea in the dark after the French fleet. Here I could have exclaimed with Ajax,

> Oh Jove! O father! if it be thy will
> That we must perish, we thy will obey,
> But let us perish by the light of day.[1]

They had got the start of us so far that we were not able to come up with them during the night; but at day-light we saw seven sail of the line of battle some miles ahead. We immediately chased them till about four o'clock in the evening, when our ships came up with them; and, though we were about fifteen large ships, our gallant admiral only fought them with his own division, which consisted of seven; so that we were just ship for ship. We passed by the whole of the enemy's fleet in

---

1 Alexander Pope (1688-1744); Equiano alters the quote from Pope's translation of Homer's *Iliad* (1720), 17.728-32.

order to come at their commander, Mons. La Clue, who was in the Ocean, an eighty-four gun ship: as we passed they all fired on us; and at one time three of them fired together, continuing to do so for some time. Notwithstanding which our admiral would not suffer a gun to be fired at any of them, to my astonishment; but made us lie on our bellies on the deck till we came quite close to the Ocean, who was ahead of them all; when we had orders to pour the whole three tiers into her at once.

The engagement now commenced with great fury on both sides: the Ocean immediately returned our fire, and we continued engaged with each other for some time; during which I was frequently stunned with the thundering of the great guns, whose dreadful contents hurried many of my companions into awful eternity. At last the French line was entirely broken, and we obtained the victory, which was immediately proclaimed with loud huzzas and acclamations. We took three prizes, La Modeste, of sixty-four guns, and Le Temeraire and Centaur, of seventy-four guns each. The rest of the French ships took to flight with all the sail they could crowd. Our ship being very much damaged, and quite disabled from pursuing the enemy, the admiral immediately quitted her, and went in the broken and only boat we had left on board the Newark, with which, and some other ships, he went after the French. The Ocean, and another large French ship, called the Redoubtable, endeavouring to escape, ran ashore at Cape Logas, on the coast of Portugal; and the French admiral and some of the crew got ashore; but we, finding it impossible to get the ships off, set fire to them both. About midnight I saw the Ocean blow up, with a most dreadful explosion. I never beheld a more awful scene. In less than a minute the midnight for a certain space seemed turned into day by the blaze, which was attended with a noise louder and more terrible than thunder, that seemed to rend every element around us.

My station during the engagement was on the middle-deck, where I was quartered with another boy, to bring powder to the aftermost gun; and here I was a witness of the dreadful fate of many of my companions, who, in the twinkling of an eye, were dashed in pieces, and launched into eternity. Happily I escaped unhurt, though the shot and splinters flew thick about me during the whole fight. Towards the latter part of it my master was wounded, and I saw him carried down to the surgeon; but though I was much alarmed for him and wished to assist him I dared not leave my post. At this station my gun-mate (a partner in bringing powder for the same gun) and I ran a very great risk for more than half an hour of blowing up the ship. For, when we had taken the cartridges out of the boxes, the bottoms of many of them proving rotten, the powder ran all about the deck, near the match tub: we scarcely had water enough at the last to throw on it. We were also, from our employment, very much exposed to the enemy's shots; for we had to go through nearly the whole length of the ship to bring the powder. I expected therefore every minute to be my last; especially when I saw our men fall so thick about me; but, wishing to guard as much against the dangers as possible, at first I thought it would be safest not to go for the powder till the Frenchmen had fired their broadside; and then, while they were charging, I could go and come with my powder: but immediately afterwards I thought this caution was fruitless; and, cheering myself with the reflection that there was a time allotted for me to die as well as to be born, I instantly cast off all fear or thought whatever of death, and went through the whole of my duty with alacrity; pleasing myself with the hope, if I survived the battle, of relating it and the dangers I had escaped to the dear Miss Guerin, and others, when I should return to London.

Our ship suffered very much in this engagement; for, besides the number of our killed and wounded, she was almost torn to pieces, and our rigging so much shattered, that our mizen-mast and main-yard, &c. hung over the side of the ship; so that we were obliged to get many carpenters, and others from some of the ships of the fleet, to assist in setting us in some tolerable order; and, notwithstanding, it took us some time before we were completely refitted; after which we left Admiral Broder-ick to command, and we, with the prizes, steered for England. On the passage, and as soon as my master was something recovered of his wounds, the admiral appointed him captain of the

Ætna fire-ship, on which he and I left the Namur, and went on board of her at sea. I liked this little ship very much. I now became the captain's steward, in which situation I was very happy: for I was extremely well treated by all on board; and I had leisure to improve myself in reading and writing. The latter I had learned a little of before I left the Namur, as there was a school on board. When we arrived at Spithead the Ætna went into Portsmouth harbour to refit, which being done, we returned to Spithead and joined a large fleet that was thought to be intended against the Havannah; but about that time the king died:[1] whether that prevented the expedition I know not; but it caused our ship to be stationed at Cowes, in the isle of Wight, till the beginning of the year sixty-one. Here I spent my time very pleasantly; I was much on shore all about this delightful island, and found the inhabitants very civil.

While I was here, I met with a trifling incident, which surprised me agreeably. I was one day in a field belonging to a gentleman who had a black boy about my own size; this boy having observed me from his master's house, was transported at the sight of one of his own countrymen, and ran to meet me with the utmost haste. I not knowing what he was about turned a little out of his way at first, but to no purpose: he soon came close to me and caught hold of me in his arms as if I had been his brother, though we had never seen each other before. After we had talked together for some time he took me to his master's house, where I was treated very kindly. This benevolent boy and I were very happy in frequently seeing each other till about the month of March 1761, when our ship had orders to fit out again for another expedition. When we got ready, we joined a very large fleet at Spithead, commanded by Commodore Keppel, which was destined against Belle-Isle, and with a number of transport ships with troops on board to make a descent on the place. We sailed once more in quest of fame. I longed to engage in new adventures and see fresh wonders.

I had a mind on which every thing uncommon made its full impression, and every event which I considered as marvellous.

---

1 King George II died on October 25, 1760, and was succeeded by his grandson King George III.

Every extraordinary escape, or signal deliverance, either of myself or others, I looked upon to be effected by the interposition of Providence. We had not been above ten days at sea before an incident of this kind happened; which, whatever credit it may obtain from the reader, made no small impression on my mind.

We had on board a gunner, whose name was John Mondle; a man of very indifferent morals. This man's cabin was between the decks, exactly over where I lay, abreast of the quarter-deck ladder. One night, the 20th of April, being terrified with a dream, he awoke in so great a fright that he could not rest in his bed any longer, nor even remain in his cabin; and he went upon deck about four o'clock in the morning extremely agitated. He immediately told those on the deck of the agonies of his mind, and the dream which occasioned it; in which he said he had seen many things very awful, and had been warned by St. Peter to repent, who told him time was short. This he said had greatly alarmed him, and he was determined to alter his life. People generally mock the fears of others when they are themselves in safety; and some of his shipmates who heard him only laughed at him. However, he made a vow that he never would drink strong liquors again; and he immediately got a light, and gave away his sea-stores of liquor. After which, his agitation still continuing, he began to read the Scriptures, hoping to find some relief; and soon afterwards he laid himself down again on his bed, and endeavoured to compose himself to sleep, but to no purpose; his mind still continuing in a state of agony. By this time it was exactly half after seven in the morning: I was then under the half-deck at the great cabin door; and all at once I heard the people in the waist cry out, most fearfully – "The Lord have mercy upon us! We are all lost! The Lord have mercy upon us!" Mr. Mondle hearing the cries, immediately ran out of his cabin; and we were instantly struck by the Lynne, a forty-gun ship, Captain Clark, which nearly ran us down. This ship had just put about, and was by the wind, but had not got full headway, or we must all have perished; for the wind was brisk. However, before Mr. Mondle had got four steps from his cabin-door, she struck our ship with her cut-water right in the middle of his bed and cabin, and ran it up to the combings of the quarter-deck hatchway, and above three feet below water, and in a minute there was not a bit of wood to be seen where Mr. Mondle's cabin stood; and he was so near being killed that some of the splinters tore his face. As Mr. Mondle must inevitably have perished from this accident had he not been alarmed in the very extraordinary way I have related, I could not help regarding this as an awful interposition of Providence for his preservation. The two ships for some time swinged alongside of each other; for ours being a fireship, our grappling-irons caught the Lynne every way, and the yards and rigging went at an astonishing rate. Our ship was in such a shocking condition that we all thought she would instantly go down, and every one ran for their lives, and got as well as they could on board the Lynne; but our lieutenant being the aggressor, he never quitted the ship. However, when we found she did not sink immediately, the captain came on board again, and encouraged our people to return and try to save her. Many on this came back, but some would not venture. Some of the ships in the fleet, seeing our situation, immediately sent their boats to our assistance; but it took us the whole day to save the ship with all their help. And by using every possible means, particularly frapping her together with many hawsers, and putting a great quantity of tallow below water where she was damaged, she was kept together: but it was well we did not meet with any gales of wind, or we must have gone to pieces; for we were in such a crazy condition that we had ships to attend us till we arrived at Belle-Isle, the place of our destination; and then we had all things taken out of the ship, and she was properly repaired. This escape of Mr. Mondle, which he, as well as myself, always considered as a singular act of Providence, I believe had a great influence on his life and conduct ever afterwards.

Now that I am on this subject I beg leave to relate another instance or two which strongly raised my belief of the particular interposition of Heaven, and which might not otherwise have found a place here, from their insignificance. I belonged for a few days in the year 1758 to the Jason, of fifty-four guns, at

Plymouth; and one night, when I was on board, a woman, with a child at her breast, fell from the upper-deck down into the hold, near the keel. Every one thought that the mother and child must be both dashed to pieces; but, to our great surprise, neither of them was hurt. I myself one day fell headlong from the upper deck of the Etna down the after-hold, when the ballast was out; and all who saw me fall cried out I was killed: but I received not the least injury. And in the same ship a man fell from the mast-head on the deck without being hurt. In these, and in many more instances, I thought I could plainly trace the hand of God, without whose permission a sparrow cannot fall. I began to raise my fear from man to him alone, and to call daily on his holy name with fear and reverence: and I trust he heard my supplications, and graciously condescended to answer me according to his holy word, and to implant the seeds of piety in me, even one of the meanest of his creatures.

When we had refitted our ship, and all things were in readiness for attacking the place, the troops on board the transports were ordered to disembark; and my master, as a junior captain, had a share in the command of the landing. This was on the 8th of April. The French were drawn up on the shore, and had made every disposition to oppose the landing of our men, only a small part of them this day being able to effect it; most of them, after fighting with great bravery, were cut off; and General Crawford, with a number of others, were taken prisoners. In this day's engagement we had also our lieutenant killed.

On the 21st of April we renewed our efforts to land the men, while all the men of war were stationed along the shore to cover it, and fired at the French batteries and breastworks from early in the morning till about four o'clock in the evening, when our soldiers effected a safe landing. They immediately attacked the French; and, after a sharp encounter, forced them from the batteries. Before the enemy retreated they blew up several of them, lest they should fall into our hands. Our men now proceeded to besiege the citadel, and my master was ordered on shore to superintend the landing of all the materials necessary for carrying on the siege; in which service I mostly attended him. While I was there I went about to different parts of the island; and one day, particularly, my curiosity almost cost me my life. I wanted very much to see the mode of charging the mortars and letting off the shells, and for that purpose I went to an English battery that was but a very few yards from the walls of the citadel. There, indeed, I had the opportunity of completely gratifying myself in seeing the whole operation, and that not without running a very great risk, both from the English shells that burst while I was there, but likewise from those of the French. One of the largest of their shells bursted within nine or ten yards of me: there was a single rock close by, about the size of a butt; and I got instant shelter under it in time to avoid the fury of the shell. Where it burst the earth was torn in such a manner that two or three butts might easily have gone into the hole it made, and it threw great quantities of stones and dirt to a considerable distance. Three shot were also fired at me and another boy who was along with me, one of them in particular seemed

Wing'd with red lightning and impetuous rage;[1]

for with a most dreadful sound it hissed close by me, and struck a rock at a little distance, which it shattered to pieces. When I saw what perilous circumstances I was in, I attempted to return the nearest way I could find, and thereby I got between the English and the French centinels. An English serjeant, who commanded the outposts, seeing me, and surprised how I came there, (which was by stealth along the seashore), reprimanded me very severely for it, and instantly took the centinel off his post into custody, for his negligence in suffering me to pass the lines. While I was in this situation I observed at a little distance a French horse, belonging to some islanders, which I thought I would now mount, for the greater expedition of getting off. Accordingly I took some cord which I had about me, and making a kind of bridle of it, I put it round the horse's head, and the tame beast very quietly suffered me to tie him thus and mount him. As soon as I was on the horse's back I began to kick and

---

1   John Milton (1608-1674), *Paradise Lost*, l.175 (London, 1674).

beat him, and try every means to make him go quick, but all to very little purpose: I could not drive him out of a slow pace. While I was creeping along, still within reach of the enemy's shot, I met with a servant well mounted on an English horse. I immediately stopped; and, crying, told him my case; and begged of him to help me, and this he effectually did; for, having a fine large whip, he began to lash my horse with it so severely, that he set off full speed with me towards the sea, while I was quite unable to hold or manage him. In this manner I went along till I came to a craggy precipice. I now could not stop my horse; and my mind was filled with apprehensions of my deplorable fate should he go down the precipice, which he appeared fully disposed to do: I therefore thought I had better throw myself off him at once, which I did immediately with a great deal of dexterity, and fortunately escaped unhurt. As soon as I found myself at liberty I made the best of my way for the ship, determined I would not be so fool-hardy again in a hurry.

We continued to besiege the citadel till June, when it surrendered. During the siege I have counted above sixty shells and carcases in the air at once. When this place was taken I went through the citadel, and in the bomb-proofs under it, which were cut in the solid rock; and I thought it a surprising place, both for strength and building: notwithstanding which our shots and shells had made amazing devastation, and ruinous heaps all around it.

After the taking of this island our ships, with some others commanded by Commodore Stanhope in the Swiftsure, went to Basse-road, where we blocked up a French fleet. Our ships were there from June till February following; and in that time I saw a great many scenes of war, and stratagems on both sides to destroy each others fleet. Sometimes we would attack the French with some ships of the line; at other times with boats; and frequently we made prizes. Once or twice the French attacked us by throwing shells with their bomb-vessels: and one day as a French vessel was throwing shells at our ships she broke from her springs, behind the isle of I de Re: the tide being complicated, she came within a gun shot of the Nassau; but the

Nassau could not bring a gun to bear upon her, and thereby the Frenchman got off. We were twice attacked by their fire-floats, which they chained together, and then let them float down with the tide; but each time we sent boats with graplings, and towed them safe out of the fleet.

We had different commanders while we were at this place, Commodores Stanhope, Dennis, Lord Howe, &c. From hence, before the Spanish war began, our ship and the Wasp sloop were sent to St. Sebastian in Spain, by Commodore Stanhope; and Commodore Dennis afterwards sent our ship as a cartel to Bayonne in France,[1] after which[2] we went in February in 1762 to Belle-Isle, and there stayed till the summer, when we left it, and returned to Portsmouth.

After our ship was fitted out again for service, in September she went to Guernsey, where I was very glad to see my old hostess, who was now a widow, and my former little charming companion, her daughter. I spent some time here very happily with them, till October, when we had orders to repair to Portsmouth. We parted from each other with a great deal of affection; and I promised to return soon, and see them again, not knowing what all-powerful fate had determined for me. Our ship having arrived at Portsmouth, we went into the harbour, and remained there till the latter end of November, when we heard great talk about peace; and, to our very great joy, in the beginning of December we had orders to go up to London with our ship to be paid off. We received this news with loud

---

1 [Equiano's note] Among others whom we brought from Bayonne, were two gentleman, who had been in the West Indies, where they sold slaves; and they confessed they had made at one time a false bill of sale, and sold two Portuguese white men among a lot of slaves.

2 [Equiano's note] Some people have it, that sometimes shortly before persons die their ward has been seen; that is, some spirit exactly in their likeness, though they are themselves at other places at the same time. One day while we were at Bayonne Mr. Mondle saw one of our men, as he thought, in the gun-room; and a little after, coming on the quarter-deck, he spoke of some circumstances of this man to some of the officers. They told him that the man was then out of the ship, in one of the boats with the Lieutenant: but Mr. Mondle would not believe it, and we searched the ship, when he found the man was actually out of her; and when the boat returned some time afterwards, we found the man had been drowned at the very time Mr. Mondle thought he saw him.

huzzas, and every other demonstration of gladness; and nothing but mirth was to be seen throughout every part of the ship. I too was not without my share of the general joy on this occasion. I thought now of nothing but being freed, and working for myself, and thereby getting money to enable me to get a good education; for I always had a great desire to be able at least to read and write; and while I was on ship-board I had endeavoured to improve myself in both. While I was in the Ætna particularly, the captain's clerk taught me to write, and gave me a smattering of arithmetic as far as the rule of three. There was also one Daniel Queen, about forty years of age, a man very well educated, who messed with me on board this ship, and he likewise dressed and attended the captain. Fortunately this man soon became very much attached to me, and took very great pains to instruct me in many things. He taught me to shave and dress hair a little, and also to read in the Bible, explaining many passages to me, which I did not comprehend. I was wonderfully surprised to see the laws and rules of my country written almost exactly here; a circumstance which I believe tended to impress our manners and customs more deeply on my memory. I used to tell him of this resemblance; and many a time we have sat up the whole night together at this employment. In short, he was like a father to me; and some even used to call me after his name; they also styled me the black Christian. Indeed I almost loved him with the affection of a son. Many things I have denied myself that he might have them; and when I used to play at marbles or any other game, and won a few halfpence, or got any little money, which I sometimes did, for shaving any one, I used to buy him a little sugar or tobacco, as far as my stock of money would go. He used to say, that he and I never should part; and that when our ship was paid off, as I was as free as himself or any other man on board, he would instruct me in his business, by which I might gain a good livelihood. This gave me new life and spirits; and my heart burned within me, while I thought the time long till I obtained my freedom. For though my master had not promised it to me, yet, besides the assurances I had received that he had no right to detain me, he always treated me with the greatest kindness, and reposed in me an unbounded confidence; he even paid attention to my morals; and would never suffer me to deceive him, or tell lies, of which he used to tell me the consequences; and that if I did so God would not love me; so that, from all this tenderness, I had never once supposed, in all my dreams of freedom, that he would think of detaining me any longer than I wished.

In pursuance of our orders we sailed from Portsmouth for the Thames, and arrived at Deptford the 10th of December, where we cast anchor just as it was high water. The ship was up about half an hour, when my master ordered the barge to be manned; and all in an instant, without having before given me the least reason to suspect any thing of the matter, he forced me into the barge; saying, I was going to leave him, but he would take care I should not. I was so struck with the unexpectedness of this proceeding, that for some time I did not make a reply, only I made an offer to go for my books and chest of clothes, but he swore I should not move out of his sight; and if I did he would cut my throat, at the same time taking his hanger.[1] I began, however, to collect myself; and, plucking up courage, I told him I was free, and he could not by law serve me so. But this only enraged him the more; and he continued to swear, and said he would soon let me know whether he would or not, and at that instant sprung himself into the barge from the ship, to the astonishment and sorrow of all on board. The tide, rather unluckily for me, had just turned downward, so that we quickly fell down the river along with it, till we came among some outward-bound West Indiamen; for he was resolved to put me on board the first vessel he could get to receive me. The boat's crew, who pulled against their will, became quite faint different times, and would have gone ashore; but he would not let them. Some of them strove then to cheer me, and told me he could not sell me, and that they would stand by me, which revived me a little; and I still entertained hopes; for as they pulled along he asked some vessels to receive me, but they could not. But, just as we had got a little below Gravesend, we came alongside of a

---

1 Hanger: a short sword.

ship which was going away the next tide for the West Indies; her name was the Charming Sally, Captain James Doran; and my master went on board and agreed with him for me; and in a little time I was sent for into the cabin. When I came there Captain Doran asked me if I knew him; I answered that I did not; "Then," said he "you are now my slave." I told him my master could not sell me to him, nor to any one else. "Why," said he, "did not your master buy you?" I confessed he did. "But I have served him," said I, "many years, and he has taken all my wages and prize-money, for I only got one sixpence during the war; besides this I have been baptized; and by the laws of the land no man has a right to sell me:" And I added, that I had heard a lawyer and others at different times tell my master so. They both then said that those people who told me so were not my friends; but I replied – it was very extraordinary that other people did not know the law as well as they. Upon this Captain Doran said I talked too much English; and if I did not behave myself well, and be quiet, he had a method on board to make me. I was too well convinced of his power over me to doubt what he said; and my former sufferings in the slave-ship presenting themselves to my mind, the recollection of them made me shudder. However, before I retired I told them that as I could not get any right among men here I hoped I should hereafter in Heaven; and I immediately left the cabin, filled with resentment and sorrow. The only coat I had with me my master took away with him, and said if my prize-money had been £10,000 he had a right to it all, and would have taken it. I had about nine guineas, which, during my long sea-faring life, I had scraped together from trifling perquisites and little ventures; and I hid it that instant, lest my master should take that from me likewise, still hoping that by some means or other I should make my escape to the shore; and indeed some of my old shipmates told me not to despair, for they would get me back again; and that, as soon as they could get their pay, they would immediately come to Portsmouth to me, where this ship was going: but, alas! all my hopes were baffled, and the hour of my deliverance was yet far off. My master, having soon concluded his bargain with the captain, came out of the cabin, and

he and his people got into the boat and put off; I followed
them with aching eyes as long as I could, and when they were
out of sight I threw myself on the deck, while my heart was
ready to burst with sorrow and anguish.

CHAP. V.

The author's reflections on his situation – Is deceived by a promise of being delivered – His despair at sailing for the West Indies – Arrives at Montserrat, where he is sold to Mr. King – Various interesting instances of oppression, cruelty, and extortion, which the author saw practiced upon the slaves in the West Indies during his captivity from the year 1763 to 1766 – Address on it to the planters.

THUS, at the moment I expected all my toils to end, was I plunged, as I supposed, in a new slavery; in comparison of which all my service hitherto had been "perfect freedom;" and whose horrors, always present to my mind, now rushed on it with tenfold aggravation. I wept very bitterly for some time: and began to think that I must have done something to displease the Lord, that he thus punished me so severely. This filled me with painful reflections on my past conduct; I recollected that on the morning of our arrival at Deptford I had rashly sworn that as soon as we reached London I would spend the day in rambling and sport. My conscience smote me for this unguarded expression: I felt that the Lord was able to disappoint me in all things, and immediately considered my present situation as a judgment of Heaven on account of my presumption in swearing: I therefore, with contrition of heart, acknowledged my transgression to God, and poured out my soul before him with unfeigned repentance, and with earnest supplications I besought him not to abandon me in my distress, nor cast me from his mercy for ever. In a little time my grief, spent with its own violence, began to subside; and after the first confusion of my thoughts was over I reflected with more calmness on my present condition: I considered that trials and disappointments are sometimes for our good, and I thought God might perhaps have permitted this in order to teach me wisdom and resignation; for he had hitherto shadowed me with the wings of his mercy, and by his invisible but powerful hand brought me the way I knew not. These reflections gave me a little comfort, and I rose at last from the deck with dejection and sorrow in my countenance, yet mixed with some faint hope that the *Lord would appear* for my deliverance.

Soon afterwards, as my new master was going ashore, he called me to him, and told me to behave myself well, and do the business of the ship the same as any of the rest of the boys, and that I should fare the better for it; but I made him no answer. I was then asked if I could swim, and I said, No. However I was made to go under the deck, and was well watched. The next tide the ship got under way, and soon after arrived at the Mother Bank, Portsmouth; where she waited a few days for some of the West India convoy. While I was here I tried every means I could devise amongst the people of the ship to get me a boat from the shore, as there was none suffered to come alongside of the ship; and their own, whenever it was used, was hoisted in again immediately. A sailor on board took a guinea from me on pretence of getting me a boat; and promised me, time after time, that it was hourly to come off. When he had the watch upon deck I watched also; and looked long enough, but all in vain; I could never see either the boat or my guinea again. And what I thought was still the worst of all, the fellow gave information, as I afterwards found, all the while to the mates, of my intention to go off, if I could in any way do it; but, rogue like, he never told them he had got a guinea from me to procure my escape. However, after we had sailed, and his trick was made known to the ship's crew, I had some satisfaction in seeing him detested and despised by them all for his behaviour to me. I was still in hopes that my old shipmates would not forget their promise to come for me to Portsmouth: and, indeed, at last, but not till the day before we sailed, some of them did come there, and sent me off some oranges, and other tokens of their regard. They also sent me word they would come off to me themselves the next day or the day after; and a lady also, who lived in Gosport, wrote to me that she would come and take me out of the ship at the same time. This lady had been once very intimate with my former master: I used to sell and take care of a great deal of property for her, in different ships; and in return she always shewed great friendship for me, and used to tell my master that she would take me away to live with her: but, unfortunately for me, a disagreement soon afterwards took place between them; and she was succeeded in my master's good graces by another lady, who appeared sole mistress of the Ætna, and mostly lodged on board. I was not so great a favourite with this lady as with the former; she had conceived a pique against me on some occasion when she was on board, and she did not fail to instigate my master to treat me in the manner he did.[1]

However, the next morning, the 30th of December, the wind being brisk and easterly, the OEolus frigate, which was to escort the convoy, made a signal for sailing. All the ships then got up their anchors; and, before any of my friends had an opportunity to come off to my relief, to my inexpressible anguish our ship had got under way. What tumultuous emotions agitated my soul when the convoy got under sail, and I a prisoner on board, now without hope! I kept my swimming eyes upon the land in a state of unutterable grief; not knowing what to do, and despairing how to help myself. While my mind was in this situation the fleet sailed on, and in one day's time I lost sight of the wished-for land. In the first expressions of my grief I reproached my fate, and wished I had never been born. I was ready to curse the tide that bore us, the gale that wafted my prison, and even the ship that conducted us; and I called on death to relieve me from the horrors I felt and dreaded, that I might be in that place

> Where slaves are free, and men oppress no more.
> Fool that I was, inur'd so long to pain,
> To trust to hope, or dream of joy again.

> * * * * * * * * * * * *

> Now dragg'd once more beyond the western main,

---

1   [Equiano's note] Thus was I sacrificed to the envy and resentment of this woman for knowing that the lady whom she had succeeded in my master's good graces designed to take me into her service; which, had I once got on shore, she would not have been able to prevent. She felt her pride alarmed at the superiority of her rival in being attended by a black servant: it was not less to prevent this than to be revenged on me, that she caused the captain to treat me thus cruelly.

To groan beneath some dastard planter's chain;
Where my poor countrymen in bondage wait
The long enfrachisement of ling'ring fate:
Hard ling'ring fate! while, ere the dawn of day,
Rous'd by the lash they go their cheerless way;
And as their souls with shame and anguish burn,
Salute with groans unwelcome morn's return,
And, chiding ev'ry hour the slow-pac'd sun,
Pursue their toils till all his race is run.
No eye to mark their suff'rings with a tear;
No friend to comfort, and no hope to cheer:
Then, like the dull unpity'd brutes, repair
To stalls as wretched, and as coarse a fare;
Thank heaven one day of mis'ry was o'er,
Then sink to sleep, and wish to wake no more.[1]

The turbulence of my emotions however naturally gave way to calmer thoughts, and I soon perceived what fate had decreed no mortal on earth could prevent. The convoy sailed on without any accident, with a pleasant gale and smooth sea, for six weeks, till February, when one morning the OEolus ran down a brig, one of the convoy, and she instantly went down and was ingulfed in the dark recesses of the ocean. The convoy was immediately thrown into great confusion till it was day-light; and the OEolus was illumined with lights to prevent any farther mischief. On the 13th of February 1763, from the masthead, we descried our destined island Montserrat; and soon after I beheld those

Regions of sorrow, doleful shades, where peace
And rest can rarely dwell. Hope never comes

---

1   [Equiano's note] "The Dying Negro," a poem originally published in 1773. Perhaps it may not be deemed impertinent here to add, that this elegant and pathetic little poem was occasioned, as appears by the advertisement prefixed to it, by the following incident. "A black, who, a few days before had ran away from his master, and got himself christened, with intent to marry a white woman his fellow-servant, being taken and sent on board a ship in the Thames, took an opportunity of shooting himself through the head." [Equiano does not quote exactly the lines from *The Dying Negro* by Thomas Day and John Bicknell (London, 1773).]

That comes to all, but torture without end
Still urges.[1]

At the sight of this land of bondage, a fresh horror ran through all my frame, and chilled me to the heart. My former slavery now rose in dreadful review to my mind, and displayed nothing but misery, stripes, and chains; and, in the first paroxysm of my grief, I called upon God's thunder, and his avenging power, to direct the stroke of death to me, rather than permit me to become a slave, and be sold from lord to lord.

In this state of my mind our ship came to an anchor, and soon after discharged her cargo. I now knew what it was to work hard; I was made to help to unload and load the ship. And, to comfort me in my distress in that time, two of the sailors robbed me of all my money, and ran away from the ship. I had been so long used to an European climate that at first I felt the scorching West India sun very painful, while the dashing surf would toss the boat and the people in it frequently above high water mark. Sometimes our limbs were broken with this, or even attended with instant death, and I was day by day mangled and torn.

About the middle of May, when the ship was got ready to sail for England, I all the time believing that Fate's blackest clouds were gathering over my head, and expecting their bursting would mix me with the dead, Captain Doran sent for me ashore one morning, and I was told by the messenger that my fate was then determined. With trembling steps and fluttering heart I came to the captain, and found with him one Mr. Robert King, a quaker, and the first merchant in the place. The captain then told me my former master has sent me there to be sold; but that he had desired him to get me the best master he could, as he told him I was a very deserving boy, which Captain Doran said he found to be true; and if he were to stay in the West Indies he would be glad to keep me himself; but he could not venture to take me to London, for he was very sure that when I came there I would leave him. I at that instant burst out

---

1   Milton, *Paradise Lost*, l.65–68.

a crying, and begged much of him to take me to England with him, but all to no purpose. He told me he had got me the very best master in the whole island, with whom I should be as happy as if I were in England, and for that reason he chose to let him have me, though he could sell me to his own brother-in-law for a great deal more money than what he got from this gentleman. Mr. King, my new master, then made a reply, and said the reason he had bought me was on account of my good character; and, as he had not the least doubt of my good behaviour, I should be very well off with him. He also told me he did not live in the West Indies, but at Philadelphia, where he was going soon; and, as I understood something of the rules of arithmetic, when we got there he would put me to school, and fit me for a clerk. This conversation relieved my mind a little, and I left those gentlemen considerably more at ease in myself than when I came to them; and I was very grateful to Captain Doran, and even to my old master, for the character they had given me; a character which I afterwards found of infinite service to me. I went on board again, and took leave of all my shipmates; and the next day the ship sailed. When she weighed anchor I went to the waterside and looked at her with a very wishful and aching heart, and followed her with my eyes and tears until she was totally out of sight. I was so bowed down with grief that I could not hold up my head for many months; and if my new master had not been kind to me I believe I should have died under it at last. And indeed I soon found that he fully deserved the good character which Captain Doran had given me of him; for he possessed a most amiable disposition and temper, and was very charitable and humane. If any of his slaves behaved amiss he did not beat or use them ill, but parted with them. This made them afraid of disobliging him; and as he treated his slaves better than any other man on the island, so he was better and more faithfully served by them in return. By this kind treatment I did at last endeavour to compose myself; and with fortitude, though moneyless, determined to face whatever fate had decreed for me. Mr. King soon asked me what I could do; and at the same time said he did not mean to treat me as a common slave. I told him I knew something of seamanship, and could shave and dress hair pretty well; and I could refine wines, which I had learned on shipboard, where I had often done it; and that I could write, and understood arithmetic tolerably well as far as the Rule of Three. He then asked me if I knew any thing of gauging; and, on my answering that I did not, he said one of his clerks should teach me to gauge.[1]

Mr. King dealt in all manner of merchandize, and kept from one to six clerks. He loaded many vessels in a year; particularly to Philadelphia, where he was born, and was connected with a great mercantile house in that city. He had besides many vessels and droggers, of different sizes, which used to go about the island; and others to collect rum, sugar, and other goods. I understood pulling and managing those boats very well; and this hard work, which was the first that he set me to, in the sugar seasons used to be my constant employment. I have rowed the boat, and slaved at the oars, from one hour to sixteen in the twenty-four; during which I had fifteen pence sterling per day to live on, though sometimes only ten pence. However this was considerably more than was allowed to other slaves that used to work with me, and belonged to other gentlemen on the island: those poor souls had never more than nine pence per day, and seldom more than six pence, from their masters or owners, though they earned them three or four pisterines:[2] for it is a common practice in the West Indies for men to purchase slaves though they have not plantations themselves, in order to let them out to planters and merchants at so much a piece by the day, and they give what allowance they chuse out of this produce of their daily work to their slaves for subsistence; this allowance is often very scanty. My master often gave the owners of these slaves two and a half of these pieces per day, and found the poor fellows in victuals himself, because he thought their owners did not feed them well enough according to the work they did. The slaves used to like this very well; and, as they knew my master to be a man of feeling, they were always glad to work for him in preference to any other gentleman: some of whom, after they had been paid for these poor people's

---

1   Gauge: measure.
2   [Equiano's note] These pisterines are of the value of a shilling.

labours, would not give them their allowance out of it. Many times have I even seen these unfortunate wretches beaten for asking for their pay; and often severely flogged by their owners if they did not bring them their daily or weekly money exactly to the time; though the poor creatures were obliged to wait on the gentlemen they had worked for sometimes for more than half the day before they could get their pay; and this generally on Sundays, when they wanted the time for themselves. In particular, I knew a countryman of mine who once did not bring the weekly money directly that it was earned; and though he brought it the same day to his master, yet he was staked to the ground for this pretended negligence, and was just going to receive a hundred lashes, but for a gentleman who begged him off fifty. This poor man was very industrious; and, by his frugality, had saved so much money by working on shipboard, that he had got a white man to buy him a boat, unknown to his master. Some time after he had this little estate the governor wanted a boat to bring his sugar from different parts of the island; and, knowing this to be a negro-man's boat, he seized upon it for himself, and would not pay the owner a farthing. The man on this went to his master, and complained to him of this act of the governor; but the only satisfaction he received was to be damned very heartily by his master, who asked him how dared any of his negroes to have a boat. If the justly-merited ruin of the governor's fortune could be any gratification to the poor man he had thus robbed, he was not without consolation. Extortion and rapine are poor providers; and some time after this the governor died in the King's Bench in England, as I was told, in great poverty. The last war favoured this poor negro-man, and he found some means to escape from his Christian master: he came to England; where I saw him afterwards several times. Such treatment as this often drives these miserable wretches to despair, and they run away from their masters at the hazard of their lives. Many of them in this place, unable to get their pay when they have earned it, and fearing to be flogged, as usual, if they return home without it, run away where they can for shelter, and a reward is often offered to bring them in dead or alive. My master used sometimes, in these cases, to agree with their owners, and to settle with them himself; and thereby he saved many of them a flogging.

Once, for a few days, I was let out to fit a vessel, and I had no victuals allowed me by either party; at last I told my master of this treatment, and he took me away from it. In many of the estates, on the different islands where I used to be sent for rum or sugar, they would not deliver it to me, or any other negro; he was therefore obliged to send a white man along with me to those places; and then he used to pay him six to ten pisterines a day. From being thus employed, during the time I served Mr. King, in going about the different estates on the island, I had all the opportunity I could wish for to see the dreadful usage of the poor men; usage that reconciled me to my situation, and made me bless God for the hands into which I had fallen.

I had the good fortune to please my master in every department in which he employed me; and there was scarcely any part of his business, or household affairs, in which I was not occasionally engaged. I often supplied the place of a clerk, in receiving and delivering cargoes to the ships, in tending stores, and delivering goods: and, besides this, I used to shave and dress my master when convenient, and take care of his horse; and when it was necessary, which was very often, I worked likewise on board of different vessels of his. By these means I became very useful to my master; and saved him, as he used to acknowledge, above a hundred pounds a year. Nor did he scruple to say I was of more advantage to him than any of his clerks; though their usual wages in the West Indies are from sixty to a hundred pounds current a year.

I have sometimes heard it asserted that a negro cannot earn his master the first cost; but nothing can be further from the truth. I suppose nine tenths of the mechanics throughout the West Indies are negro slaves; and I well know the coopers among them earn two dollars a day; the carpenters the same, and oftentimes more; as also the masons, smiths, and fishermen, &c. and I have known many slaves whose masters would not take a thousand pounds current for them. But surely this assertion refutes itself; for, if it be true, why do the planters and merchants pay such a price for slaves? And, above all, why do those who make this assertion exclaim the most loudly against the abolition of the slave trade? So much are men blinded, and to such inconsistent arguments are they driven by mistaken interest! I grant, indeed, that slaves are some times, by half-feeding, half-clothing, over-working and stripes, reduced so low, that they are turned out as unfit for service, and left to perish in the woods, or expire on a dunghill.

My master was several times offered by different gentlemen one hundred guineas for me; but he always told them he would not sell me, to my great joy: and I used to double my diligence and care for fear of getting into the hands of those men who did not allow a valuable slave the common support of life. Many of them even used to find fault with my master for feeding his slaves so well as he did; although I often went hungry, and an Englishman might think my fare very indifferent; but he used to tell them he always would do it, because the slaves thereby looked better and did more work.

While I was thus employed by my master I was often witness to cruelties of every kind, which were exercised on my unhappy fellow slaves. I used frequently to have different cargoes of new negroes in my care for sale; and it was almost a constant practice with our clerks, and other whites, to commit violent depredations on the chastity of the female slaves; and these I was, though with reluctance, obliged to submit to at all times, being unable to help them. When we have had some of these slaves on board my master's vessels to carry them to other islands, or to America, I have known our mates to commit these acts most shamefully, to the disgrace, not of Christians only, but of men. I have even known them gratify their brutal passion with females not ten years old; and these abominations some of them practised to such scandalous excess, that one of our captains discharged the mate and others on that account. And yet in Montserrat I have seen a negro man staked to the ground, and cut most shockingly, and then his ears cut off bit by bit, because he had been connected with a white woman who was a common prostitute: as if it were no crime in the whites to rob an innocent African girl of her virtue; but most heinous in a black man only to gratify a passion of nature, where the temptation was offered by one of a different colour, though the most abandoned woman of her species.[1] Another negro man was half-hanged, and then burnt, for attempting to poison a cruel overseer. Thus by repeated cruelties are the wretched first urged to despair, and then murdered, because they still retain so much of human nature about them as to wish to put an end to their misery, and retaliate on their tyrants! These overseers are indeed for the most part persons of the worst character of any denomination of men in the West Indies. Unfortunately, many humane gentlemen, by not residing on their estates, are obliged to leave the management of them in the hands of these human butchers, who cut and mangle the slaves in a shocking manner on the most trifling occasions, and altogether treat them in every respect like brutes. They pay no regard to the situation of pregnant women, nor the least attention to the lodging of the field negroes. Their huts, which ought to be well covered, and the place dry where they take their little repose, are often open sheds, built in damp places; so that, when the poor creatures return tired from the toils of the field, they contract many disorders, from being exposed to the damp air in this uncomfortable state, while they are heated, and their pores are open. This neglect certainly conspires with many others to cause a decrease in the births as well as in the lives of the grown negroes. I can quote many instances of gentlemen who reside on their estates in the West Indies, and then the scene is quite changed; the negroes are treated with lenity and proper care, by which their lives are prolonged, and their masters are profited. To the honour of humanity, I knew several gentlemen who managed their estates in this manner; and they found that benevolence was their true interest. And, among many I could mention in several of the

---

1 The following paragraph was added here by Equiano in later editions:

One Mr. D[rummond] told me that he had sold 41,000 negroes, and that he once cut off a negro-man's leg for running away. – I asked him if the man had died in the operation, how he, as a Christian, could answer for the horrid act before God? and he told me, answering was a thing of another world, but what he thought and did were policy. I told him that the Christian doctrine taught us to do unto others as we would that others should do unto us. He then said that his scheme had the desired effect – it cured that man and some others of running away.

islands, I knew one in Montserrat[1] whose slaves looked remarkably well, and never needed any fresh supplies of negroes; and there are many other estates, especially in Barbadoes, which, from such judicious treatment, need no fresh stock of negroes at any time. I have the honour of knowing a most worthy and humane gentleman, who is a native of Barbadoes, and has estates there.[2] This gentleman has written a treatise on the usage of his own slaves. He allows them two hours for refreshment at mid-day; and many other indulgencies and comforts, particularly in their lying; and, besides this, he raises more provisions on his estate than they can destroy; so that by these attentions he saves the lives of his negroes, and keeps them healthy, and as happy as the condition of slavery can admit. I myself, as shall appear in the sequel, managed an estate, where, by those attentions, the negroes were uncommonly cheerful and healthy, and did more work by half than by the common mode of treatment they usually do. For want, therefore, of such care and attention to the poor negroes, and otherwise oppressed as they are, it is no wonder that the decrease should require 20,000 new negroes annually to fill up the vacant places of the dead.

Even in Barbadoes, notwithstanding those humane exceptions which I have mentioned, and others I am acquainted with, which justly make it quoted as a place where slaves meet with the best treatment, and need fewest recruits of any in the West Indies, yet this island requires 1000 negroes annually to keep up the original stock, which is only 80,000. So that the whole term of a negro's life may be said to be there but sixteen years![3] And yet the climate here is in every respect the same as that from which they are taken, except in being more wholesome. Do the British colonies decrease in this manner? And yet what a prodigious difference is there between an English and West India climate?

While I was in Montserrat I knew a negro man, named

---

1   [Equiano's note] Mr. Dubury, and many others, Montserrat.
2   [Equiano's note] Sir Philip Gibbes, Baronet, Barbadoes.
3   [Equiano's note] Benezet's "Account of Guinea," p. 16.

Emanuel Sankey, who endeavoured to escape from his miserable bondage, by concealing himself on board of a London ship: but fate did not favour the poor oppressed man; for, being discovered when the vessel was under sail, he was delivered up again to his master. This *Christian master* immediately pinned the wretch down to the ground at each wrist and ancle, and then took some sticks of sealing wax, and lighted them, and dropped it all over his back. There was another master who was noted for cruelty; and I believe he had not a slave but what had been cut, and had pieces fairly taken out of the flesh: and, after they had been punished thus, he used to make them get into a long wooden box or case he had for that purpose, in which he shut them up during pleasure. It was just about the height and breadth of a man; and the poor wretches had no room, when in the case, to move.

It was very common in several of the islands, particularly in St. Kitt's, for the slaves to be branded with the initial letters of their master's name; and a load of heavy iron hooks hung about their necks. Indeed on the most trifling occasions they were loaded with chains; and often instruments of torture were added. The iron muzzle, thumb-screws, &c. are so well known, as not to need a description, and were sometimes applied for the slightest faults. I have seen a negro beaten till some of his bones were broken, for even letting a pot boil over.[1] Is it surprising that usage like this should drive the poor creatures to despair, and make them seek a refuge in death from those evils which render their lives intolerable – while,

With shudd'ring horror pale, and eyes aghast,

---

1 The following lines appear in later editions:
It is not uncommon after a flogging, to make slaves go on their knees, and thank their owners, and pray, or rather say, God bless them. I have often asked many of the men slaves (who used to go several miles to their wives, and late in the night, after having been wearied with a hard day's labour) why they went so far for wives, and why they did not take them of their own master's negro women, and particularly those who lived together as household slaves? Their answers have ever been – "Because when the master or mistress choose to punish the women, they make the husbands flog their own wives, and that they could not bear to do."

They view their lamentable lot, and find
No rest![1]

This they frequently do. A negro-man on board a vessel of
my master, while I belonged to her, having been put in irons
for some trifling misdemeanor, and kept in that state for some
days, being weary of life, took an opportunity of jumping overboard into the sea; however, he was picked up without being
drowned. Another, whose life was also a burden to him,
resolved to starve himself to death, and refused to eat any victuals; this procured him a severe flogging: and he also, on the
first occasion which offered, jumped overboard at Charles
Town,[2] but was saved.

Nor is there any greater regard shewn to the little property
than there is to the persons and lives of the negroes. I have
already related an instance or two of particular oppression out
of many which I have witnessed; but the following is frequent
in all the islands. The wretched field-slaves, after toiling all the
day for an unfeeling owner, who gives them but little victuals,
steal sometimes a few moments from rest or refreshment to
gather some small portion of grass, according as their time will
admit. This they commonly tie up in a parcel; (either a bit,
worth six pence; or half a bit's worth) and bring it to town, or
to the market, to sell. Nothing is more common than for the
white people on this occasion to take the grass from them
without paying for it; and not only so, but too often also, to my
knowledge, our clerks, and many others, at the same time have
committed acts of violence on the poor, wretched, and helpless
females; whom I have seen for hours stand crying to no purpose, and get no redress or pay of any kind. Is not this one
common and crying sin enough to bring down God's judgment on the islands? He tells us the oppressor and the
oppressed are both in his hands; and if these are not the poor,
the broken-hearted, the blind, the captive, the bruised, which
our Saviour speaks of, who are they? One of these depredators
once, in St. Eustatia, came on board of our vessel, and bought

---

1   Milton, *Paradise Lost*, 2.616-18.
2   Charles Town: Charleston, South Carolina. Equiano at times spells it Charlestown.

some fowls and pigs of me; and a whole day after his departure with the things he returned again and wanted his money back: I refused to give it; and, not seeing my captain on board, he began the common pranks with me; and swore he would even break open my chest and take my money. I therefore expected, as my captain was absent, that he would be as good as his word: and he was just proceeding to strike me, when fortunately a British seaman on board, whose heart had not been debauched by a West India climate, interposed and prevented him. But had the cruel man struck me I certainly should have defended myself at the hazard of my life; for what is life to a man thus oppressed? He went away, however, swearing; and threatened that whenever he caught me on shore he would shoot me, and pay for me afterwards.

The small account in which the life of a negro is held in the West Indies is so universally known, that it might seem impertinent to quote the following extract, if some people had not been hardy enough of late to assert that negroes are on the same footing in that respect as Europeans. By the 329th Act, page 125, of the Assembly of Barbadoes, it is enacted "That if any negro, or other slave, under punishment by his master, or his order, for running away, or any other crime or misdemeanor towards his said master, unfortunately shall suffer in life or member, no person whatsoever shall be liable to a fine; but if any man shall out of *wantonness, or only of bloody-mindedness, or cruel intention, wilfully kill a negro, or other slave, of his own, he shall pay into the public treasury fifteen pounds sterling.*" And it is the same in most, if not all, of the West India islands. Is not this one of the many acts of the islands which call loudly for redress? And do not the assembly which enacted it deserve the appellation of savages and brutes rather than of Christians and men? It is an act at once unmerciful, unjust, and unwise; which for cruelty would disgrace an assembly of those who are called barbarians; and for its injustice and *insanity* would shock the morality and common sense of a Samaide or a Hottentot.[1]

Shocking as this and many more acts of the bloody West

---

1 Samaide: Samoyeds are inhabitants of the Ural regions of Siberia; Hottentots were considered to be barbaric natives living in South Africa.

India code at first view appear, how is the iniquity of it heightened when we consider to whom it may be extended! Mr. James Tobin, a zealous labourer in the vineyard of slavery, gives an account of a French planter of his acquaintance, in the island of Martinico,[1] who shewed him many mulattoes working in the fields like beasts of burden; and he told Mr Tobin these were all the produce of his own loins! And I myself have known similar instances. Pray, reader, are these sons and daughters of the French planter less his children by being begotten on a black woman? And what must be the virtue of those legislators, and the feelings of those fathers, who estimate the lives of their sons, however begotten, at no more than fifteen pounds; though they should be murdered, as the act says, *out of wantonness and bloody-mindedness!* But is not the slave trade entirely a war with the heart of man? And surely that which is begun by breaking down the barriers of virtue involves in its continuance destruction to every principle, and buries all sentiments in ruin!

I have often seen slaves, particularly those who were meagre, in different islands, put into scales and weighed; and then sold from three pence to six pence or nine pence a pound. My master, however, whose humanity was shocked at this mode, used to sell such by the lump. And at or after a sale it was not uncommon to see negroes taken from their wives, wives taken from their husbands, and children from their parents, and sent off to other islands, and wherever else their merciless lords chose; and probably never more during life to see each other! Oftentimes my heart has bled at these partings; when the friends of the departed have been at the water side, and, with sighs and tears, have kept their eyes fixed on the vessel till it went out of sight.

A poor Creole negro I knew well, who, after having been often thus transported from island to island, at last resided in Montserrat. This man used to tell me many melancholy tales of himself. Generally, after he had done working for his master, he used to employ his few leisure moments to go a fishing. When he had caught any fish, his master would frequently take them from him without paying him; and at other times some other

---

1   Martinico: the West Indian island of Martinique.

white people would serve him in the same manner. One day he said to me, very movingly, "Sometimes when a white man take away my fish I go to my master, and he get me my right; and when my master by strength take away my fishes, what me must do? I can't go to any body to be righted; then" said the poor man, looking up above "I must look up to God Mighty in the top for right." This artless tale moved me much, and I could not help feeling the just cause Moses had in redressing his brother against the Egyptian. I exhorted the man to look up still to the God on the top, since there was no redress below. Though I little thought then that I myself should more than once experience such imposition, and need the same exhortation hereafter, in my own transactions in the islands; and that even this poor man and I should some time after suffer together in the same manner, as shall be related hereafter.

Nor was such usage as this confined to particular places or individuals; for, in all the different islands in which I have been (and I have visited no less than fifteen) the treatment of the slaves was nearly the same; so nearly indeed, that the history of an island, or even a plantation, with a few such exceptions as I have mentioned, might serve for a history of the whole. Such a tendency has the slave-trade to debauch men's minds, and harden them to every feeling of humanity! For I will not suppose that the dealers in slaves are born worse than other men – No; it is the fatality of this mistaken avarice, that it corrupts the milk of human kindness and turns it into gall. And, had the pursuits of those men been different, they might have been as generous, as tender-hearted and just, as they are unfeeling, rapacious and cruel. Surely this traffic cannot be good, which spreads like a pestilence, and taints what it touches! which violates that first natural right of mankind, equality and independency, and gives one man a dominion over his fellows which God could never intend! For it raises the owner to a state as far above man as it depresses the slave below it; and, with all the presumption of human pride, sets a distinction between them, immeasurable in extent, and endless in duration! Yet how mistaken is the avarice even of the planters? Are slaves more useful by being thus humbled to the condition of brutes, than they would be if suffered to enjoy the privileges of men? The freedom which diffuses health and prosperity throughout Britain answers you – No. When you make men slaves you deprive them of half their virtue, you set them in your own conduct an example of fraud, rapine, and cruelty, and compel them to live with you in a state of war; and yet you complain that they are not honest or faithful! You stupify them with stripes, and think it necessary to keep them in a state of ignorance; and yet you assert that they are incapable of learning; that their minds are such a barren soil or moor, that culture would be lost on them; and that they come from a climate, where nature, though prodigal of her bounties in a degree unknown to yourselves, has left man alone scant and unfinished, and incapable of enjoying the treasures she has poured out for him! – An assertion at once impious and absurd. Why do you use those instruments of torture? Are they fit to be applied by one rational being to another? And are ye not struck with shame and mortification, to see the partakers of your nature reduced so low? But, above all, are there no dangers attending this mode of treatment? Are you not hourly in dread of an insurrection? Nor would it be surprising: for when

> —No peace is given
> To us enslav'd, but custody severe;
> And stripes and arbitrary punishment
> Inflicted – What peace can we return?
> But to our power, hostility and hate;
> Untam'd reluctance, and revenge, though slow,
> Yet ever plotting how the conqueror least
> May reap his conquest, and may least rejoice
> In doing what we most in suffering feel.[1]

But by changing your conduct, and treating your slaves as men, every cause of fear would be banished. They would be faithful, honest, intelligent and vigorous; and peace, prosperity, and happiness, would attend you.

---

1 Milton, *Paradise Lost*, 2.332–40.

CHAP. VI.

Some account of Brimstone-Hill in Montserrat — Favourable change in the author's situation — He commences merchant with three pence — His various success in dealing in the different islands, and America, and the impositions he meets with in his transactions with Europeans — A curious imposition on human nature — Danger of the surfs in the West Indies — Remarkable instance of kidnapping a free mulatto — The author is nearly murdered by Doctor Perkins in Savannah.

In the preceding chapter I have set before the reader a few of those many instances of oppression, extortion, and cruelty, which I have been a witness to in the West Indies: but, were I to enumerate them all, the catalogue would be tedious and disgusting. The punishments of the slaves on every trifling occasion are so frequent, and so well known, together with the different instruments with which they are tortured, that it cannot any longer afford novelty to recite them; and they are too shocking to yield delight either to the writer or the reader. I shall therefore hereafter only mention such as incidentally befel myself in the course of my adventures.

In the variety of departments in which I was employed by my master, I had an opportunity of seeing many curious scenes in different islands; but, above all, I was struck with a celebrated curiosity called Brimstone-Hill, which is a high and steep mountain, some few miles from the town of Plymouth in Montserrat. I had often heard of some wonders that were to be seen on this hill, and I went once with some white and black people to visit it. When we arrived at the top, I saw under different cliffs great flakes of brimstone, occasioned by the steams of various little ponds, which were then boiling naturally in the earth. Some of these ponds were as white as milk, some quite blue, and many others of different colours. I had taken some potatoes with me, and I put them into different ponds, and in a few minutes they were well boiled. I tasted some of them, but they were very sulphurous; and the silver shoe buckles, and all the other things of that metal we had among us, were, in a little time, turned as black as lead.[1]

Some time in the year 1763 kind Providence seemed to appear rather more favourable to me. One of my master's vessels, a Bermudas sloop, about sixty tons, was commanded by one Captain Thomas Farmer, an Englishman, a very alert and active man, who gained my master a great deal of money by his good management in carrying passengers from one island to another; but very often his sailors used to get drunk and run away from the vessel, which hindered him in his business very much. This man had taken a liking to me; and many different times begged of my master to let me go a trip with him as a sailor; but he would tell him he could not spare me, though the vessel sometimes could not go for want of hands, for sailors were generally very scarce in the island. However, at last, from necessity or force, my master was prevailed on, though very reluctantly, to let me go with this captain; but he gave great charge to him to take care that I did not run away, for if I did he would make him pay for me. This being the case, the captain had for some time a sharp eye upon me whenever the vessel anchored; and as soon as she returned I was sent for on shore again. Thus was I slaving as it were for life, sometimes at one thing, and sometimes at another; so that the captain and I

---

1   Equiano later added these paragraphs here:

Whilst I was on the island, one night I felt a strange sensation, viz. I was told that the house where I lived was haunted by spirits. And once, at midnight, as I was sleeping on a large chest, I felt the whole building shake in an uncommon and astonishing manner; so much so, that it shook me off the chest where I then lay; I was exceedingly frightened, and thought it was the visitation of the spirits. It threw me into such a tremor as is not to be described. I instantly covered my head all over as I lay, and did not know what to think or do; and in this consternation, a gentleman, who lay in the next room just by me came out, and I was glad to hear him, and made a sham cough, and he asked me, if I felt the earthquake. I told him I was shook off the chest where I lay, but did not know what occasioned it; and he told me it was an earthquake, and shook him out of his bed. At hearing this I became easy in my mind.

At another time a circumstance of this kind happened, when I was on board of a vessel in Montserrat-road, at midnight, as we were asleep, and it shook the vessel in the most unaccountable manner imaginable, and to me it seemed as when a vessel or a boat runs on gravel, as near as I can describe it. Many things on board were moved out of their places, but happily no damage was done.

were nearly the most useful men in my master's employment. I also became so useful to the captain on shipboard, that many times, when he used to ask for me to go with him, though it should be but for twenty-four hours, to some of the islands near us, my master would answer he could not spare me, at which the captain would swear, and would not go the trip; and tell my master I was better to him on board than any three white men he had; for they used to behave ill in many respects, particularly in getting drunk; and then they frequently got the boat stove, so as to hinder the vessel from coming back as soon as she might have done. This my master knew very well; and at last, by the captain's constant entreaties, after I had been several times with him, one day, to my great joy, my master told me the captain would not let him rest, and asked me whether I would go aboard as a sailor, or stay on shore and mind the stores, for he could not bear any longer to be plagued in this manner. I was very happy at this proposal, for I immediately thought I might in time stand some chance by being on board to get a little money, or possibly make my escape if I should be used ill: I also expected to get better food, and in greater abundance; for I had felt much hunger oftentimes, though my master treated his slaves, as I have observed, uncommonly well. I therefore, without hesitation, answered him, that I would go and be a sailor if he pleased. Accordingly I was ordered on board directly. Nevertheless, between the vessel and the shore, when she was in port, I had little or no rest, as my master always wished to have me along with him. Indeed he was a very pleasant gentleman, and but for my expectations on shipboard I should not have thought of leaving him. But the captain liked me also very much, and I was entirely his right-hand man. I did all I could to deserve his favour, and in return I received better treatment from him than any other I believe ever met with in the West Indies in my situation.

After I had been sailing for some time with this captain, at length I endeavoured to try my luck and commence merchant. I had but a very small capital to begin with; for one single half bit, which is equal to three pence in England, made up my whole stock. However I trusted to the Lord to be with me; and at one of our trips to St. Eustatia, a Dutch island, I bought a glass tumbler with my half bit, and when I came to Montserrat I sold it for a bit, or sixpence. Luckily we made several successive trips to St. Eustatia (which was a general mart for the West Indies, about twenty leagues from Montserrat); and in our next, finding my tumbler so profitable, with this one bit I bought two tumblers more; and when I came back I sold them for two bits, equal to a shilling sterling. When we went again I bought with these two bits four more of these glasses, which I sold for four bits on our return to Montserrat: and in our next voyage to St. Eustatia I bought two glasses with one bit, and with the other three I bought a jug of Geneva, nearly about three pints in measure. When we came to Montserrat I sold the gin for eight bits, and the tumblers for two, so that my capital now amounted in all to a dollar, well husbanded and acquired in the space of a month or six weeks, when I blessed the Lord that I was so rich. As we sailed to different islands, I laid this money out in various things occasionally, and it used to turn out to very good account, especially when we went to Guadaloupe, Grenada, and the rest of the French islands. Thus was I going all about the islands upwards of four years, and ever trading as I went, during which I experienced many instances of ill usage, and have seen many injuries done to other negroes in our dealings with Europeans: and, amidst our recreations, when we have been dancing and merry-making, they, without cause, have molested and insulted us. Indeed I was more than once obliged to look up to God on high, as I had advised the poor fisherman some time before. And I had not been long trading for myself in the manner I have related above, when I experienced the like trial in company with him as follows: This man being used to the water, was upon an emergency put on board of us by his master to work as another hand, on a voyage to Santa Cruz; and at our sailing he had brought his little all for a venture, which consisted of six bits' worth of limes and oranges in a bag; I had also my whole stock, which was about twelve bits' worth of the same kind of goods, separate in two bags; for we had heard these fruits sold well in that island. When we came there, in some little convenient time he and I went ashore with our fruits to sell them; but we had scarcely landed when we were met by two white men, who presently took our three bags from us. We could not at first guess what they meant to do; and for some time we thought they were jesting with us; but they too soon let us know otherwise, for they took our ventures immediately to a house hard by, and adjoining the fort, while we followed all the way begging of them to give us our fruits, but in vain. They not only refused to return them, but swore at us, and threatened if we did not immediately depart they would flog us well. We told them these three bags were all we were worth in the world, and that we brought them with us to sell when we came from Montserrat, and shewed them the vessel. But this was rather against us, as they now saw we were strangers as well as slaves. They still therefore swore, and desired us to be gone, and even took sticks to beat us; while we, seeing they meant what they said, went off in the greatest confusion and despair. Thus, in the very minute of gaining more by three times than I ever did by any venture in my life before, was I deprived of every farthing I was worth. An insupportable misfortune! but how to help ourselves we knew not. In our consternation we went to the commanding officer of the fort and told him how we had been served by some of his people; but we obtained not the least redress: he answered our complaints only by a volley of imprecations against us, and immediately took a horse-whip, in order to chastise us, so that we were obliged to turn out much faster than we came in. I now, in the agony of distress and indignation, wished that the ire of God in his forked lightning might transfix these cruel oppressors among the dead. Still however we persevered; went back again to the house, and begged and besought them again and again for our fruits, till at last some other people that were in the house asked if we would be contented if they kept one bag and gave us the other two. We, seeing no remedy whatever, consented to this; and they, observing one bag to have both kinds of fruit in it, which belonged to my companions, kept that; and the other two, which were mine, they gave us back. As soon as I got them, I ran as fast as I could, and got the first negro man I could to help me off; my companion, however, stayed a little longer to plead; he told them the bag they had was his, and likewise all that he was worth in the world; but this was of no avail, and he was obliged to return without it. The poor old man, wringing his hands, cried bitterly for his loss; and, indeed, he then did look up to God on high, which so moved me with pity for him, that I gave him nearly one third of my fruits. We then proceeded to the markets to sell them; and Providence was more favourable to us than we could have expected, for we sold our fruits uncommonly well; I got for mine about thirty-seven bits. Such a surprising reverse of fortune in so short a space of time seemed like a dream to me, and proved no small encouragement for me to trust the Lord in any situation. My captain afterwards frequently used to take my part, and get me my right, when I have been plundered or used ill by these tender Christian depredators; among whom I have shuddered to observe the unceasing blasphemous execrations which are wantonly thrown out by persons of all ages and conditions, not only without occasion, but even as if they were indulgences and pleasure.

At one of our trips to St. Kitt's I had eleven bits of my own; and my friendly captain lent me five bits more, with which I bought a Bible. I was very glad to get this book, which I scarcely could meet with any where. I think there was none sold in Montserrat; and, much to my grief, from being forced out of the Ætna in the manner I have related, my Bible, and the Guide to the Indians, the two books I loved above all others, were left behind.

While I was in this place, St. Kitt's, a very curious imposition on human nature took place: – A white man wanted to marry in the church a free black woman that had land and slaves in Montserrat: but the clergyman told him it was against the law of the place to marry a white and a black in the church. The man then asked to be married on the water, to which the parson consented, and the two lovers went in one boat, and the parson and clerk in another, and thus the ceremony was performed. After this the loving pair came on board our vessel, and my captain treated them extremely well, and brought them safe to Montserrat.

The reader cannot but judge of the irksomeness of this situation to a mind like mine, in being daily exposed to new hardships and impositions, after having seen many better days, and having been as it were in a state of freedom and plenty; added to which, every part of the world I had hitherto been in seemed to me a paradise in comparison of the West Indies. My mind was therefore hourly replete with inventions and thoughts of being freed, and, if possible, by honest and honourable means; for I always remembered the old adage; and I trust it has ever been my ruling principle, that honesty is the best policy; and likewise that other golden precept – to do unto all men as I would they should do unto me. However, as I was from early years a predestinarian,[1] I thought whatever fate had determined must ever come to pass; and therefore, if ever it were my lot to be freed nothing could prevent me, although I should at present see no means or hope to obtain my freedom; on the other hand, if it were my fate not to be freed I never should be so, and all my endeavours for that purpose would be fruitless. In the midst of these thoughts I therefore looked up with prayers anxiously to God for my liberty; and at the same time I used every honest means, and endeavoured all that was possible on my part to obtain it. In process of time I became master of a few pounds, and in a fair way of making more, which my friendly captain knew very well; this occasioned him sometimes to take liberties with me: but whenever he treated me waspishly I used plainly to tell him my mind, and that I would die before I would be imposed on as other negroes were, and that to me life had lost its relish when liberty was gone. This I said although I foresaw my then well-being or future hopes of freedom (humanly speaking) depended on this man. However, as he could not bear the thoughts of my not sailing with him, he always became mild on my threats. I therefore continued with him; and, from my great attention to his orders and his business, I gained him credit, and through his kindness to me I at last procured my liberty. While I thus went on, filled with the thoughts of freedom, and resisting oppres-

---

1 Predestinarian: the belief that God foreordained everything that would happen.

sion as well as I was able, my life hung daily in suspense, particularly in the surfs I have formerly mentioned, as I could not swim. These are extremely violent throughout the West Indies, and I was ever exposed to their howling rage and devouring fury in all the islands. I have seen them strike and toss a boat right up an end, and maim several on board. Once in the Grenada islands, when I and about eight others were pulling a large boat with two puncheons of water in it, a surf struck us, and drove the boat and all in it about half a stone's throw, among some trees, and above the high water mark. We were obliged to get all the assistance we could from the nearest estate to mend the boat, and launch it into the water again. At Montserrat one night, in pressing hard to get off the shore on board, the punt was overset with us four times; the first time I was very near being drowned; however the jacket I had on kept me up above water a little space of time, while I called on a man near me who was a good swimmer, and told him I could not swim; he then made haste to me, and, just as I was sinking, he caught hold of me, and brought me to sounding, and then he went and brought the punt also. As soon as we had turned the water out of her, lest we should be used ill for being absent, we attempted again three times more, and as often the horrid surfs served us as at first; but at last, the fifth time we attempted, we gained our point, at the imminent hazard of our lives. One day also, at Old Road in Montserrat, our captain, and three men besides myself, were going in a large canoe in quest of rum and sugar, when a single surf tossed the canoe an amazing distance from the water, and some of us near a stone's throw from each other: most of us were very much bruised; so that I and many more often said, and really thought, that there was not such another place under the heavens as this. I longed therefore much to leave it, and daily wished to see my master's promise performed of going to Philadelphia. While we lay in this place a very cruel thing happened on board of our sloop which filled me with horror; though I found afterwards such practices were frequent. There was a very clever and decent free young mulatto-man who sailed a long time with us: he had a free woman for his wife, by whom he had a child; and she was then living on shore, and all very happy. Our captain and mate, and other people on board, and several elsewhere, even the natives of Bermudas, all knew this young man from a child that he was always free, and no one had ever claimed him as their property: however, as might too often overcomes right in these parts, it happened that a Bermudas captain, whose vessel lay there for a few days in the road, came on board of us, and seeing the mulatto-man, whose name was Joseph Clipson, he told him he was not free, and that he had orders from his master to bring him to Bermudas. The poor man could not believe the captain to be in earnest; but he was very soon undeceived, his men laying violent hands on him: and although he shewed a certificate of his being born free in St. Kitt's, and most people on board knew that he served his time to boat-building, and always passed for a free man, yet he was taken forcibly out of our vessel. He then asked to be carried ashore before the secretary or magistrates, and these infernal invaders of human rights promised him he should; but, instead of that, they carried him on board of the other vessel: and the next day, without giving the poor man any hearing on shore, or suffering him even to see his wife or child, he was carried away, and probably doomed never more in this world to see them again. Nor was this the only instance of this kind of barbarity I was a witness to. I have since often seen in Jamaica and other islands free men, whom I have known in America, thus villainously trepanned and held in bondage. I have heard of two similar practices even in Philadelphia: and were it not for the benevolence of the quakers in that city many of the sable race, who now breathe the air of liberty, would, I believe, be groaning indeed under some planter's chains. These things opened my mind to a new scene of horror to which I had been before a stranger. Hitherto I had thought only slavery dreadful; but the state of a free negro appeared to me now equally so at least, and in some respects even worse, for they live in constant alarm for their liberty; and even this is but nominal, for they are universally insulted and plundered without the possibility of redress; for such is the equity of the West Indian laws, that no free negro's evidence will be admitted in their courts of justice. In this situation is it surprising that slaves, when mildly treated, should prefer even the misery of slavery to such a mockery of freedom? I was now completely disgusted with the West Indies, and thought I never should be entirely free until I had left them.

> With thoughts like these my anxious boding mind
> Recall'd those pleasing scenes I left behind;
> Scenes where fair Liberty in bright array
> Makes darkness bright, and e'en illumines day;
> Where nor complexion, wealth, or station, can
> Protect the wretch who makes a slave of man.[1]

I determined to make every exertion to obtain any freedom and to return to Old England. For this purpose I thought a knowledge of navigation might be of use to me; for, though I did not intend to run away unless I should be ill used, yet, in such a case, if I understood navigation, I might attempt my escape in our sloop, which was one of the swiftest sailing vessels in the West Indies, and I could be at no loss for hands to join me: and if I should make this attempt, I had intended to have gone for England; but this, as I said, was only to be in the event of my meeting with any ill usage. I therefore employed the mate of our vessel to teach me navigation, for which I agreed to give him twenty-four dollars, and actually paid him part of the money down; though when the captain, some time after, came to know that the mate was to have such a sum for teaching me, he rebuked him, and said it was a shame for him to take any money from me. However, my progress in this useful art was much retarded by the constancy of our work. Had I wished to run away I did not want opportunities, which frequently presented themselves; and particularly at one time, soon after this. When we were at the island of Gaurdeloupe there was a large fleet of merchantmen bound for Old France; and, seamen then being very scarce, they gave from fifteen to twenty pounds a man for the run. Our mate, and all the white sailors,

---

1   These lines were probably written by Equiano.

left our vessel on this account, and went on board of the French ships. They would have had me also to go with them, for they regarded me; and they swore to protect me, if I would go: and, as the fleet was to sail the next day, I really believe I could have got safe to Europe at that time. However, as my master was kind, I would not attempt to leave him; and remembering the old maxim, that "honesty is the best policy," I suffered them to go without me. Indeed my captain was much afraid of my leaving him and the vessel at that time, as I had so fair an opportunity: but, I thank God, this fidelity of mine turned out much to my advantage hereafter, when I did not in the least think of it; and made me so much in favour with the captain, that he used now and then to teach me some parts of navigation himself: but some of our passengers, and others, seeing this, found much fault with him for it, saying it was a very dangerous thing to let a negro know navigation; thus I was hindered again in my pursuits. About the latter end of the year 1764 my master bought a larger sloop, called the Providence, about seventy or eighty tons, of which my captain had the command. I went with him into this vessel, and we took a load of new slaves for Georgia and Charles Town. My master now left me entirely to the captain, though he still wished for me to be with him; but I, who always much wished to lose sight of the West Indies, was not a little rejoiced at the thoughts of seeing any other country. Therefore, relying on the goodness of my captain, I got ready all the little venture I could; and, when the vessel was ready, we sailed, to my great joy. When we got to our destined places, Georgia and Charles Town, I expected I should have an opportunity of selling my little property to advantage: but here, particularly in Charles Town, I met with buyers, white men, who imposed on me as in other places. Notwithstanding, I was resolved to have fortitude; thinking no lot or trial is too hard when kind Heaven is the rewarder. We soon got loaded again, and returned to Montserrat; and there, amongst the rest of the islands, I sold my goods well; and in this manner I continued trading during the year 1764; meeting with various scenes of imposition, as usual. After this, my master fitted out his vessel for Philadelphia, in the year

1765; and during the time we were loading her, and getting ready for the voyage, I worked with redoubled alacrity, from the hope of getting money enough by these voyages to buy my freedom in time, if it should please God; and also to see the town of Philadelphia, which I had heard a great deal about for some years past; besides which, I had always longed to prove my master's promise the first day I came to him. In the midst of these elevated ideas, and while I was about getting my little merchandize in readiness, one Sunday my master sent for me to his house. When I came there I found him and the captain together; and, on my going in, I was struck with astonishment at his telling me he heard that I meant to run away from him when I got to Philadelphia: "And therefore," said he, "I must sell you again: you cost me a great deal of money, no less than forty pounds sterling; and it will not do to lose so much. You are a valuable fellow," continued he; "and I can get any day for you one hundred guineas, from many gentlemen in this island." And then he told me of Captain Doran's brother-in-law, a severe master, who ever wanted to buy me to make me his overseer. My captain also said he could get much more than a hundred guineas for me in Carolina. This I knew to be a fact; for the gentleman that wanted to buy me came off several times on board of us, and spoke to me to live with him, and said he would use me well. When I asked what work he would put me to he said, as I was a sailor, he would make me a captain of one of his rice vessels. But I refused: and fearing, at the same time, by a sudden turn I saw in the captain's temper, he might mean to sell me, I told the gentleman I would not live with him on any condition, and that I certainly would run away with his vessel: but he said he did not fear that, as he would catch me again; and then he told me how cruelly he would serve me if I should do so. My captain, however, gave him to understand that I knew something of navigation: so he thought better of it; and, to my great joy, he went away. I now told my master I did not say I would run away in Philadelphia; neither did I mean it, as he did not use me ill, nor yet the captain: for if they did I certainly would have made some attempts before now; but as I thought that if it were God's will I ever should be freed it would be so, and, on the contrary, if it was not his will it would not happen; so I hoped, if ever I were freed, whilst I was used well, it should be by honest means; but, as I could not help myself, he must do as he pleased; I could only hope and trust to the God of Heaven; and at that instant my mind was big with inventions and full of schemes to escape. I then appealed to the captain whether he ever saw any sign of my making the least attempt to run away; and asked him if I did not always come on board according to the time for which he gave me liberty; and, more particularly, when all our men left us at Gaurdeloupe and went on board of the French fleet, and advised me to go with them, whether I might not, and that he could not have got me again. To my no small surprise, and very great joy, the captain confirmed every syllable that I had said: and even more; for he said he had tried different times to see if I would make any attempt of this kind, both at St. Eustatia and in America, and he never found that I made the smallest; but, on the contrary, I always came on board according to his orders; and he did really believe, if I ever meant to run away, that, as I could never have had a better opportunity, I would have done it the night the mate and all the people left our vessel at Gaurdeloupe. The captain then informed my master, who had been thus imposed on by our mate, though I did not know who was my enemy, the reason the mate had for imposing this lie upon him; which was, because I had acquainted the captain of the provisions the mate had given away or taken out of the vessel. This speech of the captain was like life to the dead to me, and instantly my soul glorified God; and still more so on hearing my master immediately say that I was a sensible fellow, and he never did intend to use me as a common slave; and that but for the entreaties of the captain, and his character of me, he would not have let me go from the stores about as I had done; that also, in so doing, he thought by carrying one little thing or other to different places to sell I might make money. That he also intended to encourage me in this by crediting me with half a puncheon of rum and half a hogshead of sugar at a time; so that, from being careful, I might have money enough, in some time, to purchase my freedom; and, when that was the case, I might depend upon it he would let me have it for forty pounds sterling money, which was only the same price he gave for me.

This sound gladdened my poor heart beyond measure; though indeed it was no more than the very idea I had formed in my mind of my master long before, and I immediately made him this reply: "Sir, I always had that very thought of you, indeed I had, and that made me so diligent in serving you." He then gave me a large piece of silver coin, such as I never had seen or had before, and told me to get ready for the voyage, and he would credit me with a tierce of sugar, and another of rum; he also said that he had two amiable sisters in Philadelphia, from whom I might get some necessary things. Upon this my noble captain desired me to go aboard; and, knowing the African metal, he charged me not to say any thing of this matter to any body; and he promised that the lying mate should not go with him any more. This was a change indeed; in the same hour to feel the most exquisite pain, and in the turn of a moment the fullest joy. It caused in me such sensations as I was only able to express in my looks; my heart was so overpowered with gratitude that I could have kissed both of their feet. When I left the room I immediately went, or rather flew, to the vessel, which being loaded, my master, as good as his word, trusted me with a tierce of rum, and another of sugar, when we sailed, and arrived safe at the elegant town of Philadelphia. I soon sold my goods here pretty well; and in this charming place I found every thing plentiful and cheap.

While I was in this place a very extraordinary occurrence befell me. I had been told one evening of a *wise* woman, a Mrs. Davis, who revealed secrets, foretold events, &c. I put little faith in this story at first, as I could not conceive that any mortal could foresee the future disposals of Providence, nor did I believe in any other revelation than that of the Holy Scriptures; however, I was greatly astonished at seeing this woman in a dream that night, though a person I never before beheld in my life; this made such an impression on me, that I could not get the idea the next day out of my mind, and I then became as anxious to see her as I was before indifferent; accordingly in the evening, after we left off working, I inquired where she lived, and being directed to her, to my inexpressible surprise, beheld the very woman in the very same dress she appeared to me to wear in the vision. She immediately told me I had dreamed of her the preceding night; related to me many things that had happened with a correctness that astonished me; and finally told me I should not be long a slave: this was the more agreeable news, as I believed it the more readily from her having so faithfully related the past incidents of my life. She said I should be twice in very great danger of my life within eighteen months, which, if I escaped, I should afterwards go on well; so, giving me her blessing, we parted. After staying here some time till our vessel was loaded, and I had bought in my little traffic, we sailed from this agreeable spot for Montserrat, once more to encounter the raging surfs.

We arrived safe at Montserrat, where we discharged our cargo; and soon after that we took slaves on board for St. Eustatia, and from thence to Georgia. I had always exerted myself and did double work, in order to make our voyages as short as possible; and from thus overworking myself while we were at Georgia I caught a fever and ague. I was very ill for eleven days and near dying; eternity was now exceedingly impressed on my mind, and I feared very much that awful event. I prayed the Lord therefore to spare me; and I made a promise in my mind to God, that I would be good if ever I should recover. At length, from having an eminent doctor to attend me, I was restored again to health; and soon after we got the vessel loaded, and set off for Montserrat. During the passage, as I was perfectly restored, and had much business of the vessel to mind, all my endeavours to keep up my integrity, and perform my promise to God, began to fail; and, in spite of all I could do, as we drew nearer and nearer to the islands, my resolutions more and more declined, as if the very air of that country or climate seemed fatal to piety. When we were safe arrived at Montserrat, and I had got ashore, I forgot my former resolutions. – Alas! how prone is the heart to leave that God it wishes to love! and how strongly do the things of this world strike the senses and captivate the soul! – After our vessel was discharged, we soon got her ready, and took in, as usual, some of the poor oppressed natives of Africa, and other negroes; we then set off again for Georgia and Charlestown. We arrived at Georgia, and having landed part of our cargo, proceeded to Charlestown with the remainder. While we were there I saw the town illuminated;

the guns were fired, and bonfires and other demonstrations of joy shewn, on account of the repeal of the stamp act. Here I disposed of some goods on my own account; the white men buying them with smooth promises and fair words, giving me however but very indifferent payment. There was one gentleman particularly who bought a puncheon of rum of me, which gave me a great deal of trouble; and, although I used the interest of my friendly captain, I could not obtain any thing for it; for, being a negro man, I could not oblige him to pay me. This vexed me much, not knowing how to act; and I lost some time in seeking after this Christian; and though, when the Sabbath came (which the negroes usually make their holiday) I was much inclined to go to public worship, I was obliged to hire some black men to help to pull a boat across the water to go in quest of this gentleman. When I found him, after much entreaty, both from myself and my worthy captain, he at last paid me in dollars; some of them, however, were copper, and of consequence of no value; but he took advantage of my being a negro man, and obliged me to put up with those or none, although I objected to them. Immediately after, as I was trying to pass them in the market, amongst other white men, I was abused for offering to pass bad coin; and, though I shewed them the man I got them from, I was within one minute of being tied up and flogged without either judge or jury; however, by the help of a good pair of heels, I ran off, and so escaped the bastinadoes I should have received. I got on board as fast as I could, but still continued in fear of them until we sailed, which I thanked God we did not long after; and I have never been amongst them since.

We soon came to Georgia, where we were to complete our lading; and here worse fate than ever attended me: for one Sunday night, as I was with some negroes in their master's yard in the town of Savannah, it happened that their master, one Doctor Perkins, who was a very severe and cruel man, came in drunk; and, not liking to see any strange negroes in his yard, he and a ruffian of a white man he had in his service beset me in an instant, and both of them struck me with the first weapons they could get hold of. I cried out as long as I could for help and mercy; but, though I gave a good account of myself, and he knew my captain, who lodged hard by him, it was to no purpose. They beat and mangled me in a shameful manner, leaving me near dead. I lost so much blood from the wounds I received, that I lay quite motionless, and was so benumbed that I could not feel any thing for many hours. Early in the morning they took me away to the jail. As I did not return to the ship all night, my captain, not knowing where I was, and being uneasy that I did not then make my appearance, he made inquiry after me; and, having found where I was, immediately came to me. As soon as the good man saw me so cut and mangled, he could not forbear weeping; he soon got me out of jail to his lodgings, and immediately sent for the best doctors in the place, who at first declared it as their opinion that I could not recover. My captain on this went to all the lawyers in the town for their advice, but they told him they could do nothing for me as I was a negro. He then went to Doctor Perkins, the hero who had vanquished me, and menaced him, swearing he would be revenged of him, and challenged him to fight. – But cowardice is ever the companion of cruelty – and the Doctor refused. However, by the skilfulness of one Doctor Brady of that place, I began at last to amend; but, although I was so sore and bad with the wounds I had all over me that I could not rest in any posture, yet I was in more pain on account of the captain's uneasiness about me than I otherwise should have been. The worthy man nursed and watched me all the hours of the night; and I was, through his attention and that of the doctor, able to get out of bed in about sixteen or eighteen days. All this time I was very much wanted on board, as I used frequently to go up and down the river for rafts, and other parts of our cargo, and stow them when the mate was sick or absent. In about four weeks I was able to go on duty; and in a fortnight after, having got in all our lading, our vessel set sail for Montserrat; and in less than three weeks we arrived there safe towards the end of the year. This ended my adventures in 1764 [1765]; for I did not leave Montserrat again till the beginning of the following year.

END OF THE FIRST VOLUME.

Engraving of the storm-wrecked slave ship *Nancy* on the Bahama Banks in 1767.

THE

INTERESTING NARRATIVE

OF

THE LIFE

OF

OLAUDAH EQUIANO,

OR

GUSTAVUS VASSA,

THE AFRICAN.

WRITTEN BY HIMSELF.

VOL. II.

Behold, God is my salvation; I will trust and not be afraid, for the Lord Jehovah is my strength and my song; he also is become my salvation.

And in that day shall ye say, Praise the Lord, call upon his name, declare his doings among the people.

Isaiah xii. 2, 4.

LONDON:

Printed for and sold by the AUTHOR, No. 10, Union-Street, Middlesex-Hospital.

Sold also by Mr. Johnson, St. Paul's Church-Yard; Mr. Murray, Fleet-Street; Messrs. Robson and Clark, Bond-Street; Mr. Davis, opposite Gray's-Inn, Holborn; Messrs. Shepperson and Reynolds, and Mr. Jackson. Oxford-Street; Mr. Lackington, Chifwell-Street; Mr. Mathews, Strand; Mr. Murray, Prince's-Street, Soho; Mess. Taylor and Co. South Arch, Royal Exchange; Mr. Button, Newington-Causeway; Mr. Parsons, Paternofter-Row; and may be had of all the Bookfellers in Town and Country.

[Entered at Stationer's Hall.]

They ran the ship aground: and the forepart stuck fast, and remained unmoveable, but the hinder part was broken with the violence of the waves.

ACTS xxvii. 41.

Howbeit, we must be cast upon a certain island;
Wherefore, sirs, be of good cheer: for I believe God, that it shall be even as it was told me.

ACTS xxvii. 26, 25.

Now a thing was secretly brought to me, and mine ear received a little thereof.
In thoughts from the visions of the night, when deep sleep falleth on men.

JOB iv. 12, 13.

Lo, all these *things* worketh God oftentimes with man,
To bring back his soul from the pit, to be enlightened with the light of the living.

JOB xxxiii. 29, 30.

CONTENTS OF VOLUME II.

THE LIFE, &C.

CHAP. VII.

The author's disgust at the West Indies — Forms schemes to obtain his freedom — Ludicrous disappointment he and his Captain meet with in Georgia — At last, by several successful voyages, he acquires a sum of money sufficient to purchase it — Applies to his master, who accepts it, and grants his manumission, to his great joy — He afterwards enters as a freeman on board one of Mr. King's ships, and sails for Georgia — Impositions on free negroes as usual — His venture of turkies — Sails for Montserrat, and on his passage his friend, the Captain, falls ill and dies.

EVERY day now brought me nearer my freedom, and I was impatient till we proceeded again to sea, that I might have an opportunity of getting a sum large enough to purchase it. I was not long ungratified; for, in the beginning of the year 1766, my master bought another sloop, named the Nancy, the largest I had ever seen. She was partly laden, and was to proceed to Philadelphia; our Captain had his choice of three, and I was well pleased he chose this, which was the largest; for, from his having a large vessel, I had more room, and could carry a larger quantity of goods with me. Accordingly, when we had delivered our old vessel, the Prudence, and completed the lading of the Nancy, having made near three hundred per cent, by four barrels of pork I brought from Charlestown, I laid in as large a cargo as I could, trusting to God's providence to prosper my undertaking. With these views I sailed for Philadelphia. On our passage, when we drew near the land, I was for the first time surprised at the sight of some whales, having never seen any such large sea monsters before; and as we sailed by the land one morning I saw a puppy whale close by the vessel; it was about the length of a wherry boat, and it followed us all the day till we got within the Capes. We arrived safe and in good time at Philadelphia, and I sold my goods there chiefly to the quakers. They always appeared to be a very honest discreet sort of people, and never attempted to impose on me; I therefore liked them, and ever after chose to deal with them in preference to any others. One Sunday morning while I was here, as I was going to church, I chanced to pass a meeting-house. The doors being open, and the house full of people, it excited my curiosity to go in. When I entered the house, to my great surprise, I saw a very tall woman standing in the midst of them, speaking in an audible voice something which I could not understand. Having never seen any thing of this kind before, I stood and stared about me for some time, wondering at this odd scene. As soon as it was over I took an opportunity to make inquiry about the place and people, when I was informed they were called Quakers. I particularly asked what that woman I saw in the midst of them had said, but none of them were pleased to satisfy me; so I quitted them, and soon after, as I was returning, I came to a church crowded with people; the church-yard was full likewise, and a number of people were even mounted on ladders, looking in at the windows. I thought this a strange sight, as I had never seen churches, either in England or the West Indies, crowded in this manner before. I therefore made bold to ask some people the meaning of all this, and they told me the Rev. Mr. George Whitfield was preaching.[1] I had often heard of this gentleman, and had wished to see and hear him; but I had never before had an opportunity. I now therefore resolved to gratify myself with the sight, and I pressed in amidst the multitude. When I got into the church I saw this pious man exhorting the people with the greatest fervour and earnestness, and sweating as much as I ever did while in slavery on Montserrat beach. I was very much struck and impressed with this; I thought it strange I had never seen divines exert themselves in this manner before, and I was no longer at a loss

---

1 George Whitefield (1714-70) was a British Methodist clergyman well-known for his fervent evangelical preaching in America, especially during the religious revival of the late 1730s and early 1740s known as the Great Awakening. Equiano was mistaken about seeing him in Philadelphia. He probably heard Whitefield speak in Savannah, Georgia, or in London at another time.

to account for the thin congregations they preached to. When we had discharged our cargo here, and were loaded again, we left this fruitful land once more, and set sail for Montserrat. My traffic had hitherto succeeded so well with me, that I thought, by selling my goods when we arrived at Montserrat, I should have enough to purchase my freedom. But, as soon as our vessel arrived there, my master came on board, and gave orders for us to go to St. Eustatia, and discharge our cargo there, and from thence proceed for Georgia. I was much disappointed at this; but thinking, as usual, it was of no use to encounter with the decrees of fate, I submitted without repining, and we went to St. Eustatia. After we had discharged our cargo there we took in a live cargo, as we call a cargo of slaves. Here I sold my goods tolerably well; but, not being able to lay out all my money in this small island to as much advantage as in many other places, I laid out only part, and the remainder I brought away with me neat. We sailed from hence for Georgia, and I was glad when we got there, though I had not much reason to like the place from my last adventure in Savannah; but I longed to get back to Montserrat and procure my freedom, which I expected to be able to purchase when I returned. As soon as we arrived here I waited on my careful doctor, Mr. Brady, to whom I made the most grateful acknowledgments in my power for his former kindness and attention during my illness. While we were here an odd circumstance happened to the Captain and me, which disappointed us both a good deal. A silversmith, whom we had brought to this place some voyages before, agreed with the Captain to return with us to the West Indies, and promised at the same time to give the Captain a great deal of money, having pretended to take a liking to him, and being, as we thought, very rich. But while we stayed to load our vessel this man was taken ill in a house where he worked, and in a week's time became very bad. The worse he grew the more he used to speak of giving the Captain what he had promised him, so that he expected something considerable from the death of this man, who had no wife or child, and he attended him day and night. I used also to go with the Captain, at his own desire, to attend him; especially when we saw there was no appearance of his recovery: and, in order to recompense me for my trouble, the Captain promised me ten pounds, when he should get the man's property. I thought this would be of great service to me, although I had nearly money enough to purchase my freedom, if I should get safe this voyage to Montserrat. In this expectation I laid out above eight pounds of my money for a suit of superfine clothes to dance in at my freedom, which I hoped was then at hand. We still continued to attend this man, and were with him even on the last day he lived, till very late at night, when we went on board. After we were got to bed, about one or two o'clock in the morning, the Captain was sent for, and informed the man was dead. On this he came to my bed, and, waking me, informed me of it, and desired me to get up and procure a light, and immediately go to him. I told him I was very sleepy, and wished he would take somebody else with him; or else, as the man was dead, and could want no farther attendance, to let all things remain as they were till the next morning. "No, no," said he, "we will have the money to-night, I cannot wait till to-morrow; so let us go." Accordingly I got up and struck a light, and away we both went and saw the man as dead as we could wish. The Captain said he would give him a grand burial, in gratitude for the promised treasure; and desired that all the things belonging to the deceased might be brought forth. Among others, there was a nest of trunks of which he had kept the keys whilst the man was ill, and when they were produced we opened them with no small eagerness and expectation; and as there were a great number within one another, with much impatience we took them one out of the other. At last, when we came to the smallest, and had opened it, we saw it was full of papers, which we supposed to be notes; at the sight of which our hearts leapt for joy; and that instant the Captain, clapping his hands, cried out, "Thank God, here it is." But when we took up the trunk, and began to examine the supposed treasure and long-looked-for bounty, (alas! alas! how uncertain and deceitful are all human affairs!) what had we found! While we thought we were embracing a substance we grasped an empty nothing. The whole amount that was in the nest of trunks was only one dollar and a half; and all that the man possessed would not pay for his coffin. Our sudden and exquisite joy was now succeeded by as sudden and exquisite pain; and my Captain and I exhibited, for some time, most ridiculous figures – pictures of chagrin and disappointment! We went away greatly mortified, and left the deceased to do as well as he could for himself, as we had taken so good care of him when alive for nothing. We set sail once more for Montserrat, and arrived there safe; but much out of humour with our friend the silversmith. When we had unladed the vessel, and I had sold my venture, finding myself master of about forty-seven pounds, I consulted my true friend, the Captain, how I should proceed in offering my master the money for my freedom. He told me to come on a certain morning, when he and my master would be at breakfast together. Accordingly, on that morning I went, and met the Captain there, as he had appointed. When I went in I made my obeisance to my master, and with my money in my hand, and many fears in my heart, I prayed him to be as good as his offer to me, when he was pleased to promise me my freedom as soon as I could purchase it. This speech seemed to confound him; he began to recoil: and my heart that instant sunk within me. "What," said he, "give you your freedom? Why, where did you get the money? Have you got forty pounds sterling?" "Yes, sir," I answered. "How did you get it?" replied he. I told him, very honestly. The Captain then said he knew I got the money very honestly and with much industry, and that I was particularly careful. On which my master replied, I got money much faster than he did: and said he would not have made me the promise he did if he had thought I should have got money so soon. "Come, come," said my worthy Captain, clapping my master on the back, "Come, Robert, (which was his name) I think you must let him have his freedom; you have laid your money out very well; you have received good interest for it all this time, and here is now the principal at last. I know Gustavus has earned you more than an hundred a-year, and he will still save you money, as he will not leave you: – Come, Robert, take the money." My master then said, he would not be worse than his promise; and, taking the money, told me to go to the Secretary at the Register Office, and get my manumission drawn up. These words of my master were like a voice from heaven to me: in an instant all my trepidation was turned into unutterable bliss; and I most reverently bowed myself with gratitude, unable to express my feelings, but by the overflowing of my eyes, while my true and worthy friend, the Captain, congratulated us both with a peculiar degree of heart-felt pleasure. As soon as the first transports of my joy were over, and that I had expressed my thanks to these my worthy friends in the best manner I was able, I rose with a heart full of affection and reverence, and left the room, in order to obey my master's joyful mandate of going to the Register Office. As I was leaving the house I called to mind the words of the Psalmist, in the 126th Psalm, and like him, "I glorified God in my heart, in whom I trusted."[1] These words had been impressed on my mind from the very day I was forced from Deptford to the present hour, and I now saw them, as I thought, fulfilled and verified. My imagination was all rapture as I flew to the Register Office, and, in this respect, like the apostle Peter,[2] (whose deliverance from prison was so sudden and extraordinary, that he thought he was in a vision) I could scarcely believe I was awake. Heavens! who could do justice to my feelings at this moment! Not conquering heroes them-selves, in the midst of a triumph – Not the tender mother who has just regained her long-lost infant, and presses it to her heart – Not the weary hungry mariner, at the sight of the desired friendly port – Not the lover, when he once more embraces his beloved mistress, after she had been ravished from his arms! – All within my breast was tumult, wildness, and delirium! My feet scarcely touched the ground, for they were winged with joy, and, like Elijah, as he rose to heaven, they "were with light-ning sped as I went on."[3] Every one I met I told of my happi-ness, and blazed about the virtue of my amiable master and cap-tain.

---

1 Psalm 126 dwells on release from captivity. Equiano's quote does not appear in the biblical psalm.
2 [Equiano's note] Acts, chap. xii. ver. 9.
3 The biblical story of Elijah taken up into heaven on a fiery chariot with horses of fire appears in 2 Kings 2.1-18. Equiano's quote is his own.

When I got to the office and acquainted the Register with my errand he congratulated me on the occasion, and told me he would draw up my manumission for half price, which was a guinea. I thanked him for his kindness; and, having received it and paid him, I hastened to my master to get him to sign it, that I might be fully released. Accordingly he signed the manumission that day, so that, before night, I who had been a slave in the morning, trembling at the will of another, was become my own master, and completely free. I thought this was the happiest day I had ever experienced; and my joy was still heightened by the blessings and prayers of the sable race, particularly the aged, to whom my heart had ever been attached with reverence.

As the form of my manumission has something peculiar in it, and expresses the absolute power and dominion one man claims over his fellow, I shall beg leave to present it before my readers at full length:

Montserrat. – To all men unto whom these presents shall come: I Robert King, of the parish of St. Anthony in the said island, merchant, send greeting: Know ye, that I the aforesaid Robert King, for and in consideration of the sum of seventy pounds current money of the said island, to me in hand paid, and to the intent that a negro manslave, named Gustavus Vassa, shall and may become free, have manumitted, emancipated, enfranchised, and set free, and by these presents do manumit, emancipate, enfranchise, and set free, the aforesaid negro man-slave, named Gustavus Vassa, for ever, hereby giving, granting, and releasing unto him, the said Gustavus Vassa, all right, title, dominion, sovereignty, and property, which, as lord and master over the aforesaid Gustavus Vassa, I had, or now I have, or by any means whatsoever I may or can hereafter possibly have over him the aforesaid negro, for ever. In witness whereof I the above-said Robert King have unto these presents set my hand and seal, this tenth day of July,

in the year of our Lord one thousand seven hundred and
sixty-six.

ROBERT KING.

Signed, sealed, and delivered in the presence of
  Terrylegay, Montserrat.
Registered the within manumission at full length, this
eleventh day of July, 1766, in liber D.

TERRYLEGAY, Register.

In short, the fair as well as black people immediately styled
me by a new appellation, to me the most desirable in the world,
which was Freeman, and at the dances I gave, my Georgia
superfine blue clothes made no indifferent appearance, as I
thought. Some of the sable females, who formerly stood aloof,
now began to relax and appear less coy; but my heart was still
fixed on London, where I hoped to be ere long. So that my
worthy captain and his owner, my late master, finding that the
bent of my mind was towards London, said to me, "We hope
you won't leave us, but that you will still be with the vessels."
Here gratitude bowed me down; and none but the generous
mind can judge of my feelings, struggling between inclination
and duty. However, notwithstanding my wish to be in London,
I obediently answered my benefactors that I would go in the
vessel, and not leave them; and from that day I was entered on
board as an able-bodied sailor, at thirty-six shillings per month,
besides what perquisites I could make. My intention was to
make a voyage or two, entirely to please these my honoured
patrons; but I determined that the year following, if it pleased
God, I would see Old England once more, and surprise my old
master, Capt. Pascal, who was hourly in my mind; for I still
loved him, notwithstanding his usage of me, and I pleased
myself with thinking of what he would say when he saw what
the Lord had done for me in so short a time, instead of being, as
he might perhaps suppose, under the cruel yoke of some

planter. With these kind of reveries I used often to entertain myself, and shorten the time till my return; and now, being as in my original free African state, I embarked on board the Nancy, after having got all things ready for our voyage. In this state of serenity we sailed for St. Eustatia; and, having smooth seas and calm weather, we soon arrived there: after taking our cargo on board, we proceeded to Savannah in Georgia, in August, 1766. While we were there, as usual, I used to go for the cargo up the rivers in boats; and on this business I have been frequently beset by alligators, which were very numerous on that coast, and I have shot many of them when they have been near getting into our boats; which we have with great difficulty sometimes prevented, and have been very much frightened at them. I have seen a young one sold in Georgia alive for six pence. During our stay at this place, one evening a slave belonging to Mr. Read, a merchant of Savannah, came near our vessel, and began to use me very ill. I entreated him, with all the patience I was master of, to desist, as I knew there was little or no law for a free negro here; but the fellow, instead of taking my advice, persevered in his insults, and even struck me. At this I lost all temper, and I fell on him and beat him soundly. The next morning his master came to our vessel as we lay alongside the wharf, and desired me to come ashore that he might have me flogged all round the town, for beating his negro slave. I told him he had insulted me, and had given the provocation, by first striking me. I had told my captain also the whole affair that morning, and wished him to have gone along with me to Mr. Read, to prevent bad consequences; but he said that it did not signify, and if Mr. Read said any thing he would make matters up, and had desired me to go to work, which I accordingly did. The Captain being on board when Mr. Read came, he told him I was a free man; and when Mr. Read applied to him to deliver me up, he said he knew nothing of the matter. I was astonished and frightened at this, and thought I had better keep where I was than go ashore and be flogged round the town, without judge or jury. I therefore refused to stir; and Mr. Read went away, swearing he would bring all the constables in the town, for he would have me out of the vessel. When he was gone, I thought his threat might prove too true to my sorrow; and I was confirmed in this belief, as well by the many instances I had seen of the treatment of free negroes, as from a fact that had happened within my own knowledge here a short time before. There was a free black man, a carpenter, that I knew, who, for asking a gentleman that he worked for, for the money he had earned, was put into gaol; and afterwards this oppressed man was sent from Georgia, with false accusations, of an intention to set the gentleman's house on fire, and run away with his slaves. I was therefore much embarrassed, and very apprehensive of a flogging at least. I dreaded, of all things, the thoughts of being striped, as I never in my life had the marks of any violence of that kind. At that instant a rage seized my soul, and for a little I determined to resist the first man that should offer to lay violent hands on me, or basely use me without a trial; for I would sooner die like a free man, than suffer myself to be scourged by the hands of ruffians, and my blood drawn like a slave. The captain and others, more cautious, advised me to make haste and conceal myself; for they said Mr. Read was a very spiteful man, and he would soon come on board with constables and take me. At first I refused this counsel, being determined to stand my ground; but at length, by the prevailing entreaties of the captain and Mr. Dixon, with whom he lodged, I went to Mr. Dixon's house, which was a little out of town, at a place called Yea-ma-chra. I was but just gone when Mr. Read, with the constables, came for me, and searched the vessel; but, not finding me there, he swore he would have me dead or alive. I was secreted about five days; however, the good character which my captain always gave me as well as some other gentlemen who also knew me, procured me some friends. At last some of them told my captain that he did not use me well, in suffering me thus to be imposed upon, and said they would see me redressed, and get me on board some other vessel. My captain, on this, immediately went to Mr. Read, and told him, that ever since I eloped from the vessel his work had been neglected, and he could not go on with her loading, himself and mate not being well; and, as I had managed things on board for them, my absence must retard his voyage, and consequently hurt the owner; he therefore begged of him to forgive me, as he said he never had any complaint of me before, for the many years that I had been with him. After repeated entreaties, Mr. Read said I might go to hell, and that he would not meddle with me; on which my captain came immediately to me at his lodging, and telling me how pleasantly matters had gone on, he desired me to go on board. Some of my other friends then asked him if he had got the constable's warrant from them; the captain said, No. On this I was desired by them to stay in the house; and they said they would get me on board of some other vessel before the evening. When the captain heard this he became almost distracted. He went immediately for the warrant, and, after using every exertion in his power, he at last got it from my hunters; but I had all the expenses to pay. After I had thanked all my friends for their attention, I went on board again to my work, of which I had always plenty. We were in haste to complete our lading, and were to carry twenty head of cattle with us to the West Indies, where they are a very profitable article. In order to encourage me in working, and to make up for the time I had lost, my captain promised me the privilege of carrying two bullocks of my own with me; and this made me work with redoubled ardour. As soon as I had got the vessel loaded, in doing which I was obliged to perform the duty of the mate as well as my own work, and that the bullocks were near coming on board, I asked the captain leave to bring my two, according to his promise; but, to my great surprise, he told me there was no room for them. I then asked him to permit me to take one; but he said he could not. I was a good deal mortified at this usage, and told him I had no notion that he intended thus to impose on me; nor could I think well of any man that was so much worse than his word. On this we had some disagreement, and I gave him to understand, that I intended to leave the vessel. At this he appeared to be very much dejected; and our mate, who had been very sickly, and whose duty had long devolved upon me, advised him to persuade me to stay: in consequence of which he spoke very kindly to me, making many fair promises, telling me that, as the mate was so sickly, he could not do without me, and that, as the safety of the vessel and cargo depended greatly upon me, he therefore hoped that I would not be offended at what had passed between us, and swore he would make up all matters when we arrived in the West Indies; so I consented to slave on as before. Soon after this, as the bullocks were coming on board, one of them ran at the captain, and butted him so furiously in the breast, that he never recovered of the blow. In order to make me some amends for his treatment about the bullocks, the captain now pressed me very much to take some turkeys, and other fowls, with me, and gave me liberty to take as many as I could find room for; but I told him he knew very well I had never carried any turkeys before, as I always thought they were such tender birds that they were not fit to cross the seas. However, he continued to press me to buy them for once; and, what was very surprising to me, the more I was against it, the more he urged my taking them, insomuch that he ensured me from all losses that might happen by them, and I was prevailed on to take them; but I thought this very strange, as he had never acted so with me before. This, and not being able to dispose of my paper-money in any other way, induced me at length to take four dozen. The turkeys, however, I was so dissatisfied about that I determined to make no more voyages to this quarter, nor with this captain; and was very apprehensive that my free voyage would be the worst I had ever made. We set sail for Montserrat. The captain and mate had been both complaining of sickness when we sailed, and as we proceeded on our voyage they grew worse. This was about November, and we had not been long at sea before we began to meet with strong northerly gales and rough seas; and in about seven or eight days all the bullocks were near being drowned, and four or five of them died. Our vessel, which had not been tight at first, was much less so now; and, though we were but nine in the whole, including five sailors and myself, yet we were obliged to attend to the pumps every half or three quarters of an hour. The captain and mate came on deck as often as they were able, which was now but seldom; for they declined so fast, that they were not well enough to make observations above four or five times the whole voyage. The whole care of the vessel rested, therefore, upon me, and I was obliged to direct her by my former experience, not being able to work a traverse. The captain was now very sorry he had not taught me navigation, and protested, if ever he should get well again, he would not fail to do so; but in about seventeen days his illness increased so much, that he was obliged to keep his bed, continuing sensible, however, till the last, constantly having the owner's interest at heart; for this just and benevolent man ever appeared much concerned about the welfare of what he was intrusted with. When this dear friend found the symptoms of death approaching, he called me by my name; and, when I came to him, he asked (with almost his last breath) if he had ever done me any harm? "God forbid I should think so," I replied, "I should then be the most ungrateful of wretches to the best of benefactors." While I was thus expressing my affection and sorrow by his bedside, he expired without saying another word; and the day following we committed his body to the deep. Every man on board loved this man, and regretted his death; but I was exceedingly affected at it, and I found that I did not know, till he was gone, the strength of my regard for him. Indeed I had every reason in the world to be attached to him; for, besides that he was in general mild, affable, generous, faithful, benevolent, and just, he was to me a friend and a father; and, had it pleased Providence that he had died but five months before, I verily believe I should not have obtained my freedom when I did; and it is not improbable that I might not have been able to get it at any rate afterwards. The captain being dead, the mate came on the deck, and made such observations as he was able, but to no purpose. In the course of a few days more, the few bullocks that remained were found dead; but the turkies I had, though on the deck, and exposed to so much wet and bad weather, did well, and I afterwards gained near three hundred per cent. on the sale of them; so that in the event it proved a happy circumstance for me that I had not bought the bullocks I intended, for they must have perished with the rest; and I could not help looking on this, otherwise trifling circumstance, as a particular providence of God, and I was thankful accordingly. The care of the vessel took up all my time, and engaged my attention entirely. As we were not out of the variable winds, I thought I should not be much puzzled to hit upon the islands. I was persuaded I steered right for Antigua, which I wished to reach, as the nearest to us; and in the course of nine or ten days we made this island, to our great joy; and the next day after we came safe to Montserrat. Many were surprised when they heard of my conducting the sloop into the port, and I now obtained a new appelation, and was called Captain. This elated me not a little, and it was quite flattering to my vanity to be thus styled by as high a title as any free man in this place possessed. When the death of the captain became known, he was much regretted by all who knew him; for he was a man universally respected. At the same time the sable captain lost no fame; for the success I had met with increased the affection of my friends in no small measure.

CHAP. VIII.

The author, to oblige Mr. King, once more embarks for Georgia in one of his vessels — A new captain is appointed — They sail, and steer a new course — Three remarkable dreams — The vessel is shipwrecked on the Bahama bank, but the crew are preserved, principally by means of the author — He sets out from the island with the captain, in a small boat, in quest of a ship — Their distress — Meet with a wrecker — Sail for Providence — Are overtaken again by a terrible storm, and are all near perishing — Arrive at New Providence — The author, after some time, sails from thence to Georgia — Meets with another storm, and is obliged to put back and refit — Arrives at Georgia — Meets new impositions — Two white men attempt to kidnap him — Officiates as a parson at a funeral ceremony — Bids adieu to Georgia, and sails for Martinico.

As I had now, by the death of my captain, lost my great benefactor and friend, I had little inducement to remain longer in the West Indies, except my gratitude to Mr. King, which I thought I had pretty well discharged in bringing back his vessel safe, and delivering his cargo to his satisfaction. I began to think of leaving this part of the world, of which I had been long tired, and returning to England, where my heart had always been; but Mr. King still pressed me very much to stay with his vessel; and he had done so much for me that I found myself unable to refuse his requests, and consented to go another voyage to Georgia, as the mate, from his ill state of health, was quite useless in the vessel. Accordingly a new captain was appointed, whose name was William Phillips, an old acquaintance of mine; and, having refitted our vessel, and taken several slaves on board, we set sail for St. Eustatia, where we stayed but a few days; and on the 30th of January 1767 we steered for Georgia. Our new captain boasted strangely of his skill in navigating and conducting a vessel; and in consequence of this he steered a new course, several points more to the westward than we ever did before; this appeared to me very extraordinary.

On the fourth of February, which was soon after we had got into our new course, I dreamt the ship was wrecked amidst the surfs and rocks, and that I was the means of saving every one on board; and on the night following I dreamed the very same dream. These dreams however made no impression on my mind; and the next evening, it being my watch below, I was pumping the vessel a little after eight o'clock, just before I went off the deck, as is the custom; and being weary with the duty of the day, and tired at the pump, (for we made a good deal of water) I began to express my impatience, and I uttered with an oath, "Damn the vessel's bottom out." But my conscience instantly smote me for the expression. When I left the deck I went to bed, and had scarcely fallen asleep when I dreamed the same dream again about the ship that I had dreamt the two pre-ceeding nights. At twelve o'clock the watch was changed; and, as I had always the charge of the captain's watch, I then went upon deck. At half after one in the morning the man at the helm saw something under the lee-beam that the sea washed against; and he immediately called to me that there was a gram-pus, and desired me to look at it. Accordingly I stood up and observed it for some time; but, when I saw the sea wash up against it again and again, I said it was not a fish but a rock. Being soon certain of this, I went down to the captain, and, with some confusion, told him the danger we were in, and desired him to come upon deck immediately. He said it was very well, and I went up again. As soon as I was upon deck the wind, which had been pretty high, having abated a little, the vessel began to be carried sideways towards the rock, by means of the current. Still the captain did not appear. I therefore went to him again, and told him the vessel was then near a large rock, and desired he would come up with speed. He said he would, and I returned to the deck. When I was upon the deck again I saw we were not above a pistol shot from the rock, and I heard the noise of the breakers all around us. I was exceeding-ly alarmed at this; and the captain having not yet come on the deck I lost all patience; and, growing quite enraged, I ran down to him again, and asked him why he did not come up, and what he could mean by all this? "The breakers," said I, "are round us, and the vessel is almost on the rock." With that he came on the deck with me, and we tried to put the vessel about, and get her out of the current, but all to no purpose, the wind being very small. We then called all hands up immediately; and after a little we got up one end of a cable, and fastened it to the anchor. By this time the surf was foaming round us, and made a dreadful noise on the breakers, and the very moment we let the anchor go the vessel struck against the rocks. One swell now succeeded another, as it were one wave calling on its fellow: the roaring of the billows increased, and, with one single heave of the swells, the sloop was pierced and transfixed among the rocks! In a moment a scene of horror presented itself to my mind, such as I never had conceived or experienced before. All my sins stared me in the face; and especially, I thought that God had hurled his direful vengeance on my guilty head for cursing the vessel on which my life depended. My spirits at this forsook me, and I expected every moment to go to the bottom: I determined if I should still be saved that I would never swear again. And in the midst of my distress, while the dreadful surfs were dashing with unremitting fury among the rocks, I remembered the Lord, though fearful that I was undeserving of forgiveness, and I thought that as he had often delivered he might yet deliver; and, calling to mind the many mercies he had shewn me in times past, they gave me some small hope that he might still help me. I then began to think how we might be saved; and I believe no mind was ever like mine so replete with inventions and confused with schemes, though how to escape death I knew not. The captain immediately ordered the hatches to be nailed down on the slaves in the hold, where there were above twenty, all of whom must unavoidably have perished if he had been obeyed. When he desired the man to nail down the hatches I thought that my sin was the cause of this, and that God would charge me with these people's blood. This thought rushed upon my mind that instant with such violence, that it quite overpowered me, and I fainted. I recovered just as the people were about to nail down the hatches; perceiving which, I desired them to stop. The captain then said it must be done: I asked him why? He said that every one would endeavour to get into the boat, which was but small, and thereby we should be drowned; for it would not have carried above ten at the most. I could no longer restrain my emotion, and I told him he deserved drowning for not knowing how to navigate the vessel; and I believe the people would have tossed him overboard if I had given them the least hint of it. However the hatches were not nailed down; and, as none of us could leave the vessel then on account of the darkness, and as we knew not where to go, and were convinced besides that the boat could not survive the surfs, we all said we would remain on the dry part of the vessel, and trust to God till daylight appeared, when we should know better what to do.

I then advised to get the boat prepared against morning, and some of us began to set about it; but some abandoned all care of the ship and themselves, and fell to drinking. Our boat had a piece out of her bottom near two feet long, and we had no materials to mend her; however, necessity being the mother of invention, I took some pump leather and nailed it to the broken part, and plastered it over with tallow-grease. And, thus prepared, with the utmost anxiety of mind we watched for daylight, and thought every minute an hour till it appeared. At last it saluted our longing eyes, and kind Providence accompanied its approach with what was no small comfort to us; for the dreadful swell began to subside; and the next thing that we discovered to raise our drooping spirits, was a small key or island, about five or six miles off; but a barrier soon presented itself; for there was not water enough for our boat to go over the reefs, and this threw us again into a sad consternation; but there was no alternative, we were therefore obliged to put but few in the boat at once; and, what is still worse, all of us were frequently under the necessity of getting out to drag and lift it over the reefs. This cost us much labour and fatigue; and, what was yet more distressing, we could not avoid having our legs cut and torn very much with the rocks. There were only four people that would work with me at the oars; and they consisted of three black men and a Dutch creole sailor; and, though we went with the boat five times that day, we had no others to assist us. But, had we not worked in this manner, I really believe the people could not have been saved; for not one of the white men did any thing to preserve their lives; and indeed they soon got so drunk that they were not able, but lay about the deck like swine, so that we were at last obliged to lift them into the boat and carry them on shore by force. This want of assistance made our labour intolerably severe; insomuch, that, by putting on shore so often that day, the skin was entirely stript off my hands. However, we continued all the day to toil and strain our exertions, till we had brought all on board safe to the shore; so that out of thirty-two people we lost not one. My dream now returned upon my mind with all its force; it was fulfilled in every part; for our danger was the same I had dreamt of: and I could not help looking on myself as the principal instrument in effecting our deliverance; for, owing to some of our people getting drunk, the rest of us were obliged to double our exertions; and it was fortunate we did, for in a very little time longer the patch of leather on the boat would have been worn out, and she would have been no longer fit for service. Situated as we were, who could think that men should be so careless of the danger they were in? for, if the wind had but raised the swell as it was when the vessel struck, we must have bid a final farewell to all hopes of deliverance; and though, I warned the people who were drinking and entreated them to embrace the moment of deliverance, nevertheless they persisted, as if not possessed of the least spark of reason. I could not help thinking, that, if any of these people had been lost, God would charge me with their lives, which, perhaps, was one cause of my labouring so hard for their preservation, and indeed every one of them afterwards seemed so sensible of the service I had rendered them; that while we were on the key I was a kind of chieftain amongst them. I brought some limes, oranges, and lemons ashore; and, finding it to be a good soil where we were, I planted several of them as a token to any one that might be cast away hereafter. This key, as we afterwards found, was one of the Bahama islands, which consist of a cluster of large islands, with smaller ones or keys, as they are called, interspersed among them. It was about a mile in circumference, with a white sandy beach running in a regular order along it. On that part of it where we first attempted to land there stood some very large birds, called flamingoes: these, from the reflection of the sun, appeared to us at a little distance as large as men; and, when they walked backwards and forwards, we could not conceive what they were: our captain swore they were cannibals. This created a great panic among us; and we held a consultation how to act. The captain wanted to go to a key that was within sight, but a great way off; but I was against it, as in so doing we should not be able to save all the people; "And therefore," said I, "let us go on shore here, and perhaps these cannibals may take to the water." Accordingly we steered towards them; and when we approached them, to our very great joy and no less wonder, they walked off one after the other very deliberately; and at last they took flight and relieved us entirely from our fears. About the key there were turtles and several sorts of fish in such abundance that we caught them without bait, which was a great relief to us after the salt provisions on board. There was also a large rock on the beach, about ten feet high, which was in the form of a punch-bowl at the top; this we could not help thinking Providence had ordained to supply us with rain-water; and it was something singular that, if we did not take the water when it rained, in some little time after it would turn as salt as sea-water.

Our first care, after refreshment, was to make ourselves tents to lodge in, which we did as well as we could with some sails we had brought from the ship. We then began to think how we might get from this place, which was quite uninhabited; and we determined to repair our boat, which was very much shattered, and to put to sea in quest of a ship or some inhabited island. It took us up however eleven days before we could get the boat ready for sea in the manner we wanted it, with a sail and other necessaries. When we had got all things prepared the captain wanted me to stay on shore while he went to sea in quest of a vessel to take all the people off the key; but this I refused; and the captain and myself, with five more, set off in the boat towards New Providence. We had no more than two musket load of gun-powder with us if any thing should happen; and our stock of provisions consisted of three gallons of rum, four of water, some salt beef, some biscuit; and in this manner we proceeded to sea.

On the second day of our voyage we came to an island called Obbico, the largest of the Bahama islands. We were much in want of water; for by this time our water was expended, and we were exceedingly fatigued in pulling two days in the heat of the sun; and it being late in the evening, we hauled the boat ashore to try for water and remain during the night: when we came ashore we searched for water, but could find none. When it was dark, we made a fire around us for fear of the wild beasts, as the place was an entire thick wood, and we took it by turns to watch. In this situation we found very little rest, and waited with impatience for the morning. As soon as the light appeared we set off again with our boat, in hopes of finding assistance during the day. We were now much dejected and weakened by pulling the boat; for our sail was of no use, and we were almost famished for want of fresh water to drink. We had nothing left to eat but salt beef, and that we could not use without water. In this situation we toiled all day in sight of the island, which was very long; in the evening, seeing no relief, we made ashore again, and fastened our boat. We then went to look for fresh water, being quite faint for the want of it; and we dug and searched about for some all the remainder of the evening, but could not find one drop, so that our dejection at this period became excessive, and our terror so great, that we expected nothing but death to deliver us. We could not touch our beef, which was as salt as brine, without fresh water; and we were in the greatest terror from the apprehension of wild beasts. When unwelcome night came we acted as on the night before; and the next morning we set off again from the island in hopes of seeing some vessel. In this manner we toiled as well as we were able till four o'clock, during which we passed several keys, but could not meet with a ship; and, still famishing with thirst, went ashore on one of the those keys again in hopes of finding some water. Here we found some leaves with a few drops of water in them, which we lapped with much eagerness; we then dug in several places, but without success. As we were digging holes in search of water there came forth some very thick and black stuff; but none of us could touch it, except the poor Dutch Creole, who drank above a quart of it as eagerly as if it had been wine. We tried to catch fish, but could not; and we now began to repine at our fate, and abandon ourselves to despair; when, in the midst of our murmuring, the captain all at once cried out "A sail! a sail! a sail!" This gladdening sound was like a reprieve to a convict, and we all instantly turned to look at it; but in a little time some of us began to be afraid it was not a sail. However, at a venture, we embarked and steered after it; and, in half an hour, to our unspeakable joy, we plainly saw that it was a vessel. At this our drooping spirits revived, and we made towards her with all the speed imaginable. When we came near to her, we found she was a little sloop, about the size of a Gravesend hoy,[1] and quite full of people; a circumstance which we could not make out the meaning of. Our captain, who was a Welchman, swore that they were pirates, and would kill us. I said, be that as it might, we must board her if we were to die for it; and, if they should not receive us kindly, we must oppose them as well as we could; for there was no alternative between their perishing and ours. This counsel was immediately taken; and I really believe that the captain, myself, and the Dutchman, would then have faced twenty men. We had two cutlasses and a musquet, that I brought in the boat; and, in this situation, we rowed alongside, and immediately boarded her. I believe there were about forty hands on board; but how great was our surprise, as soon as we got on board, to find that the major part of them were in the same predicament as ourselves!

They belonged to a whaling schooner that was wrecked two days before us about nine miles to the north of our vessel. When she was wrecked some of them had taken to their boats and had left some of their people and property on a key, in the same manner as we had done; and were going, like us, to New Providence in quest of a ship, when they met with this little sloop, called a wrecker; their employment in those seas being to look after wrecks. They were then going to take the remainder of the people belonging to the schooner; for which the wrecker was to have all things belonging to the vessel, and likewise their people's help to get what they could out of her, and were then to carry the crew to New Providence.

---

1 Hoy: a small passenger boat.

We told the people of the wrecker the condition of our vessel, and we made the same agreement with them as the schooner's people; and, on their complying, we begged of them to go to our key directly, because our people were in want of water. They agreed, therefore, to go along with us first; and in two days we arrived at the key, to the inexpressible joy of the people that we had left behind, as they had been reduced to great extremities for want of water in our absence. Luckily for us, the wrecker had now more people on board than she could carry or victual for any moderate length of time; they therefore hired the schooner's people to work on our wreck, and we left them our boat, and embarked for New Providence.

Nothing could have been more fortunate than our meeting with this wrecker, for New Providence was at such a distance that we never could have reached it in our boat. The island of Abbico was much longer than we expected; and it was not till after sailing for three or four days that we got safe to the farther end of it, towards New Providence. When we arrived there we watered, and got a good many lobsters and other shellfish; which proved a great relief to us, as our provisions and water were almost exhausted. We then proceeded on our voyage; but the day after we left the island, late in the evening, and whilst we were yet amongst the Bahama keys, we were overtaken by a violent gale of wind, so that we were obliged to cut away the mast. The vessel was very near foundering; for she parted from her anchors, and struck several times on the shoals. Here we expected every minute that she would have gone to pieces, and each moment to be our last; so much so that my old captain and sickly useless mate, and several others, fainted; and death stared us in the face on every side. All the swearers on board now began to call on the God of Heaven to assist them: and, sure enough, beyond our comprehension he did assist us, and in a miraculous manner delivered us! In the very height of our extremity the wind lulled for a few minutes; and, although the swell was high beyond expression, two men, who were expert swimmers, attempted to go to the buoy of the anchor, which we still saw on the water, at some distance, in a little punt that belonged to the wrecker, which was not large enough to carry more than two. She filled different times in their endeavours to get into her alongside of our vessel; and they saw nothing but death before them, as well as we; but they said they might as well die that way as any other. A coil of very small rope, with a little buoy, was put in along with them; and, at last, with great hazard, they got the punt clear from the vessel; and these two intrepid water heroes paddled away for life towards the buoy of the anchor. The eyes of us all were fixed on them all the time, expecting every minute to be their last: and the prayers of all those that remained in their senses were offered up to God, on their behalf, for a speedy deliverance; and for our own, which depended on them; and he heard and answered us! These two men at last reached the buoy; and, having fastened the punt to it, they tied one end of their rope to the small buoy that they had in the punt, and sent it adrift towards the vessel. We on board observing this threw out boat-hooks and leads fastened to lines, in order to catch the buoy: at last we caught it, and fastened a hawser to the end of the small rope; we then gave them a sign to pull, and they pulled the hawser to them, and fastened it to the buoy: which being done we hauled for our lives; and, through the mercy of God, we got again from the shoals into deep water, and the punt got safe to the vessel. It is impossible for any to conceive our heart-felt joy at this second deliverance from ruin, but those who have suffered the same hardships. Those whose strength and senses were gone came to themselves, and were now as elated as they were before depressed. Two days after this the wind ceased, and the water became smooth. The punt then went on shore, and we cut down some trees; and having found our mast and mended it we brought it on board, and fixed it up. As soon as we had done this we got up the anchor, and away we went once more for New Providence, which in three days more we reached safe, after having been above three weeks in a situation in which we did not expect to escape with life. The inhabitants here were very kind to us; and, when they learned our situation, shewed us a great deal of hospitality and friendship. Soon after this every one of my old fellow-sufferers that were free parted from us, and shaped their course where their inclination led them. One merchant, who had a large sloop, seeing our condition, and knowing we wanted to go to Georgia, told four of us that his vessel was going there; and, if we would work on board and load her, he would give us our passage free. As we could not get any wages whatever, and found it very hard to get off the place, we were obliged to consent to his proposal; and we went on board and helped to load the sloop, though we had only our victuals allowed us. When she was entirely loaded he told us she was going to Jamaica first, where we must go if we went in her. This, however, I refused; but my fellow-sufferers not having any money to help themselves with, necessity obliged them to accept of the offer, and to steer that course, though they did not like it.

We stayed in New Providence about seventeen or eighteen days; during which time I met with many friends, who gave me encouragement to stay there with them: but I declined it; though, had not my heart been fixed on England, I should have stayed, as I liked the place extremely, and there were some free black people here who were very happy, and we passed our time pleasantly together, with the melodious sound of the catguts, under the lime and lemon trees. At length Captain Phillips hired a sloop to carry him and some of the slaves that he could not sell to Georgia; and I agreed to go with him in this vessel, meaning now to take my farewell of that place. When the vessel was ready we all embarked; and I took my leave of New Providence, not without regret. We sailed about four o'clock in the morning, with a fair wind, for Georgia; and about eleven o'clock the same morning a short and sudden gale sprung up and blew away most of our sails; and, as we were still amongst the keys, in a very few minutes it dashed the sloop against the rocks. Luckily for us the water was deep; and the sea was not so angry but that, after having for some time laboured hard, and being many in number, we were saved through God's mercy; and, by using our greatest exertions, we got the vessel off. The next day we returned to Providence, where we soon got her again refitted. Some of the people swore that we had spells set upon us by somebody in Montserrat; and others that we had witches and wizzards amongst the poor helpless slaves;

and that we never should arrive safe at Georgia. But these things did not deter me; I said, "Let us again face the winds and seas, and swear not, but trust to God, and he will deliver us." We therefore once more set sail; and, with hard labour, in seven days' time arrived safe at Georgia.

After our arrival we went up to the town of Savannah; and the same evening I went to a friend's house to lodge, whose name was Mosa, a black man. We were very happy at meeting each other; and after supper we had a light till it was between nine and ten o'clock at night. About that time the watch or patrol came by; and, discerning a light in the house, they knocked at the door: we opened it; and they came in and sat down, and drank some punch with us: they also begged some limes of me, as they understood I had some, which I readily gave them. A little after this they told me I must go to the watch-house with them: this surprised me a good deal, after our kindness to them; and I asked them, Why so? They said that all negroes who had light in their houses after nine o'clock were to be taken into custody, and either pay some dollars or be flogged. Some of those people knew that I was a free man; but, as the man of the house was not free, and had his master to protect him, they did not take the same liberty with him they did with me. I told them that I was a free man, and just arrived from Providence; that we were not making any noise, and that I was not a stranger in that place, but was very well known there: "Besides," said I, "what will you do with me?" – "That you shall see," replied they, "but you must go to the watch-house with us." Now whether they meant to get money from me or not I was at a loss to know; but I thought immediately of the oranges and limes at Santa Cruz: and seeing that nothing would pacify them I went with them to the watch-house, where I remained during the night. Early the next morning these imposing ruffians flogged a negro-man and woman that they had in the watch-house, and then they told me that I must be flogged too. I asked why? and if there was no law for free men? And told them if there was I would have it put in force against them. But this only exasperated them the more; and instantly they swore they would serve me as Doctor Perkins had done; and they were going to lay violent hands on me; when one of them, more humane than the rest, said that as I was a free man they could not justify stripping me by law. I then immediately sent for Doctor Brady, who was known to be an honest and worthy man; and on his coming to my assistance they let me go.

This was not the only disagreeable incident I met with while I was in this place; for, one day, while I was a little way out of the town of Savannah, I was beset by two white men, who meant to play their usual tricks with me in the way of kidnapping. As soon as these men accosted me, one of them said to the other, "This is the very fellow we are looking for that you lost:" and the other swore immediately that I was the identical person. On this they made up to me, and were about to handle me; but I told them to be still and keep off; for I had seen those kind of tricks played upon other free blacks, and they must not think to serve me so. At this they paused a little, and one said to the other – it will not do; and the other answered that I talked too good English. I replied, I believed I did; and I had also with me a revengeful stick equal to the occasion; and my mind was likewise good. Happily however it was not used; and, after we had talked together a little in this manner, the rogues left me. I stayed in Savannah some time, anxiously trying to get to Montserrat once more to see Mr. King, my old master, and then to take a final farewell of the American quarter of the globe. At last I met with a sloop called the Speedwell, Captain John Bunton, which belonged to Grenada, and was bound to Martinico, a French island, with a cargo of rice, and I shipped myself on board of her. Before I left Georgia a black woman, who had a child lying dead, being very tenacious of the church burial service, and not able to get any white person to perform it, applied to me for that purpose. I told her I was no parson; and besides, that the service over the dead did not affect the soul. This however did not satisfy her; she still urged me very hard: I therefore complied with her earnest entreaties, and at last consented to act the parson for the first time in my life. As she was much respected, there was a great company both of white and black people at the grave. I then accordingly assumed my new vocation, and performed the funeral ceremony to the satisfaction of all present; after which I bade adieu to Georgia, and sailed for Martinico.

CHAP. IX.

The author arrives at Martinico – Meets with new difficulties – Gets to Montserrat, where he takes leave of his old master, and sails for England – Meets Capt. Pascal – Learns the French horn – Hires himself with Doctor Irving, where he learns to freshen sea water – Leaves the doctor, and goes a voyage to Turkey and Portugal; and afterwards goes a voyage to Grenada, and another to Jamaica – Returns to the Doctor, and they embark together on a voyage to the North Pole, with the Hon. Capt. Phipps – Some account of that voyage, and the dangers the author was in – He returns to England.

I THUS took a final leave of Georgia; for the treatment I had received in it disgusted me very much against the place; and when I left it and sailed for Martinico I determined never more to revisit it. My new captain conducted his vessel safer than my former one; and, after an agreeable voyage, we got safe to our intended port. While I was on this island I went about a good deal, and found it very pleasant, in particular I admired the town of St. Pierre, which is the principal one in the island, and built more like an European town than any I had seen in the West Indies. In general also, slaves were better treated, had more holidays, and looked better than those in the English islands. After we had done our business here, I wanted my discharge, which was necessary; for it was then the month of May, and I wished much to be at Montserrat to bid farewell to Mr. King, and all my other friends there, in time to sail for Old England in the July fleet. But, alas! I had put a great stumbling block in my own way, by which I was near losing my passage that season to England. I had lent my captain some money, which I now wanted to enable me to prosecute my intentions. This I told him; but when I applied for it, though I urged the necessity of my occasion, I met with so much shuffling from him, that I began at last to be afraid of losing my money, as I could not recover it by law: for I have already mentioned, that throughout the West Indies no black man's testimony is admitted, on any occasion, against any white person whatever, and therefore my own oath would have been of no use. I was obliged, therefore, to remain with him till he might be disposed to return it to me. Thus we sailed from Martinico for the Grenades,[1] I frequently pressing the captain for my money to no purpose; and, to render my condition worse, when we got there, the captain and his owners quarrelled; so that my situation became daily more irksome: for besides that we on board had little or no victuals allowed us, and I could not get my money nor wages, I could then have gotten my passage free to Montserrat had I been able to accept it. The worst of all was, that it was growing late in July, and the ships in the islands must sail by the 26th of that month. At last, however, with a great many entreaties, I got my money from the captain, and took the first vessel I could meet with for St. Eustatia. From thence I went in another to Basseterre in St. Kitts, where I arrived on the 19th of July. On the 22d, having met with a vessel bound to Montserrat, I wanted to go in her; but the captain and others would not take me on board until I should advertise myself, and give notice of my going off the island. I told them of my haste to be in Montserrat, and that the time then would not admit of advertising, it being late in the evening, and the captain about to sail; but he insisted it was necessary, and otherwise he said he would not take me. This reduced me to great perplexity; for if I should be compelled to submit to this degrading necessity, which every black freeman is under, of advertising himself like a slave, when he leaves an island, and which I thought a gross imposition upon any freeman, I feared I should miss that opportunity of going to Montserrat, and then I could not get to England that year. The vessel was just going off, and no time could be lost; I immediately therefore set about, with a heavy heart, to try who I could get to befriend me in complying with the demands of the captain. Luckily I found, in a few minutes, some gentlemen of Montserrat whom I knew; and, having told them my situation, I requested their friendly assistance in helping me off the island. Some of them, on this, went with me to the captain, and satisfied him of my freedom; and, to my very great joy, he desired me to go on board. We then set sail, and the next day,

---

1   Grenades: the Grenadines; a small group of islands in the British West Indies.

the 23d, I arrived at the wished-for place, after an absence of six months, in which I had more than once experienced the delivering hand of Providence, when all human means of escaping destruction seemed hopeless. I saw my friends with a gladness of heart which was increased by my absence and the dangers I had escaped, and I was received with great friendship by them all, but particularly by Mr. King, to whom I related the fate of his sloop, the Nancy, and the causes of her being wrecked. I now learned with extreme sorrow, that his house was washed away during my absence, by the bursting of a pond at the top of a mountain that was opposite the town of Plymouth. It swept great part of the town away, and Mr. King lost a great deal of property from the inundation, and nearly his life. When I told him I intended to go to London that season, and that I had come to visit him before my departure, the good man expressed a great deal of affection for me, and sorrow that I should leave him, and warmly advised me to stay there; insisting, as I was much respected by all the gentlemen in the place, that I might do very well, and in a short time have land and slaves of my own. I thanked him for this instance of his friendship; but, as I wished very much to be in London, I declined remaining any longer there, and begged he would excuse me. I then requested he would be kind enough to give me a certificate of my behaviour while in his service, which he very readily complied with, and gave me the following:

Montserrat, January 26, 1767.
The bearer hereof, Gustavus Vassa, was my slave for upwards of three years, during which he has always behaved himself well, and discharged his duty with honesty and assiduity.

ROBERT KING.
To all whom this may concern.

Having obtained this, I parted from my kind master, after many sincere professions of gratitude and regard, and prepared for my departure for London. I immediately agreed to go with one Capt. John Hamer, for seven guineas, the passage to London, on board a ship called the Andromache; and on the 24th and 25th I had free dances as they are called, with some of my countrymen, previous to my setting off; after which I took leave of all my friends, and on the 26th I embarked for London, exceedingly glad to see myself once more on board of a ship; and still more so, in steering the course I had long wished for. With a light heart I bade Montserrat farewell, and never had my feet on it since; and with it I bade adieu to the sound of the cruel whip, and all other dreadful instruments of torture; adieu to the offensive sight of the violated chastity of the sable females, which has too often accosted my eyes; adieu to oppressions (although to me less severe than most of my countrymen); and adieu to the angry howling, dashing surfs. I wished for a grateful and thankful heart to praise the Lord God on high for all his mercies!

We had a most prosperous voyage, and, at the end of seven weeks, arrived at Cherry-Garden stairs.[1] Thus were my longing eyes once more gratified with a sight of London, after having been absent from it above four years. I immediately received my wages, and I never had earned seven guineas so quick in my life before; I had thirty-seven guineas in all, when I got cleared of the ship. I now entered upon a scene, quite new to me, but full of hope. In this situation my first thoughts were to look out for some of my former friends, and amongst the first of those were the Miss Guerins. As soon, therefore, as I had regaled myself I went in quest of those kind ladies, whom I was very impatient to see; and with some difficulty and perseverance, I found them at May's-hill, Greenwich. They were most agreeably surprised to see me, and I quite overjoyed at meeting with them. I told them my history, at which they expressed great wonder, and freely acknowledged it did their cousin, Capt. Pascal, no honour. He then visited there frequently; and I met him four or five days after in Greenwich park. When he saw me he appeared a good deal surprised, and asked me how I came back? I answered, "In a ship." To which he replied dryly, "I suppose you did not walk back to London on the water." As I saw,

---

1 Cherry-Garden stairs: a landing area on the bank of the Thames.

by his manner, that he did not seem to be sorry for his behaviour to me, and that I had not much reason to expect any favour from him, I told him that he had used me very ill, after I had been such a faithful servant to him for so many years; on which, without saying any more, he turned about and went away. A few days after this I met Capt. Pascal at Miss Guerin's house, and asked him for my prize-money. He said there was none due to me; for, if my prize money had been £10,000 he had a right to it all. I told him I was informed otherwise; on which he bade me defiance; and, in a bantering tone, desired me to commence a lawsuit against him for it: ".There are lawyers enough," said he, "that will take the cause in hand, and you had better try it." I told him then that I would try it, which enraged him very much; however, out of regard to the ladies, I remained still, and never made any farther demand of my right. Some time afterwards these friendly ladies asked me what I meant to do with myself, and how they could assist me. I thanked them, and said, if they pleased. I would be their servant; but if not, as I had thirty-seven guineas, which would support me for some time, I would be much obliged to them to recommend me to some person who would teach me a business whereby I might earn my living. They answered me very politely, that they were sorry it did not suit them to take me as their servant, and asked me what business I should like to learn? I said, hair-dressing. They then promised to assist me in this; and soon after they recommended me to a gentleman whom I had known before, one Capt. O'Hara, who treated me with much kindness, and procured me a master, a hair-dresser, in Coventry-court, Haymarket, with whom he placed me. I was with this man from September till the February following. In that time we had a neighbour in the same court who taught the French horn. He used to blow it so well that I was charmed with it, and agreed with him to teach me to blow it. Accordingly he took me in hand, and began to instruct me, and I soon learned all the three parts. I took great delight in blowing on this instrument, the evenings being long; and besides that I was fond of it, I did not like to be idle, and it filled up my vacant hours innocently. At this time also I agreed with the Rev. Mr.

Gregory, who lived in the same court, where he kept an academy and an evening-school, to improve me in arithmetic. This he did as far as barter and alligation; so that all the time I was there I was entirely employed. In February 1768 I hired myself to Dr. Charles Irving, in Pall-mall, so celebrated for his successful experiments in making sea water fresh; and here I had plenty of hair-dressing to improve my hand. This gentleman was an excellent master; he was exceedingly kind and good tempered; and allowed me in the evenings to attend my schools, which I esteemed a great blessing; therefore I thanked God and him for it, and used all my diligence to improve the opportunity. This diligence and attention recommended me to the notice and care of my three preceptors, who on their parts bestowed a great deal of pains in my instruction, and besides were all very kind to me. My wages, however, which were by two thirds less than I ever had in my life (for I had only £12 per annum) I soon found would not be sufficient to defray this extraordinary expense of masters, and my own necessary expenses; my old thirty-seven guineas had by this time worn all away to one. I thought it best, therefore, to try the sea again in quest of more money, as I had been bred to it, and had hitherto found the profession of it successful. I had also a very great desire to see Turkey, and I now determined to gratify it. Accordingly, in the month of May, 1768, I told the doctor my wish to go to sea again, to which he made no opposition; and we parted on friendly terms. The same day I went into the city in quest of a master. I was extremely fortunate in my inquiry; for I soon heard of a gentleman who had a ship going to Italy and Turkey, and he wanted a man who could dress hair well. I was overjoyed at this, and went immediately on board of his ship, as I had been directed, which I found to be fitted up with great taste, and I already foreboded no small pleasure in sailing in her. Not finding the gentleman on board, I was directed to his lodgings, where I met with him the next day, and gave him a specimen of my dressing. He liked it so well that he hired me immediately, so that I was perfectly happy; for the ship, master, and voyage, were entirely to my mind. The ship was called the Delawar, and my master's name was John Jolly, a neat smart good humoured man, just such an one as I wished to serve. We sailed from England in July following, and our voyage was extremely pleasant. We went to Villa Franca, Nice, and Leghorn, and in all these places I was charmed with the richness and beauty of the countries, and struck with the elegant buildings with which they abound. We had always in them plenty of extraordinary good wines and rich fruits, which I was very fond of; and I had frequent occasions of gratifying both my taste and curiosity; for my captain always lodged on shore in those places, which afforded me opportunities to see the country around. I also learned navigation of the mate, which I was very fond of. When we left Italy we had delightful sailing among the Archipelago islands, and from thence to Smyrna in Turkey. This is a very ancient city; the houses are built of stone, and most of them have graves adjoining to them; so that they sometimes present the appearance of church-yards. Provisions are very plentiful in this city, and good wine less than a penny a pint. The grapes, pomegranates, and many other fruits, were also the richest and largest I ever tasted. The natives are well looking and strong made, and treated me always with great civility. In general I believe they are fond of black people; and several of them gave me pressing invitations to stay amongst them, although they keep the franks, or Christians, separate, and do not suffer them to dwell immediately amongst them. I was astonished in not seeing women in any of their shops, and very rarely any in the streets; and whenever I did they were covered with a veil from head to foot, so that I could not see their faces, except when any of them out of curiosity uncovered them to look at me, which they sometimes did. I was surprised to see how the Greeks are, in some measure, kept under by the Turks, as the negroes are in the West Indies by the white people. The less refined Greeks, as I have already hinted, dance here in the same manner as we do in my nation. On the whole, during our stay here, which was about five months, I liked the place and the Turks extremely well. I could not help observing one very remarkable circumstance there: the tails of the sheep are flat, and so very large, that I have known the tail even of a lamb to weigh from eleven to thirteen pounds. The fat of them is very white and rich, and is excellent in puddings, for which it is much used. Our ship being at length richly loaded with silk, and other articles, we sailed for England.

In May 1769, soon after our return from Turkey, our ship made a delightful voyage to Oporto in Portugal, where we arrived at the time of the carnival. On our arrival, there were sent on board to us thirty-six articles to observe, with very heavy penalties if we should break any of them; and none of us even dared to go on board any other vessel or on shore till the Inquisition[1] had sent on board and searched for every thing illegal, especially bibles. Such as were produced, and certain other things, were sent on shore till the ships were going away; and any person in whose custody a bible was found concealed was to be imprisoned and flogged, and sent into slavery for ten years. I saw here many very magnificent sights, particularly the garden of Eden, where many of the clergy and laity went in procession in their several orders with the host, and sung Te Deum.[2] I had a great curiosity to go into some of their churches, but could not gain admittance without using the necessary sprinkling of holy water at my entrance. From curiosity, and a wish to be holy, I therefore complied with this ceremony, but its virtues were lost on me, for I found myself nothing the better for it. This place abounds with plenty of all kinds of provisions. The town is well built and pretty, and commands a fine prospect. Our ship having taken in a load of wine, and other commodities, we sailed for London, and arrived in July following. Our next voyage was to the Mediterranean. The ship was again got ready, and we sailed in September for Genoa. This is one of the finest cities I ever saw; some of the edifices were of beautiful marble, and made a most noble appearance; and many had very curious fountains before them. The churches were rich and magnificent, and curiously adorned both in the inside and out. But all this grandeur was in my eyes disgraced by the galley slaves, whose condition both there and in other parts of Italy is truly piteous and wretched. After we had stayed there

---

1   Inquisition: officials who carried out the Roman Catholic Church's persecution of persons suspected or actually accused of committing heresy.
2   Te Deum: a Latin hymn of praise to God sung during the Roman Catholic Mass.

some weeks, during which we bought many different things which we wanted, and got them very cheap, we sailed to Naples, a charming city, and remarkably clean. The bay is the most beautiful I ever saw; the moles for shipping are excellent. I thought it extraordinary to see grand operas acted here on Sunday nights, and even attended by their majesties. I too, like these great ones, went to those sights, and vainly served God in the day while I thus served mammon effectually at night. While we remained here there happened an eruption of mount Vesuvius, of which I had a perfect view. It was extremely awful; and we were so near that the ashes from it used to be thick on our deck. After we had transacted our business at Naples we sailed with a fair wind once more for Smyrna, where we arrived in December. A seraskier or officer took a liking to me here, and wanted me to stay, and offered me two wives; however I refused the temptation. The merchants here travel in caravans or large companies. I have seen many caravans from India, with some hundreds of camels, laden with different goods. The people of these caravans are quite brown. Among other articles, they brought with them a great quantity of locusts, which are a kind of pulse, sweet and pleasant to the palate, and in shape resembling French beans, but longer. Each kind of goods is sold in a street by itself, and I always found the Turks very honest in their dealings. They let no Christians into their mosques or churches, for which I was very sorry; as I was always fond of going to see the different modes of worship of the people wherever I went. The plague broke out while we were in Smyrna, and we stopped taking goods into the ship till it was over. She was then richly laden, and we sailed in about March 1770 for England. One day in our passage we met with an accident which was near burning the ship. A black cook, in melting some fat, overset the pan into the fire under the deck, which immediately began to blaze, and the flame went up very high under the foretop. With the fright the poor cook became almost white, and altogether speechless. Happily however we got the fire out without doing much mischief. After various delays in this passage, which was tedious, we arrived in Standgate creek in July; and, at the latter end of the year, some new event occurred, so that my noble captain, the ship, and I all separated.

In April 1771 I shipped myself as a steward with Capt. Wm. Robertson of the ship Grenada Planter, once more to try my fortune in the West Indies; and we sailed from London for Madeira, Barbadoes, and the Grenades. When we were at this last place, having some goods to sell, I met once more with my former kind of West India customers. A white man, an islander, bought some goods of me to the amount of some pounds, and made me many fair promises as usual, but without any intention of paying me. He had likewise bought goods from some more of our people, whom he intended to serve in the same manner; but he still amused us with promises. However, when our ship was loaded, and near sailing, this honest buyer discovered no intention or sign of paying for any thing he had bought of us; but on the contrary, when I asked him for my money he threatened me and another black man he had bought goods of, so that we found we were like to get more blows than payment. On this we went to complain to one Mr. M'Intosh, a justice of the peace; we told his worship of the man's villainous tricks, and begged that he would be kind enough to see us redressed: but being negroes, although free, we could not get any remedy; and our ship being then just upon the point of sailing, we knew not how to help ourselves, though we thought it hard to lose our property in this manner. Luckily for us however, this man was also indebted to three white sailors, who could not get a farthing from him; they therefore readily joined us, and we all went together in search of him. When we found where he was, I took him out of a house and threatened him with vengeance; on which, finding he was likely to be handled roughly, the rogue offered each of us some small allowance, but nothing near our demands. This exasperated us much more; and some were for cutting his ears off; but he begged hard for mercy, which was at last granted him, after we had entirely stripped him. We then let him go, for which he thanked us, glad to get off so easily, and ran into the bushes, after having wished us a good voyage. We then repaired on board, and shortly after set sail for England. I cannot help remarking here a very narrow escape we had from being blown up, owing to a piece of negligence of mine. Just as our ship was under sail, I went down into the cabin to do some business, and had a lighted candle in my hand, which, in my hurry, without thinking, I held in a barrel of gunpowder. It remained in the powder until it was near catching fire, when fortunately I observed it and snatched it out in time, and providentially no harm happened; but I was so overcome with terror that I immediately fainted at this deliverance.

In twenty-eight days time we arrived in England, and I got clear of this ship. But, being still of a roving disposition, and desirous of seeing as many different parts of the world as I could, I shipped myself soon after, in the same year, as steward on board of a fine large ship, called the Jamaica, Captain David Watt; and we sailed from England in December 1771 for Nevis and Jamaica. I found Jamaica to be a very fine large island, well peopled, and the most considerable of the West India islands. There was a vast number of negroes here, whom I found as usual exceedingly imposed upon by the white people, and the slaves punished as in the other islands. There are negroes whose business it is to flog slaves; they go about to different people for employment, and the usual pay is from one to four bits. I saw many cruel punishments inflicted on the slaves in the short time I stayed here. In particular I was present when a poor fellow was tied up and kept hanging by the wrists at some distance from the ground, and then some half hundred weights were fixed to his ancles, in which posture he was flogged most unmercifully. There were also, as I heard, two different masters noted for cruelty on the island, who had staked up two negroes naked, and in two hours the vermin stung them to death. I heard a gentleman I well knew tell my captain that he passed sentence on a negro man to be burnt alive for attempting to poison an overseer. I pass over numerous other instances, in order to relieve the reader by a milder scene of roguery. Before I had been long on the island, one Mr. Smith at Port Morant bought goods of me to the amount of twenty-five pounds sterling; but when I demanded payment from him, he was going each time to beat me, and threatened that he would put me in gaol. One time he would say I was going to set his house on fire, at another he would swear I was going to run away with his slaves. I was astonished at this usage from a person who was in the situation of a gentleman, but I had no alternative; I was therefore obliged to submit. When I came to Kingston, I was surprised to see the number of Africans who were assembled together on Sundays; particularly at a large commodious place, called Spring Path. Here each different nation of Africa meet and dance after the manner of their own country. They still retain most of their native customs: they bury their dead, and put victuals, pipes and tobacco, and other things, in the grave with the corpse, in the same manner as in Africa. Our ship having got her loading we sailed for London, where we arrived in the August following. On my return to London, I waited on my old and good master, Dr. Irving, who made me an offer of his service again. Being now tired of the sea I gladly accepted it. I was very happy in living with this gentleman once more; during which time we were daily employed in reducing old Neptune's dominions by purifying the briny element and making it fresh. Thus I went on till May 1773, when I was roused by the sound of fame, to seek new adventures, and to find, towards the north pole, what our Creator never intended we should, a passage to India. An expedition was now fitting out to explore a north-east passage, conducted by the Honourable John Constantine Phipps, since Lord Mulgrave, in his Majesty's sloop of war the Race Horse. My master being anxious for the reputation of this adventure, we therefore prepared every thing for our voyage, and I attended him on board the Race Horse, the 24th day of May 1773. We proceeded to Sheerness, where we were joined by his Majesty's sloop the Carcass, commanded by Captain Lutwidge. On the 4th of June we sailed towards our destined place, the pole; and on the 15th of the same month we were off Shetland. On this day I had a great and unexpected deliverance from an accident which was near blowing up the ship and destroying the crew, which made me ever after during the voyage uncommonly cautious. The ship was so filled that there was very little room on board for any one, which placed me in a very awkward situation. I had resolved to keep a journal of this singular and interesting voyage; and I had no other place for this purpose but a little cabin, or the doctor's store-room, where I slept. This little place was stuffed with all manner of combustibles, particularly with tow and aquafortis,[1] and many other dangerous things. Unfortunately it happened in the evening as I was writing my journal, that I had occasion to take the candle out of the lanthorn, and a spark having touched a single thread of the tow, all the rest caught the flame, and immediately the whole was in a blaze. I saw nothing but present death before me, and expected to be the first to perish in the flames. In a moment the alarm was spread, and many people who were near ran to assist in putting out the fire. All this time I was in the very midst of the flames; my shirt, and the handkerchief on my neck, were burnt, and I was almost smothered with the smoke. However, through God's mercy, as I was nearly giving up all hopes, some people brought blankets and mattresses and threw them on the flames, by which means in a short time the fire was put out. I was severely reprimanded and menaced by such of the officers who knew it, and strictly charged never more to go there with a light: and, indeed, even my own fears made me give heed to this command for a little time; but at last, not being able to write my journal in any other part of the ship, I was tempted again to venture by stealth with a light in the same cabin, though not without considerable fear and dread on my mind. On the 20th of June we began to use Dr. Irving's apparatus for making salt water fresh; I used to attend the distillery: I frequently purified from twenty-six to forty gallons a day. The water thus distilled was perfectly pure, well tasted, and free from salt: and was used on various occasions on board the ship. On the 28th of June, being in lat. 78, we made Greenland, where I was surprised to see the sun did not set. The weather now became extremely cold; and as we sailed between north and east, which was our course, we saw many very high and curious mountains of ice; and also a great number of very large whales, which used to come close to our ship, and blow the water up to

---

1 Tow and aquafortis: rope and nitric acid.

a very great height in the air. One morning we had vast quantities of sea-horses about the ship, which neighed exactly like any other horses. We fired some harpoon guns amongst them, in order to take some, but we could not get any. The 30th, the captain of a Greenland ship came on board, and told us of three ships that were lost in the ice; however we still held on our course till July the 11th, when we were stopt by one compact impenetrable body of ice. We ran along it from east to west above ten degrees; and on the 27th we got as far north as 80, 37; and in 19 or 20 degrees east longitude from London. On the 29th and 30th of July we saw one continued plain of smooth unbroken ice, bounded only by the horizon; and we fastened to a piece of ice that was eight yards eleven inches thick. We had generally sunshine, and constant daylight; which gave cheerfulness and novelty to the whole of this striking, grand, and uncommon scene; and, to heighten it still more, the reflection of the sun from the ice gave the clouds a most beautiful appearance. We killed many different animals at this time, and among the rest nine bears. Though they had nothing in their paunches but water yet they were all very fat. We used to decoy them to the ship sometimes by burning feathers or skins. I thought them coarse eating, but some of the ship's company relished them very much. Some of our people once, in the boat, fired at and wounded a sea-horse, which dived immediately; and, in a little time after, brought up with it a number of others. They all joined in an attack upon the boat, and were with difficulty prevented from staving or oversetting her; but a boat from the Carcass having come to assist ours, and joined it, they dispersed, after having wrested an oar from one of the men. One of the ship's boats had before been attacked in the same manner, but happily no harm was done. Though we wounded several of these animals we never got but one. We remained hereabouts until the 1st of August; when the two ships got completely fastened in the ice, occasioned by the loose ice that set in from the sea. This made our situation very dreadful and alarming; so that on the 7th day we were in very great apprehension of having the ships squeezed to pieces. The officers now held a council to know what was best for us to do in order to save our lives; and it was determined that we should endeavour to escape by dragging our boats along the ice towards the sea; which, however, was farther off than any of us thought. This determination filled us with extreme dejection, and confounded us with despair; for we had very little prospect of escaping with life. However, we sawed some of the ice about the ships to keep it from hurting them; and thus kept them in a kind of pond. We then began to drag the boats as well as we could towards the sea; but, after two or three days labour, we made very little progress; so that some of our hearts totally failed us, and I really began to give up myself for lost, when I saw our surrounding calamities. While we were at this hard labour I once fell into a pond we had made amongst some loose ice, and was very near being drowned; but providentially some people were near who gave me immediate assistance, and thereby I escaped drowning. Our deplorable condition, which kept up the constant apprehension of our perishing in the ice, brought me gradually to think of eternity in such a manner as I never had done before. I had the fears of death hourly upon me, and shuddered at the thoughts of meeting the grim king of terrors in the *natural* state I then was in, and was exceedingly doubtful of a happy eternity if I should die in it. I had no hopes of my life being prolonged for any time; for we saw that our existence could not be long on the ice after leaving the ships, which were now out of sight, and some miles from the boats. Our appearance now became truly lamentable; pale dejection seized every countenance; many, who had been before blasphemers, in this our distress began to call on the good God of heaven for his help; and in the time of our utter need he heard us, and against hope or human probability delivered us! It was the eleventh day of the ships being thus fastened, and the fourth of our drawing the boats in this manner, that the wind changed to the E. N. E. The weather immediately became mild, and the ice broke towards the sea, which was to the S. W. of us. Many of us on this got on board again, and with all our might we hove the ships into every open water we could find, and made all the sail on them in our power; and now, having a prospect of success, we made signals for the boats and the remainder of the people. This seemed to us like a reprieve from death; and happy was the man who could first get on board of any ship, or the first boat he could meet. We then proceeded in this manner till we got into the open water again, which we accomplished in about thirty hours, to our infinite joy and gladness of heart. As soon as we were out of danger we came to anchor and refitted; and on the 19th of August we sailed from this uninhabited extremity of the world, where the inhospitable climate affords neither food nor shelter, and not a tree or shrub of any kind grows amongst its barren rocks; but all is one desolate and expanded waste of ice, which even the constant beams of the sun for six months in the year cannot penetrate or dissolve. The sun now being on the decline the days shortened as we sailed to the southward; and, on the 28th, in latitude 73, it was dark by ten o'clock at night. September the 10th, in latitude 58-59, we met a very severe gale of wind and high seas, and shipped a great deal of water in the space of ten hours. This made us work exceedingly hard at all our pumps a whole day; and one sea, which struck the ship with more force than any thing I ever met with of the kind before, laid her under water for some time, so that we thought she would have gone down. Two boats were washed from the booms, and the long-boat from the chucks: all other moveable things on the deck were also washed away, among which were many curious things of different kinds which we had brought from Greenland; and we were obliged, in order to lighten the ship, to toss some of our guns overboard. We saw a ship, at the same time, in very great distress, and her masts were gone; but we were unable to assist her. We now lost sight of the Carcass till the 26th, when we saw land about Orfordness, off which place she joined us. From thence we sailed for London, and on the 30th came up to Deptford. And thus ended our Arctic voyage, to the no small joy of all on board, after having been absent four months; in which time, at the imminent hazard of our lives, we explored nearly as far towards the Pole as 81 degrees north, and 20 degrees east longitude; being much farther, by all accounts, than any navigator had ever ventured before; in which we fully proved the impracticability of finding a passage that way to India.

CHAP. X.

The author leaves Doctor Irving and engages on board a Turkey ship –
Account of a black man's being kidnapped on board and sent to the
West Indies, and the author's fruitless endeavours to procure his freedom
– Some account of the manner of the author's conversion to the faith of
Jesus Christ.

OUR voyage to the North Pole being ended, I returned to
London with Doctor Irving, with whom I continued for some
time, during which I began seriously to reflect on the dangers I
had escaped, particularly those of my last voyage, which made a
lasting impression on my mind, and, by the grace of God,
proved afterwards a mercy to me; it caused me to reflect deeply
on my eternal state, and to seek the Lord with full purpose of
heart ere it was too late. I rejoiced greatly; and heartily thanked
the Lord for directing me to London, where I was determined
to work out my own salvation, and in so doing procure a title
to heaven, being the result of a mind blended by ignorance and
sin.

In process of time I left my master, Doctor Irving, the puri-
fier of waters, and lodged in Coventry-court, Haymarket,
where I was continually oppressed and much concerned about
the salvation of my soul, and was determined (in my own
strength) to be a first-rate Christian. I used every means for this
purpose; and, not being able to find any person amongst my
acquaintance that agreed with me in point of religion, or, in
scripture language, "that would shew me any good;" I was
much dejected, and knew not where to seek relief; however, I
first frequented the neighbouring churches, St. James's, and
others, two or three times a day, for many weeks: still I came
away dissatisfied; something was wanting that I could not
obtain, and I really found more heart-felt relief in reading my
bible at home than in attending the church; and, being resolved
to be saved, I pursued other methods still. First I went among
the quakers, where the word of God was neither read or
preached, so that I remained as much in the dark as ever. I then
searched into the Roman catholic principles, but was not in the

least satisfied. At length I had recourse to the Jews, which availed me nothing, for the fear of eternity daily harassed my mind, and I knew not where to seek shelter from the wrath to come. However this was my conclusion, at all events, to read the four evangelists, and whatever sect or party I found adhering thereto such I would join. Thus I went on heavily without any guide to direct me the way that leadeth to eternal life. I asked different people questions about the manner of going to heaven, and was told different ways. Here I was much staggered, and could not find any at that time more righteous than myself, or indeed so much inclined to devotion. I thought we should not all be saved (this is agreeable to the holy scriptures), nor would all be damned. I found none among the circle of my acquaintance that kept wholly the ten commandments. So righteous was I in my own eyes, that I was convinced I excelled many of them in that point, by keeping eight out of ten; and finding those who in general termed themselves Christians not so honest or so good in their morals as the Turks, I really thought the Turks were in a safer way of salvation than my neighbours: so that between hopes and fears I went on, and the chief comforts I enjoyed were in the musical French horn, which I then practised, and also dressing of hair. Such was my situation some months, experiencing the dishonesty of many people here. I determined at last to set out for Turkey, and there to end my days. It was now early in the spring 1774. I sought for a master, and found a captain John Hughes, commander of a ship called Anglicania, fitting out in the river Thames, and bound to Smyrna in Turkey. I shipped myself with him as a steward; at the same time I recommended to him a very clever black man, John Annis, as a cook. This man was on board the ship near two months doing his duty: he had formerly lived many years with Mr. William Kirkpatrick, a gentleman of the island of St. Kitts, from whom he parted by consent, though he afterwards tried many schemes to inveigle the poor man. He had applied to many captains who traded to St. Kitts to trepan him; and when all their attempts and schemes of kidnapping proved abortive, Mr. Kirkpatrick came to our ship at Union Stairs on Easter Monday, April the fourth, with two wherry boats and six men, having learned that the man was on board; and tied, and forcibly took him away from the ship, in the presence of the crew and the chief mate, who had detained him after he had notice to come away. I believe that this was a combined piece of business: but, at any rate, it certainly reflected great disgrace on the mate and captain also, who, although they had desired the oppressed man to stay on board, yet he did not in the least assist to recover him, or pay me a farthing of his wages, which was about five pounds. I proved the only friend he had, who attempted to regain him his liberty if possible, having known the want of liberty myself. I sent as soon as I could to Gravesend, and got knowledge of the ship in which he was; but unluckily she had sailed the first tide after he was put on board. My intention was then immediately to apprehend Mr. Kirkpatrick, who was about setting off for Scotland; and, having obtained a *habeas corpus* for him, and got a tipstaff to go with me to St. Paul's church-yard, where he lived, he, suspecting something of this kind, set a watch to look out. My being known to them occasioned me to use the following deception: I whitened my face, that they might not know me, and this had its desired effect. He did not go out of his house that night, and next morning I contrived a well plotted stratagem notwithstanding he had a gentleman in his house to personate him. My direction to the tipstaff, who got admittance into the house, was to conduct him to a judge, according to the writ. When he came there, his plea was, that he had not the body in custody, on which he was admitted to bail. I proceeded immediately to that philanthropist, Granville Sharp, Esq.[1] who received me with the utmost kindness, and gave me every instruction that was needful on the occasion. I left him in full hope that I should gain the unhappy man his liberty, with the warmest sense of gratitude towards Mr. Sharp for his kindness; but, alas! my attorney proved unfaithful; he took my money, lost me many months employ, and did not do the least good in the cause: and when the poor man arrived at St. Kitts, he was, according to custom, staked to the ground with four pins

---

1 Granville Sharp (1735-1813): English abolitionist who actively assisted many black persons.

through a cord, two on his wrists, and two on his ancles, was cut and flogged most unmercifully, and afterwards loaded cruelly with irons about his neck. I had two very moving letters from him, while he was in this situation; and also was told of it by some very respectable families now in London, who saw him in St. Kitts, in the same state in which he remained till kind death released him out of the hands of his tyrants. During this disagreeable business I was under strong convictions of sin, and thought that my state was worse than any man's; my mind was unaccountably disturbed; I often wished for death, though at the same time convinced I was altogether unprepared for that awful summons. Suffering much by villains in the late cause, and being much concerned about the state of my soul, these things (but particularly the latter) brought me very low; so that I became a burden to myself, and viewed all things around me as emptiness and vanity, which could give no satisfaction to a troubled conscience. I was again determined to go to Turkey, and resolved, at that time, never more to return to England. I engaged as steward on board a Turkeyman (the Wester Hall, Capt. Linna); but was prevented by means of my late captain, Mr. Hughes, and others. All this appeared to be against me, and the only comfort I then experienced was, in reading the holy scriptures, where I saw that "there is no new thing under the sun," Eccles. i. 9; and what was appointed for me I must submit to. Thus I continued to travel in much heaviness, and frequently murmured against the Almighty, particularly in his providential dealings; and, awful to think! I began to blaspheme, and wished often to be any thing but a human being. In these severe conflicts the Lord answered me by awful "visions of the night, when deep sleep falleth upon men, in slumberings upon the bed," Job xxxiii. 15. He was pleased, in much mercy, to give me to see, and in some measure to understand, the great and awful scene of the judgment-day, that "no unclean person, no unholy thing, can enter into the kingdom of God," Eph. v. 5.[1] I would then, if it had been possible, have

---

1 The actual passage in Ephesians 5.5 reads: "For this ye know, that no whoremonger, nor unclean person, nor covetous man, who is an idolater, hath any inheritance in the kingdom of Christ and of God."

changed my nature with the meanest worm on the earth; and was ready to say to the mountains and rocks "fall on me," Rev. vi. 16; but all in vain. I then requested the divine Creator that he would grant me a small space of time to repent of my follies and vile iniquities, which I felt were grievous. The Lord, in his manifold mercies, was pleased to grant my request, and being yet in a state of time, the sense of God's mercies was so great on my mind when I awoke, that my strength entirely failed me for many minutes, and I was exceedingly weak. This was the first spiritual mercy I ever was sensible of, and being on praying ground, as soon as I recovered a little strength, and got out of bed and dressed myself, I invoked Heaven from my inmost soul, and fervently begged that God would never again permit me to blaspheme his most holy name. The Lord, who is long-suffering, and full of compassion to such poor rebels as we are, condescended to hear and answer. I felt that I was altogether unholy, and saw clearly what a bad use I had made of the faculties I was endowed with; they were given me to glorify God with; I thought, therefore, I had better want them here, and enter into life eternal, than abuse them and be cast into hell fire. I prayed to be directed, if there were any holier than those with whom I was acquainted, that the Lord would point them out to me. I appealed to the Searcher of hearts, whether I did not wish to love him more, and serve him better. Notwithstanding all this, the reader may easily discern, if he is a believer, that I was still in nature's darkness. At length I hated the house in which I lodged, because God's most holy name was blasphemed in it; then I saw the word of God verified, viz. "Before they call, I will answer; and while they are yet speaking, I will hear."[1]

I had a great desire to read the bible the whole day at home; but not having a convenient place for retirement, I left the house in the day, rather than stay amongst the wicked ones; and that day as I was walking, it pleased God to direct me to a house where there was an old sea-faring man, who experienced much of the love of God shed abroad in his heart. He

---

1 Isaiah 65.24.

began to discourse with me; and, as I desired to love the Lord, his conversation rejoiced me greatly; and indeed I had never heard before the love of Christ to believers set forth in such a manner, and in so clear a point of view. Here I had more questions to put to the man than his time would permit him to answer; and in that memorable hour there came in a dissenting minister; he joined our discourse, and asked me some few questions; among others, where I heard the gospel preached. I knew not what he meant by hearing the gospel; I told him I had read the gospel: and he asked where I went to church, or whether I went at all or not. To which I replied, "I attended St. James's, St. Martin's, and St. Ann's, Soho;" – "So," said he, "you are a churchman." I answered, I was. He then invited me to a love-feast at his chapel that evening. I accepted the offer, and thanked him; and soon after he went away, I had some further discourse with the old Christian, added to some profitable reading, which made me exceedingly happy. When I left him he reminded me of coming to the feast; I assured him I would be there. Thus we parted, and I weighed over the heavenly conversation that had passed between these two men, which cheered my then heavy and drooping spirit more than any thing I had met with for many months. However, I thought the time long in going to my supposed banquet. I also wished much for the company of these friendly men; their company pleased me much; and I thought the gentlemen very kind, in asking me, a stranger, to a feast; but how singular did it appear to me, to have it in a chapel! When the wished-for hour came I went, and happily the old man was there, who kindly seated me, as he belonged to the place. I was much astonished to see the place filled with people, and no signs of eating and drinking. There were many ministers in the company. At last they began by giving out hymns, and between the singing the minister engaged in prayer; in short, I knew not what to make of this sight, having never seen any thing of the kind in my life before now. Some of the guests began to speak their experience, agreeable to what I read in the Scriptures; much was said by every speaker of the providence of God, and his unspeakable mercies, to each of them. This I knew in a great measure, and could most heartily join them. But when they spoke of a future state, they seemed to be altogether certain of their calling and election of God; and that no one could ever separate them from the love of Christ, or pluck them out of his hands. This filled me with utter consternation, intermingled with admiration. I was so amazed as not to know what to think of the company; my heart was attracted and my affections were enlarged. I wished to be as happy as them, and was persuaded in my mind that they were different from the world "that lieth in wickedness," 1 John v. 19. Their language and singing, &c. did well harmonize; I was entirely overcome, and wished to live and die thus. Lastly, some persons in the place produced some neat baskets full of buns, which they distributed about; and each person communicated with his neighbour, and sipped water out of different mugs, which they handed about to all who were present. This kind of Christian fellowship I had never seen, nor ever thought of seeing on earth; it fully reminded me of what I had read in the holy scriptures, of the primitive Christians, who loved each other and broke bread. In partaking of it, even from house to house, this entertainment (which lasted about four hours) ended in singing and prayer. It was the first soul feast I ever was present at. This last twenty-four hours produced me things, spiritual and temporal, sleeping and waking, judgment and mercy, that I could not but admire the goodness of God, in directing the blind, blasphemous sinner in the path that he knew not of, even among the just; and instead of judgment he has shewed mercy, and will hear and answer the prayers and supplications of every returning prodigal:

> O! to grace how great a debtor
> Daily I'm constrain'd to be![1]

After this I was resolved to win Heaven if possible; and if I perished I thought it should be at the feet of Jesus, in praying to him for salvation. After having been an eye-witness to some of the happiness which attended those who feared God, I knew

---

1   From a Methodist hymn by Robert Robinson (1735-90), "Come Thou fount of every blessing."

not how, with any propriety, to return to my lodgings, where the name of God was continually profaned, at which I felt the greatest horror. I paused in my mind for some time, not knowing what to do; whether to hire a bed elsewhere, or go home again. At last, fearing an evil report might arise, I went home, with a farewell to card-playing and vain jesting, &c. I saw that time was very short, eternity long, and very near, and I viewed those persons alone blessed who were found ready at midnight call, or when the Judge of all, both quick and dead, cometh.

The next day I took courage, and went to Holborn, to see my new and worthy acquaintance, the old man, Mr.C——; he, with his wife, a gracious woman, were at work at silk weaving; they seemed mutually happy, and both quite glad to see me, and I more so to see them. I sat down, and we conversed much about soul matters, &c. Their discourse was amazingly delightful, edifying, and pleasant. I knew not at last how to leave this agreeable pair, till time summoned me away. As I was going they lent me a little book, entitled "The Conversion of an Indian."[1] It was in questions and answers. The poor man came over the sea to London, to inquire after the Christian's God, who, (through rich mercy) he found, and had not his journey in vain. The above book was of great use to me, and at that time was a means of strengthening my faith; however, in parting, they both invited me to call on them when I pleased. This delighted me, and I took care to make all the improvement from it I could; and so far I thanked God for such company and desires. I prayed that the many evils I felt within might be done away, and that I might be weaned from my former carnal acquaintances. This was quickly heard and answered, and I was soon connected with those whom the scripture calls the excellent of the earth. I heard the gospel preached, and the thoughts of my heart and actions were laid open by the preachers, and the way of salvation by Christ alone was evidently set forth. Thus I went on happily for near two months; and I once heard, during this period, a reverend gentleman speak of a man who had departed his life in full assurance of his going to glory. I

---

1   Laurence Harlow, *The Conversion of an Indian, in a Letter to a Friend* (London, 1774).

was much astonished at the assertion; and did very deliberately inquire how he could get at this knowledge. I was answered fully, agreeable to what I read in the oracles of truth; and was told also, that if I did not experience the new birth, and the pardon of my sins, through the blood of Christ, before I died, I could not enter the kingdom of heaven. I knew not what to think of this report; as I thought I kept eight commandments out of ten; then my worthy interpreter told me I did not do it, nor could I; and he added, that no man ever did or could keep the commandments, without offending in one point. I thought this sounded very strange, and puzzled me much for many weeks; for I thought it a hard saying. I then asked my friend, Mr. L——d, who was a clerk in a chapel, why the commandments of God were given, if we could not be saved by them? To which he replied, "The law is a schoolmaster to bring us to Christ," who alone could and did keep the commandments, and fulfilled all their requirements for his elect people, even those to whom he had given a living faith, and the sins of those chosen vessels *were already* atoned for and forgiven them whilst living; and if I did not experience the same before my exit, the Lord would say at that great day to me "Go ye cursed," &c. &c. for God would appear faithful in his judgments to the wicked, as he would be faithful in shewing mercy to those who were ordained to it before the world was; therefore Christ Jesus seemed to be all in all to that man's soul. I was much wounded at this discourse, and brought into such a dilemma as I never expected. I asked him, if *he* was to die that moment, whether he was sure to enter the kingdom of God? and added, "Do you *know* that your sins are forgiven you?" He answered in the affirmative. Then confusion, anger, and discontent seized me, and I staggered much at this sort of doctrine; it brought me to a stand, not knowing which to believe, whether salvation by works or by faith only in Christ. I requested him to tell me how I might know when my sins were forgiven me. He assured me he could not, and that none but God alone could do this. I told him it was very mysterious; but he said it was really matter of fact, and quoted many portions of scripture immediately to the point, to which I could make no reply. He then desired me to pray to God to shew me these things. I answered, that I prayed to God every day. He said, "I perceive you are a churchman." I answered I was. He then entreated me to beg of God to shew me what I was, and the true state of my soul. I thought the prayer very short and odd; so we parted for that time. I weighed all these things well over, and could not help thinking how it was possible for a man to know that his sins were forgiven him in this life. I wished that God would reveal this self same thing unto me. In a short time after this I went to Westminster chapel; the Rev. Mr. P[eckwell] preached, from Lam. iii. 39. It was a wonderful sermon; he clearly shewed that a living man had no cause to complain for the punishment of his sins; he evidently justified the Lord in all his dealings with the sons of men; he also shewed the justice of God in the eternal punishment of the wicked and impenitent. The discourse seemed to me like a two-edged sword cutting all ways; it afforded me much joy, intermingled with many fears, about my soul; and when it was ended, he gave it out that he intended, the ensuing week, to examine all those who meant to attend the Lord's table. Now I thought much of my good works, and at the same time was doubtful of my being a proper object to receive the sacrament; I was full of meditation till the day of examining. However, I went to the chapel, and, though much distressed, I addressed the reverend gentleman, thinking, if I was not right, he would endeavour to convince me of it. When I conversed with him, the first thing he asked me was, what I knew of Christ? I told him I believed in him, and had been baptized in his name. "Then," said he, "when were you brought to the knowledge of God? and how were you convinced of sin?" I knew not what he meant by these questions; I told him I kept eight commandments out of ten; but that I sometimes swore on board ship, and sometimes when on shore, and broke the sabbath. He then asked me if I could read? I answered, "Yes." – "Then," said he, "do you not read in the bible, "he that offends in one point is guilty of all?" I said, "Yes." Then he assured me, that one sin unatoned for was as sufficient to damn a soul as one leak was to sink a ship. Here I was struck with awe; for the minister exhorted me much, and reminded me of the shortness of time, and the length of eternity, and that no unregenerate soul, or any thing unclean, could enter the kingdom of Heaven. He did not admit me as a communicant; but recommended me to read the scriptures, and hear the word preached, not to neglect fervent prayer to God, who has promised to hear the supplications of those who seek him in godly sincerity; so I took my leave of him, with many thanks, and resolved to follow his advice, so far as the Lord would condescend to enable me. During this time I was out of employ, nor was I likely to get a situation suitable for me, which obliged me to go once more to sea. I engaged as steward of a ship called the Hope, Capt. Richard Strange, bound from London to Cadiz in Spain. In a short time after I was on board I heard the name of God much blasphemed, and I feared greatly, lest I should catch the horrible infection. I thought if I sinned again, after having life and death set evidently before me, I should certainly go to hell. My mind was uncommonly chagrined, and I murmured much at God's providential dealings with me, and was discontented with the commandments, that I could not be saved by what I had done; I hated all things, and wished I had never been born; confusion seized me, and I wished to be annihilated. One day I was standing on the very edge of the stern of the ship, thinking to drown myself; but this scripture was instantly impressed on my mind — "that no murderer hath eternal life abiding in him," 1 John iii. 15. Then I paused, and thought myself the unhappiest man living. Again I was convinced that the Lord was better to me than I deserved, and I was better off in the world than many. After this I began to fear death; I fretted, mourned, and prayed, till I became a burden to others, but more so to myself. At length I concluded to beg my bread on shore rather than go again to sea amongst a people who feared not God, and I entreated the captain three different time to discharge me; he would not, but each time gave me greater and greater encouragement to continue with him, and all on board shewed me very great civility: notwithstanding all this I was unwilling to embark again. At last some of my religious friends advised me, by saying it was my lawful calling, consequently it was my duty to obey, and that God was not confined to place, &c. &c. particularly Mr. G. S[mith] the governor of Tothil-fields Bridewell, who pitied my case, and read the eleventh chapter of the Hebrews to me, with exhortations. He prayed for me, and I believed that he prevailed on my behalf, as my burden was then greatly removed, and I found a heartfelt resignation to the will of God. The good man gave me a pocket Bible and Allen's Alarm to the unconverted.[1] We parted, and the next day I went on board again. We sailed for Spain, and I found favour with the captain. It was the fourth of the month of September when we sailed from London; we had a delightful voyage to Cadiz, where we arrived the twenty-third of the same month. The place is strong, commands a fine prospect, and is very rich. The Spanish galleons frequent that port, and some arrived whilst we were there. I had many opportunities of reading the scriptures. I wrestled hard with God in fervent prayer, who had declared in his word that he would hear the groanings and deep sighs of the poor in spirit. I found this verified to my utter astonishment and comfort in the following manner:

On the morning of the 6th of October, (I pray you to attend) or all that day, I thought that I should either see or hear something supernatural. I had a secret impulse on my mind of something that was to take place, which drove me continually for that time to a throne of grace. It pleased God to enable me to wrestle with him, as Jacob did: I prayed that if sudden death were to happen, and I perished, it might be at Christ's feet.

In the evening of the same day, as I was reading and meditating on the fourth chapter of the Acts, twelfth verse, under the solemn apprehensions of eternity, and reflecting on my past actions, I began to think I had lived a moral life, and that I had a proper ground to believe I had an interest in the divine favour; but still meditating on the subject, not knowing whether salvation was to be had partly for our own good deeds, or solely as the sovereign gift of God; in this deep consternation the Lord was pleased to break in upon my soul with his bright beams of heavenly light; and in an instant as it were,

---

1 *An Alarme to Unconverted Sinners* (1673) was a popular religious work by Joseph Alleine (1634-68).

removing the veil, and letting light into a dark place, I saw clearly with the eye of faith the crucified Saviour bleeding on the cross on mount Calvary: the scriptures became an unsealed book, I saw myself a condemned criminal under the law, which came with its full force to my conscience, and when "the commandment came sin revived, and I died." I saw the Lord Jesus Christ in his humiliation, loaded and bearing my reproach, sin, and shame. I then clearly perceived that by the deeds of the law no flesh living could be justified. I was then convinced that by the first Adam sin came, and by the second Adam (the Lord Jesus Christ) all that are saved must be made alive. It was given me at that time to know what it was to be born again, John iii. 5. I saw the eighth chapter to the Romans, and the doctrines of God's decrees, verified agreeable to his eternal, everlasting, and unchangeable purposes. The word of God was sweet to my taste, yea sweeter than honey and the honeycomb. Christ was revealed to my soul as the chiefest among ten thousand. These heavenly moments were really as life to the dead, and what John calls an earnest of the Spirit.[1] This was indeed unspeakable, and I firmly believe undeniable by many. Now every leading providential circumstance that happened to me, from the day I was taken from my parents to that hour, was then in my view, as if it had but just then occurred. I was sensible of the invisible hand of God, which guided and protected me when in truth I knew it not: still the Lord pursued me although I slighted and disregarded it; this mercy melted me down. When I considered my poor wretched state I wept, seeing what a great debtor I was to sovereign free grace. Now the Ethiopian was willing to be saved by Jesus Christ, the sinner's only surety, and also to rely on none other person or thing for salvation. Self was obnoxious, and good works he had none, for it is God that worketh in us both to will and to do. The amazing things of that hour can never be told — it was joy in the Holy Ghost! I felt an astonishing change; the burden of sin, the gaping jaws of hell, and the fears of death, that weighed me down before, now lost their horror; indeed I thought death would now be the

---

1   [Equiano's note] John xvi. 13, 14. &c.

best earthly friend I ever had. Such were my grief and joy as I believe are seldom experienced. I was bathed in tears, and said, What am I that God should thus look on me the vilest of sinners? I felt a deep concern for my mother and friends, which occasioned me to pray with fresh ardour; and, in the abyss of thought, I viewed the unconverted people of the world in a very awful state, being without God and without hope.

It pleased God to pour out on me the Spirit of prayer and the grace of supplication, so that in loud acclamations I was enabled to praise and glorify his most holy name. When I got out of the cabin, and told some of the people what the Lord had done for me, alas, who could understand me or believe my report! – None but to whom the arm of the Lord was revealed. I became a barbarian to them in talking of the love of Christ: his name was to me as ointment poured forth; indeed it was sweet to my soul, but to them a rock of offence. I thought my case singular, and every hour a day until I came to London, for I much longed to be with some to whom I could tell of the wonders of God's love towards me, and join in prayer to him whom my soul loved and thirsted after. I had uncommon commotions within, such as few can tell aught about. Now the bible was my only companion and comfort; I prized it much, with many thanks to God that I could read it for myself, and was not left to be tossed about or led by man's devices and notions. The worth of a soul cannot be told. – May the Lord give the reader an understanding in this. Whenever I looked in the bible I saw things new, and many texts were immediately applied to me with great comfort, for I knew that to me was the word of salvation sent. Sure I was that the Spirit which indited the word opened my heart to receive the truth of it as it is in Jesus – that the same Spirit enabled me to act faith upon the promises that were so precious to me, and enabled me to believe to the salvation of my soul. By free grace I was persuaded that I had a part in the first resurrection, and was "enlightened with the light of the living," Job xxxiii. 30. I wished for a man of God with whom I might converse: my soul was like the chariots of Aminidab, Canticles vi. 12. These, among others, were the precious promises that were so powerfully applied to me: "All things whatsoever ye shall ask in prayer, believing, ye shall receive," Mat. xxi. 22. "Peace I leave with you, my peace I give unto you," John xiv. 27. I saw the blessed Redeemer to be the fountain of life, and the well of salvation. I experienced him to be all in all; he had brought me by a way that I knew not, and he had made crooked paths straight. Then in his name I set up my Ebenezer, saying, Hitherto he hath helped me: and could say to the sinners about me, Behold what a Saviour I have! Thus I was, by the teaching of that all-glorious Deity, the great One in Three, and Three in One, confirmed in the truths of the bible, those oracles of everlasting truth, on which every soul living must stand or fall eternally, agreeable to Acts iv. 12. "Neither is there salvation in any other, for there is none other name under heaven given among men whereby we must be saved, but only Christ Jesus." May God give the reader a right understanding in these facts! "To him that believeth all things are profitable, but to them that are unbelieving nothing is pure," Titus i. 15. During this period we remained at Cadiz until our ship got laden. We sailed about the fourth of November; and, having a good passage, we arrived in London the month following, to my comfort, with heartfelt gratitude to God for his rich and unspeakable mercies. On my return I had but one text which puzzled me, or that the devil endeavoured to buffet me with, viz. Rom. xi. 6. and, as I had heard of the Reverend Mr. Romaine, and his great knowledge in the scriptures, I wished much to hear him preach. One day I went to Blackfriars church, and, to my great satisfaction and surprise, he preached from that very text. He very clearly shewed the difference between human works and free election, which is according to God's sovereign will and pleasure. These glad tidings set me entirely at liberty, and I went out of the church rejoicing, seeing my spots were those of God's children. I went to Westminster Chapel, and saw some of my old friends, who were glad when they perceived the wonderful change that the Lord had wrought in me, particularly Mr. G— S[mith], my worthy acquaintance, who was a man of a choice spirit, and had great zeal for the Lord's service. I enjoyed his correspondence till he died in the year 1784. I was again examined at that same chapel, and was received into church fellowship amongst them: I rejoiced in spirit, making melody in my heart to the God of all my mercies. Now my whole wish was to be dissolved, and to be with Christ — but, alas! I must wait mine appointed time.

MICELLANEOUS VERSES

OR

Reflections on the State of my mind during my first Convictions; of the Necessity of believing the Truth, and experiencing the inestimable Benefits of Christianity.

Well may I say my life has been
One scene of sorrow and of pain;
From early days I griefs have known,
And as I grew my griefs have grown.

Dangers were always in my path;
And fear of wrath, and sometimes death;
While pale dejection in me reign'd
I often wept, by grief constrain'd.

When taken from my native land,
By an unjust and cruel band,
How did uncommon dread prevail!
My sighs no more I could conceal.

"To ease my mind I often strove,
And tried my trouble to remove:
I sung, and utter'd sighs between –
Assay'd to stifle guilt with sin.

"But O! not all that I could do
Would stop the current of my woe;
Conviction still my vileness shew'd;
How great my guilt – how lost from God!

"Prevented, that I could not die,
Nor might to one kind refuge fly;
An orphan state I had to mourn, –
Forsook by all, and left forlorn."

Those who beheld my downcast mien
Could not guess at my woes unseen:
They by appearance could not know
The troubles that I waded through.

"Lust, anger, blasphemy, and pride,
With legions of such ills beside,
Troubled my thoughts," while doubts and fears
Clouded and darken'd most my years.

"Sighs now no more would be confin'd –
They breath'd the trouble of my mind:
I wish'd for death, but check'd the word,
And often pray'd unto the Lord."

Unhappy, more than some on earth,
I thought the place that gave me birth –
Strange thoughts oppress'd – while I replied
"Why not in Ethiopia died?"

And why thus spared, nigh to hell? –
God only knew – I could not tell!
"A tott'ring sence, a bowing wall,
I thought myself ere since the fall."

"Oft times I mused, nigh despair,
While birds melodious fill'd the air:
Thrice happy songsters, ever free,
How bless'd were they compar'd to me!"

Thus all things added to my pain,
While grief compell'd me to complain;
When sable clouds began to rise
My mind grew darker than the skies.

The English nation call'd to leave,
How did my breast with sorrows heave!

I long'd for rest – cried "Help me, Lord!
"Some mitigation, Lord, afford!"

Yet on, dejected, still I went –
Heart-throbbing woes within were pent;
Nor land, nor sea, could comfort give,
Nothing my anxious mind relieve.

Weary with travail, yet unknown
To all but God and self alone,
Numerous months for peace I strove,
And numerous foes I had to prove.

Inur'd to dangers, griefs, and woes,
Train'd up 'midst perils, deaths, and foes,
I said "Must it thus ever be? –
No quiet is permitted me."

Hard hap, and more than heavy lot!
I pray'd to God "Forget me not –
What thou ordain'st willing I'll bear;
But O! deliver from despair!"

Strivings and wrestlings seem'd in vain;
Nothing I did could ease my pain:
Then gave I up my works and will,
Confess'd and own'd my doom was hell!

Like some poor pris'ner at the bar,
Conscious of guilt, of sin and fear,
Arraign'd, and self-condemned, I stood –
"Lost in the world, and in my blood!"

Yet here, 'midst blackest clouds confin'd,
A beam from Christ, the day-star, shin'd;
Surely, thought I, if Jesus please,
He can at once sign my release.

I, ignorant of his righteousness,
Set up my labours in its place;
"Forgot for why his blood was shed,
And pray'd and fasted in its stead."

He dy'd for sinners – I am one!
Might not his blood for me atone?
Tho' I am nothing else but sin,
Yet surely he can make me clean!

Thus light came in, and I believ'd;
Myself forgot, and help receiv'd!
My Saviour then I know I found,
For, eas'd from guilt, no more I groan'd.

O, happy hour, in which I ceas'd
To mourn, for then I found a rest!
My soul and Christ were now as one –
Thy light, O Jesus, in me shone!

Bless'd be thy name, for now I know
I and my works can nothing do;
"The Lord alone can ransom man –
For this the spotless Lamb was slain!"

When sacrifices, works, and pray'r,
Prov'd vain, and ineffectual were,
"Lo, then I come!" the Saviour cry'd,
And, bleeding, bow'd his head and dy'd!

He dy'd for all who ever saw
No help in them, nor by the law: –
I this have seen; and gladly own
"Salvation is by Christ alone!"[1]

---

1 [Equiano's note] Acts iv. 12.

CHAP. XI.

The author embarks on board a ship bound for Cadiz – Is near being shipwrecked – Goes to Malaga – Remarkable fine cathedral there – The author disputes with a popish priest – Picking up eleven miserable men at sea in returning to England – Engages again with Doctor Irving to accompany him to Jamaica and the Mosquito Shore – Meets with an Indian prince on board – The author attempts to instruct him in the truths of the Gospel – Frustrated by the bad example of some in the ship – They arrive on the Mosquito Shore with some slaves they purchased at Jamaica, and begin to cultivate a plantation – Some account of the manners and customs of the Mosquito Indians – Successful device of the author's to quell a riot among them – Curious entertainment given by them to Doctor Irving and the author, who leaves the shore and goes for Jamaica – Is barbarously treated by a man with whom he engaged for his passage – Escapes and goes to the Mosquito admiral, who treats him kindly – He gets another vessel and goes on board – Instances of bad treatment – Meets Doctor Irving – Gets to Jamaica – Is cheated by his captain – Leaves the Doctor and goes for England.

WHEN our ship was got ready for sea again, I was entreated by the captain to go in her once more; but, as I felt myself now as happy as I could wish to be in this life, I for some time refused; however, the advice of my friends at last prevailed; and, in full resignation to the will of God, I again embarked for Cadiz in March 1775. We had a very good passage, without any material accident, until we arrived off the Bay of Cadiz; when one Sunday, just as we were going into the harbor, the ship struck against a rock and knocked off a garboard plank, which is the next to the keel. In an instant all hands were in the greatest confusion, and began with loud cries to call on God to have mercy on them. Although I could not swim, and saw no way of escaping death, I felt no dread in my then situation, having no desire to live. I even rejoiced in spirit, thinking this death would be sudden glory. But the fulness of time was not yet come. The people near to me were much astonished in seeing me thus calm and resigned; but I told them of the peace of

God, which through sovereign grace I enjoyed, and these words
were that instant in my mind:

> Christ is my pilot wise, my compass is his word;
> My soul each storm defies, while I have such a Lord.
> I trust his faithfulness and power,
> To save me in the trying hour.
> Though rocks and quicksands deep through all
>   my passage lie,
> Yet Christ shall safely keep and guide me with his eye.
> How can I sink with such a prop,
> That bears the world and all things up?[1]

At this time there were many large Spanish flukers or pas-
sage-vessels full of people crossing the channel; who seeing our
condition, a number of them came alongside of us. As many
hands as could be employed began to work; some at our three
pumps, and the rest unloading the ship as fast as possible. There
being only a single rock called the Porpus on which we struck,
we soon got off it, and providentially it was then high water, we
therefore run the ship ashore at the nearest place to keep her
from sinking. After many tides, with a great deal of care and
industry, we got her repaired again. When we had dispatched
our business at Cadiz, we went to Gibraltar, and from thence to
Malaga, a very pleasant and rich city, where there is one of the
finest cathedrals I had ever seen. It had been above fifty years in
building, as I heard, though it was not then quite finished; great
part of the inside, however, was completed and highly decorat-
ed with the richest marble columns and many superb paintings;
it was lighted occasionally by an amazing number of wax tapers
of different sizes, some of which were as thick as a man's thigh;
these, however, were only used on some of their grand festivals.

I was very much shocked at the custom of bull-baiting, and
other diversions which prevailed here on Sunday evenings, to
the great scandal of Christianity and morals. I used to express
my abhorrence of it to a priest whom I met with. I had fre-

---

1   Taken from "The Spiritual Victory" in a 1776 collection of hymns by Augustus
Toplady.

quent contests about religion with the reverend father, in which he took great pains to make a proselyte of me to his church; and I no less to convert him to mine. On these occasions I used to produce my Bible, and shew him in what points his church erred. He then said he had been in England, and that every person there read the Bible, which was very wrong; but I answered him that Christ desired us to search the Scriptures. In his zeal for my conversion, he solicited me to go to one of the universities in Spain, and declared that I should have my education free; and told me, if I got myself made a priest, I might in time become even pope; and that Pope Benedict was a black man.[1] As I was ever desirous of learning, I paused for some time upon this temptation; and thought by being crafty I might catch some with guile; but I began to think that it would be only hypocrisy in me to embrace his offer, as I could not in conscience conform to the opinions of his church. I was therefore enabled to regard the word of God, which says, "Come out from amongst them," and refused Father Vincent's offer. So we parted without conviction on either side.

Having taken at this place some fine wines, fruits, and money, we proceeded to Cadiz, where we took about two tons more of money, &c. and then sailed for England in the month of June. When we were about the north latitude 42, we had contrary wind for several days, and the ship did not make in that time above six or seven miles straight course. This made the captain exceeding fretful and peevish: and I was very sorry to hear God's most holy name often blasphemed by him. One day, as he was in that impious mood, a young gentleman on board, who was a passenger, reproached him, and said he acted wrong; for we ought to be thankful to God for all things, as we were not in want of any thing on board; and though the wind

---

1 Pope Benedict XIV (1675-1758) served as pope from 1740 to 1758, but he was not a black man. Perhaps the priest was referring to St. Benedict the Moor, or the Black (1526-89), who was a Sicilian born of Nubian slave parents from Ethiopia. Beatified for sainthood in 1743 and canonized in 1807, Benedict was considered the patron saint of blacks in North America. Another source for the confusion might have come from the fact that at times members of the Benedictine religious order were called "black monks" because many of them wore habits of black clothing.

was contrary for us, yet it was fair for some others, who, perhaps, stood in more need of it than we. I immediately seconded this young gentleman with some boldness, and said we had not the least cause to murmur, for that the Lord was better to us than we deserved, and that he had done all things well. I expected that the captain would be very angry with me for speaking, but he replied not a word. However, before that time on the following day, being the 21st of June, much to our great joy and astonishment, we saw the providential hand of our benign Creator, whose ways with his blind creatures are past finding out. The preceeding night I dreamed that I saw a boat immediately off the starboard main shrouds; and exactly at half past one o'clock, the following day at noon, while I was below, just as we had dined in the cabin, the man at the helm cried out, A boat! which brought my dream that instant into my mind. I was the first man that jumped on the deck; and, looking from the shrouds onward, according to my dream, I descried a little boat at some distance; but, as the waves were high, it was as much as we could do sometimes to discern her; we however stopped the ship's way, and the boat, which was extremely small, came alongside with eleven miserable men, whom we took on board immediately. To all human appearance, these people must have perished in the course of one hour or less, the boat being small, it barely contained them. When we took them up they were half drowned, and had no victuals, compass, water, or any other necessary whatsoever, and had only one bit of an oar to steer with, and that right before the wind; so that they were obliged to trust entirely to the mercy of the waves. As soon as we got them all on board, they bowed themselves on their knees, and, with hands and voices lifted up to heaven, thanked God for their deliverance; and I trust that my prayers were not wanting amongst them at the same time. This mercy of the Lord quite melted me, and I recollected his words, which I saw thus verified in the 107th Psalm "O give thanks unto the Lord, for he is good, for his mercy endureth for ever. Hungry and thirsty, their souls fainted in them. They cried unto Lord in their trouble, and he delivered them out of their distresses. And he led them forth by the right way, that they might go to a city of habitation. O that men would praise the Lord for his goodness and for his wonderful works to the children of men! For he satisfieth the longing soul, and filleth the hungry soul with goodness.

"Such as sit in darkness and in the shadow of death:

"Then they cried unto the Lord in their trouble, and he saved them out of their distresses. They that go down to the sea in ships; that do business in great waters: these see the works of the Lord, and his wonders in the deep. Whoso is wise and will observe these things, even they shall understand the loving kindness of the Lord."

The poor distressed captain said, "that the Lord is good; for, seeing that I am not fit to die, he therefore gave me a space of time to repent." I was very glad to hear this expression, and took an opportunity when convenient of talking to him on the providence of God. They told us they were Portuguese, and were in a brig loaded with corn, which shifted that morning at five o'clock, owing to which the vessel sunk that instant with two of the crew; and how these eleven got into the boat (which was lashed to the deck) not one of them could tell. We provided them with every necessary, and brought them all safe to London: and I hope the Lord gave them repentance unto life eternal.

I was happy once more amongst my friends and brethren, till November, when my old friend, the celebrated Doctor Irving, bought a remarkable fine sloop, about 150 tons. He had a mind for a new adventure in cultivating a plantation at Jamaica and the Musquito Shore; asked me to go with him, and said that he would trust me with his estate in preference to any one. By the advice, therefore, of my friends, I accepted of the offer, knowing that the harvest was fully ripe in those parts, and hoped to be the instrument, under God, of bringing some poor sinner to my well beloved master, Jesus Christ. Before I embarked, I found with the Doctor four Musquito Indians, who were chiefs in their own country, and were brought here by some English traders for some selfish ends. One of them was the Musquito king's son; a youth of about eighteen years of age; and whilst he was here he was baptized by the name of George. They were going back at the government's expense, after having been in England about twelve months, during which they learned to speak pretty good English. When I came to talk to them about eight days before we sailed, I was very much mortified in finding that they had not frequented any churches since they were here, to be baptized, nor was any attention paid to their morals. I was very sorry for this mock Christianity, and had just an opportunity to take some of them once to church before we sailed. We embarked in the month of November 1775, on board of the sloop Morning Star, Captain David Miller, and sailed for Jamaica. In our passage, I took all the pains that I could to instruct the Indian prince in the doctrines of Christianity, of which he was entirely ignorant; and, to my great joy, he was quite attentive, and received with gladness the truths that the Lord enabled me to set forth to him. I taught him in the compass of eleven days all the letters, and he could put even two or three of them together and spell them. I had Fox's Martyrology with cuts,[1] and he used to be very fond of looking into it, and would ask many questions about the papal cruelties he saw depicted there, which I explained to him. I made such progress with this youth, especially in religion, that when I used to go to bed at different hours of the night, if he was in his bed, he would get up on purpose to go to prayer with me, without any other clothes than his shirt; and before he would eat any of his meals amongst the gentlemen in the cabin, he would first come to me to pray, as he called it. I was well pleased at this, and took great delight in him, and used much supplication to God for his conversion. I was in full hope of seeing daily every appearance of that change which I could wish; not knowing the devices of satan, who had many of his emissaries to sow his tares as fast as I sowed the good seed, and pull down as fast as I built up. Thus we went on nearly four fifths of our passage, when satan at last got the upper hand. Some of his messengers, seeing this poor heathen much advanced in piety, began to ask

---

1   John Foxe (1516–87), *Book of Martyrs*, originally published in 1559. This was a popular work that dwelled mostly on the Roman Catholic Church's sadistic tortures and killings of Protestants. It usually was printed with shocking woodcut illustrations.

him whether I had converted him to Christianity, laughed, and made their jest at him, for which I rebuked them as much as I could; but this treatment caused the prince to halt between two opinions. Some of the true sons of Belial,[1] who did not believe that there was any hereafter, told him never to fear the devil, for there was none existing; and if ever he came to the prince, they desired he might be sent to them. Thus they teazed the poor innocent youth, so that he would not learn his book any more! He would not drink nor carouse with these ungodly actors, nor would he be with me, even at prayers. This grieved me very much. I endeavoured to persuade him as well as I could, but he would not come; and entreated him very much to tell me his reasons for acting thus. At last he asked me, "How comes it that all the white men on board who can read and write, and observe the sun, and know all things, yet swear, lie, and get drunk, only excepting yourself?" I answered him, the reason was, that they did not fear God; and that if any one of them died so they could not go to, or be happy with God. He replied, that if these persons went to hell he would go to hell too. I was sorry to hear this; and, as he sometimes had the tooth-ach, and also some other persons in the ship at the same time, I asked him if their toothach made his easy: he said, No. Then I told him if he and these people went to hell together, their pains would not make his any lighter. This answer had great weight with him: it depressed his spirits much; and he became ever after, during the passage, fond of being alone. When we were in the latitude of Martinico, and near making the land, one morning we had a brisk gale of wind, and, carrying too much sail, the main-mast went over the side. Many people were then all about the deck, and the yards, masts, and rigging, came tumbling all about us, yet there was not one of us in the least hurt, although some were within a hair's breadth of being killed: and, particularly, I saw two men then, by the providential hand of God, most miraculously preserved from being smashed to pieces. On the fifth of January we made Antigua and Montserrat, and ran along the rest of the islands: and on the

---

1   Belial: a biblical reference to Satan.

fourteenth we arrived at Jamaica. One Sunday while we were there I took the Musquito Prince George to church, where he saw the sacrament administered. When we came out we saw all kinds of people, almost from the church door for the space of half a mile down to the waterside, buying and selling all kinds of commodities: and these acts afforded me great matter of exhortation to this youth, who was much astonished. Our vessel being ready to sail for the Musquito shore, I went with the Doctor on board a Guinea-man, to purchase some slaves to carry with us, and cultivate a plantation; and I chose them all my own countrymen. On the twelfth of February we sailed from Jamaica, and on the eighteenth arrived at the Musquito shore, at a place called Dupeupy. All our Indian guests now, after I had admonished them and a few cases of liquor given them by the Doctor, took an affectionate leave of us, and went ashore, where they were met by the Musquito king, and we never saw one of them afterwards. We then sailed to the southward of the shore, to a place called Cape Gracias a Dios, where there was a large lagoon or lake, which received the emptying of two or three very fine large rivers, and abounded much in fish and land tortoise. Some of the native Indians came on board of us here; and we used them well, and told them we were come to dwell amongst them, which they seemed pleased at. So the Doctor and I, with some others, went with them ashore; and they took us to different places to view the land, in order to choose a place to make a plantation of. We fixed on a spot near a river's bank, in a rich soil; and, having got our necessaries out of the sloop, we began to clear away the woods, and plant different kinds of vegetables, which had a quick growth. While we were employed in this manner, our vessel went northward to Black River to trade. While she was there, a Spanish guarda costa met with and took her. This proved very hurtful, and a great embarrassment to us. However, we went on with the culture of the land. We used to make fires every night all around us, to keep off wild beasts, which, as soon as it was dark, set up a most hideous roaring. Our habitation being far up in the woods, we frequently saw different kinds of animals; but none of them ever hurt us, except poisonous snakes, the bite of which the Doctor used to cure by giving to the patient, as soon as possible, about half a tumbler of strong rum, with a good deal of Cayenne pepper in it. In this manner he cured two natives and one of his own slaves. The Indians were exceedingly fond of the Doctor, and they had good reason for it; for I believe they never had such an useful man amongst them. They came from all quarters to our dwelling; and some *woolwow*, or flat-headed Indians, who lived fifty or sixty miles above our river, and this side of the South Sea, brought us a good deal of silver in exchange for our goods. The principal articles we could get from our neighbouring Indians, were turtle oil, and shells, little silk grass, and some provisions; but they would not work at any thing for us, except fishing; and a few times they assisted to cut some trees down, in order to build us houses; which they did exactly like the Africans, by the joint labour of men, women, and children. I do not recollect any of them to have had more than two wives. These always accompanied their husbands when they came to our dwelling; and then they generally carried whatever they brought to us, and always squatted down behind their husbands. Whenever we gave them any thing to eat, the men and their wives ate it separate. I never saw the least sign of incontinence amongst them. The women are ornamented with beads, and fond of painting themselves; the men also paint, even to excess, both their faces and shirts: their favourite colour is red. The women generally cultivate the ground, and the men are all fishermen and canoe makers. Upon the whole, I never met any nation that were so simple in their manners as these people, or had so little ornament in their houses. Neither had they, as I ever could learn, one word expressive of an oath. The worst word I ever heard amongst them when they were quarreling, was one that they had got from the English, which was, "you rascal." I never saw any mode of worship among them; but in this they were not worse than their European brethren or neighbours: for I am sorry to say that there was not one white person in our dwelling, nor any where else that I saw in different places I was at on the shore, that was better or more pious than those unenlightened Indians; but they either worked or slept on Sundays:

and, to my sorrow, working was too much Sunday's employment with ourselves; so much so, that in some length of time
we really did not know one day from another. This mode of
living laid the foundation of my decamping at last. The natives
are well made and warlike; and they particularly boast of having
never been conquered by the Spaniards. They are great
drinkers of strong liquors when they can get them. We used to
distil rum from pine apples, which were very plentiful here; and
then we could not get them away from our place. Yet they
seemed to be singular, in point of honesty, above any other
nation I was ever amongst. The country being hot, we lived
under an open shed, where we had all kinds of goods, without
a door or a lock to any one article; yet we slept in safety, and
never lost any thing, or were disturbed. This surprised us a
good deal; and the Doctor, myself, and others, used to say, if we
were to lie in that manner in Europe we should have our
throats cut the first night. The Indian governor goes once in a
certain time all about the province or district, and has a number
of men with him as attendants and assistants. He settles all the
differences among the people, like the judge here, and is treated
with very great respect. He took care to give us timely notice
before he came to our habitation, by sending his stick as a
token, for rum, sugar, and gunpowder, which we did not refuse
sending; and at the same time we made the utmost preparation
to receive his honour and his train. When he came with his
tribe, and all our neighbouring chieftains, we expected to find
him a grave reverend judge, solid and sagacious; but instead of
that, before he and his gang came in sight, we heard them very
clamorous; and they even had plundered some of our good
neighbouring Indians, having intoxicated themselves with our
liquor. When they arrived we did not know what to make of
our new guests, and would gladly have dispensed with the honour of their company. However, having no alternative, we feast-
ed them plentifully all the day till the evening; when the governor, getting quite drunk, grew very unruly, and struck one of
our most friendly chiefs, who was our nearest neighbour, and
also took his gold-laced hat from him. At this a great commo-
tion taken place; and the Doctor interfered to make peace, as

we could all understand one another, but to no purpose; and at last they became so outrageous that the Doctor, fearing he might get into trouble, left the house, and made the best of his way to the nearest wood, leaving me to do as well as I could among them. I was so enraged with the Governor, that I could have wished to have seen him tied fast to a tree and flogged for his behaviour; but I had not people enough to cope with his party. I therefore thought of a stratagem to appease the riot. Recollecting a passage I had read in the life of Columbus, when he was amongst the Indians in Mexico or Peru,[1] where, on some occasion, he frightened them, by telling them of certain events in the heavens, I had recourse to the same expedient; and it succeeded beyond my most sanguine expectations. When I had formed my determination, I went in the midst of them; and, taking hold of the Governor, I pointed up to the heavens. I menaced him and the rest: I told them God lived there, and that he was angry with them, and they must not quarrel so; that they were all brothers, and if they did not leave off, and go away quietly, I would take the book (pointing to the Bible), read, and *tell* God to make them dead. This was something like magic. The clamour immediately ceased, and I gave them some rum and a few other things; after which they went away peaceably; and the Governor afterwards gave our neighbour, who was called Captain Plasmyah, his hat again. When the Doctor returned, he was exceedingly glad at my success in thus getting rid of our troublesome guests. The Musquito people within our vicinity, out of respect to the Doctor, myself and

---

1   Equiano does not remember here that the incident actually took place on the island of Jamaica. Columbus used his knowledge of a lunar eclipse due on February 29, 1504, to trick the island natives into continuing to bring food to his band of shipwrecked sailors. He foretold the moon's disappearance and warned of angry retribution by the "Great Spirit who dwells in heaven, who made and governs the world." Subsequently, when the eclipse occurred, the Jamaican Indians were terrified and quickly agreed to continue to assist him and his men. Equiano probably read the story in the popular book by William Robertson (1721-93), *The History of America* (London, 1777), 1:169-71. However, since Robertson's work served as the major source for the many biographies of Columbus that appeared in England at the end of the eighteenth century, the possibility exists that Equiano could have read about Columbus in one of those texts. Equiano's error was not corrected until the ninth edition of the *Narrative* in 1794.

his people, made entertainments of the grand kind, called in their tongue *tourrie* or *dryckbot*. The English of this expression is, a feast of drinking about, of which it seems a corruption of language. The drink consisted of pine apples roasted, and casades chewed or beaten in mortars; which, after lying some time, ferments, and becomes so strong as to intoxicate, when drank in any quantity. We had timely notice given to us of the entertainment. A white family, within five miles of us, told us how the drink was made, and I and two others went before the time to the village, where the mirth was appointed to be held; and there we saw the whole art of making the drink, and also the kind of animals that were to be eaten there. I cannot say the sight of either the drink or the meat were enticing to me. They had some thousands of pine apples roasting, which they squeezed, dirt and all, into a canoe they had there for the purpose. The casade drink was in beef barrels and other vessels, and looked exactly like hog-wash. Men, women, and children, were thus employed in roasting the pine apples, and squeezing them with their hands. For food they had many land torpins or tortoises, some dried turtle, and three large alligators alive, and tied fast to the trees. I asked the people what they were going to do with these alligators; and I was told they were to be eaten. I was much surprised at this, and went home, not a little disgusted at the preparations. When the day of the feast was come, we took some rum with us, and went to the appointed place, where we found a great assemblage of these people, who received us very kindly. The mirth had begun before we came; and they were dancing with music: and the musical instruments were nearly the same as those of any other sable people; but, as I thought, much less melodious than any other nation I ever knew. They had many curious gestures in dancing, and a variety of motions and postures of their bodies, which to me were in no wise attracting. The males danced by themselves, and the females also by themselves, as with us. The Doctor shewed his people the example, by immediately joining the women's party, though not by their choice. On perceiving the women disgusted, he joined the males. At night there were great illuminations, by setting fire to many pine trees, while the dryckbot went round merrily by calabashes or gourds: but the liquor might more justly be called eating than drinking. One Owden, the oldest father in the vicinity, was dressed in a strange and terrifying form. Around his body were skins adorned with different kinds of feathers, and he had on his head a very large and high head-piece, in the form of a grenadier's cap, with prickles like a porcupine; and he made a certain noise which resembled the cry of an alligator. Our people skipped amongst them out of complaisance, though some could not drink of their tourrie; but our rum met with customers enough, and was soon gone. The alligators were killed and some of them roasted. Their manner of roasting is by digging a hole in the earth, and filling it with wood, which they burn to coal, and then they lay sticks across, on which they set the meat. I had a raw piece of the alligator in my hand: it was very rich: I thought it looked like fresh salmon, and it had a most fragrant smell, but I could not eat any of it. This merry-making at last ended without the least discord in any person in the company, although it was made up of different nations and complexions. The rainy season came on here about the latter end of May, which continued till August very heavily; so that the rivers were overflowed, and our provisions then in the ground were washed away. I thought this was in some measure a judgment upon us for working on Sundays, and it hurt my mind very much. I often wished to leave this place and sail for Europe; for our mode of procedure and living in this heathenish form was very irksome to me. The word of God saith, "What does it avail a man if he gain the whole world, and lose his own soul?"[1] This was much and heavily impressed on my mind; and, though I did not know how to speak to the Doctor for my discharge, it was disagreeable for me to stay any longer. But about the middle of June I took courage enough to ask him for it. He was very unwilling at first to grant my request; but I gave him so many reasons for it, that at last he consented to my going, and gave me the following certificate of my behaviour:

---

1 Mark 8.36; Matthew 16.26.

The bearer, Gustavus Vassa, has served me several years with strict honesty, sobriety, and fidelity. I can, therefore, with justice recommend him for these qualifications; and indeed in every respect I consider him as an excellent servant. I do hereby certify that he always behaved well, and that he is perfectly trust-worthy.

CHARLES IRVING.

Musquito Shore, June 15, 1776.

Though I was much attached to the doctor, I was happy when he consented. I got every thing ready for my departure, and hired some Indians, with a large canoe, to carry me off. All my poor countrymen, the slaves, when they heard of my leaving them, were very sorry, as I had always treated them with care and affection, and did every thing I could to comfort the poor creatures, and render their condition easy. Having taken leave of my old friends and companions, on the 18th of June, accompanied by the doctor, I left that spot of the world, and went southward above twenty miles along the river. There I found a sloop, the captain of which told me he was going to Jamaica. Having agreed for my passage with him and one of the owners, who was also on board, named Hughes, the doctor and I parted, not without shedding tears on both sides. The vessel then sailed along the river till night, when she stopped in a lagoon within the same river. During the night a schooner belonging to the same owners came in, and, as she was in want of hands, Hughes, the owner of the sloop, asked me to go in the schooner as a sailor, and said he would give me wages. I thanked him; but I said I wanted to go to Jamaica. He then immediately changed his tone, and swore, and abused me very much, and asked how I came to be freed. I told him, and said that I came into that vicinity with Dr. Irving, whom he had seen that day. This account was of no use; he still swore exceedingly at me, and cursed the master for a fool that sold me my freedom, and the doctor for another in letting me go from him. Then he desired me to go in the schooner, or else I should not go out of the sloop as a freeman. I said this was very hard, and begged to be put on shore again; but he swore that I should not. I said I had been twice amongst the Turks, yet had never seen any such usage with them, and much less could I have expected any thing of this kind amongst Christians. This incensed him exceedingly; and, with a volley of oaths and imprecations, he replied, "Christians! Damn you, you are one of St. Paul's men; but by G——, except you have St. Paul's or St. Peter's faith, and walk upon the water to the shore, you shall not go out of the vessel;" which I now found was going amongst the Spaniards towards Carthagena, where he swore he would sell me. I simply asked him what right he had to sell me? but, without another word, he made some of his people tie ropes round each of my ancles, and also to each wrist, and another rope round my body, and hoisted me up without letting my feet touch or rest upon any thing. Thus I hung, without any crime committed, and without judge or jury; merely because I was a free man, and could not by the law get any redress from a white person in those parts of the world. I was in great pain from my situation, and cried and begged very hard for some mercy; but all in vain. My tyrant, in a great rage, brought a musquet out of the cabin, and loaded it before me and the crew, and swore that he would shoot me if I cried any more. I had now no alternative; I therefore remained silent, seeing not one white man on board who said a word on my behalf. I hung in that manner from between ten and eleven o'clock at night till about one in the morning; when, finding my cruel abuser fast asleep, I begged some of his slaves to slack the rope that was round my body, that my feet might rest on something. This they did at the risk of being cruelly used by their master, who beat some of them severely at first for not tying me when he commanded them. Whilst I remained in this condition, till between five and six o'clock next morning, I trust I prayed to God to forgive this blasphemer, who cared not what he did, but when he got up out of his sleep in the morning was of the very same temper and disposition as when he left me at night. When they got up the anchor, and the vessel was getting under way, I once more cried and begged to be released; and now, being fortunately in the way of their hoisting the sails, they released me. When I was let down, I spoke to one

Mr. Cox, a carpenter, whom I knew on board, on the impropriety of this conduct. He also knew the doctor, and the good opinion he ever had of me. This man then went to the captain, and told him not to carry me away in that manner; that I was the doctor's steward, who regarded me very highly, and would resent this usage when he should come to know it. On which he desired a young man to put me ashore in a small canoe I brought with me. This sound gladdened my heart, and I got hastily into the canoe and set off, whilst my tyrant was down in the cabin; but he soon spied me out, when I was not above thirty or forty yards from the vessel, and, running upon the deck with a loaded musket in his hand, he presented it at me, and swore heavily and dreadfully, that he would shoot me that instant, if I did not come back on board. As I knew the wretch would have done as he said, without hesitation, I put back to the vessel again; but, as the good Lord would have it, just as I was alongside he was abusing the captain for letting me go from the vessel; which the captain returned, and both of them soon got into a very great heat. The young man that was with me now got out of the canoe; the vessel was sailing on fast with a smooth sea: and I then thought it was neck or nothing, so at that instant I set off again, for my life, in the canoe, towards the shore; and fortunately the confusion was so great amongst them on board, that I got out of the reach of the musquet shot unnoticed, while the vessel sailed on with a fair wind a different way; so that they could not overtake me without tacking: but even before that could be done I should have been on shore, which I soon reached, with many thanks to God for this unexpected deliverance. I then went and told the other owner, who lived near that shore (with whom I had agreed for my passage) of the usage I had met with. He was very much astonished, and appeared very sorry for it. After treating me with kindness, he gave me some refreshment, and three heads of roasted Indian corn, for a voyage of about eighteen miles south, to look for another vessel. He then directed me to an Indian chief of a district, who was also the Musquito admiral, and had once been at our dwelling; after which I set off with the canoe across a large lagoon alone (for I could not get any one to assist me), though I was much jaded, and had pains in my bowels, by means of the rope I had hung by the night before. I was therefore at different times unable to manage the canoe, for the paddling was very laborious. However, a little before dark I got to my destined place, where some of the Indians knew me, and received me kindly. I asked for the admiral; and they conducted me to his dwelling. He was glad to see me, and refreshed me with such things as the place afforded; and I had a hammock to sleep in. They acted towards me more like Christians than those whites I was amongst the last night, though they had been baptized. I told the admiral I wanted to go to the next port to get a vessel to carry me to Jamaica; and requested him to send the canoe back which I then had, for which I was to pay him. He agreed with me, and sent five able Indians with a large canoe to carry my things to my intended place, about fifty miles; and we set off the next morning. When we got out of the lagoon and went along shore, the sea was so high that the canoe was oftentimes very near being filled with water. We were obliged to go ashore and drag across different necks of land; we were also two nights in the swamps, which swarmed with musquito flies, and they proved troublesome to us. This tiresome journey of land and water ended, however, on the third day, to my great joy; and I got on board of a sloop commanded by one Captain Jenning. She was then partly loaded, and he told me he was expecting daily to sail for Jamaica; and having agreed with me to work my passage, I went to work accordingly. I was not many days on board before we sailed; but to my sorrow and disappointment, though used to such tricks, we went to the southward along the Musquito shore, instead of steering for Jamaica. I was compelled to assist in cutting a great deal of mahogany wood on the shore as we coasted along it, and load the vessel with it, before she sailed. This fretted me much; but, as I did not know how to help myself among these deceivers, I thought patience was the only remedy I had left, and even that was forced. There was much hard work and little victuals on board, except by good luck we happened to catch turtles. On this coast there was also a particular kind of fish called manatee, which is most excellent eating, and the flesh is more like beef than fish; the scales are as large as a shilling, and the skin thicker than I ever saw that of any other fish. Within the brackish waters along shore there were likewise vast numbers of alligators, which made the fish scarce. I was on board this sloop sixteen days, during which, in our coasting, we came to another place, where there was a smaller sloop called the Indian Queen, commanded by one John Baker. He also was an Englishman, and had been a long time along the shore trading for turtle shells and silver, and had got a good quantity of each on board. He wanted some hands very much; and, understanding I was a free man, and wanted to go to Jamaica, he told me if he could get one or two, that he would sail immediately for that island: he also pretended to shew me some marks of attention and respect, and promised to give me forty-five shillings sterling a month if I would go with him. I thought this much better than cutting wood for nothing. I therefore told the other captain that I wanted to go to Jamaica in the other vessel; but he would not listen to me: and, seeing me resolved to go in a day or two, he got the vessel to sail, intending to carry me away against my will. This treatment mortified me extremely. I immediately, according to an agreement I had made with the captain of the Indian Queen, called for her boat, which was lying near us, and it came alongside; and, by the means of a north-pole shipmate which I met with in the sloop I was in, I got my things into the boat, and went on board of the Indian Queen, July the 10th. A few days after I was there, we got all things ready and sailed: but again, to my great mortification, this vessel still went to the south, nearly as far as Carthagena, trading along the coast, instead of going to Jamaica, as the captain had promised me: and, what was worst of all, he was a very cruel and bloody-minded man, and was a horrid blasphemer. Among others he had a white pilot, one Stoker, whom he beat often as severely as he did some negroes he had on board. One night in particular, after he had beaten this man most cruelly, he put him into the boat, and made two negroes row him to a desolate key, or small island; and he loaded two pistols, and swore bitterly that he would shoot the negroes if they brought Stoker on board again. There was not the least doubt but that he would do as he said, and the two poor fellows were obliged to obey the cruel mandate; but, when the captain was asleep, the two negroes took a blanket and carried it to the unfortunate Stoker, which I believe was the means of saving his life from the annoyance of insects. A great deal of entreaty was used with the captain the next day, before he would consent to let Stoker come on board; and when the poor man was brought on board he was very ill, from his situation during the night, and he remained so till he was drowned a little time after. As we sailed southward we came to many uninhabited islands, which were overgrown with fine large cocoa nuts. As I was very much in want of provisions, I brought a boat load of them on board, which lasted me and others for several weeks, and afforded us many a delicious repast in our scarcity. One day, before this, I could not help observing the providential hand of God, that ever supplies all our wants, though in the ways and manner we know not. I had been a whole day without food, and made signals for boats to come off, but in vain. I therefore earnestly prayed to God for relief in my need; and at the close of the evening I went off the deck. Just as I laid down I heard a noise on the deck; and, not knowing what it meant, I went directly on the deck again, when what should I see but a fine large fish about seven or eight pounds, which had jumped aboard! I took it, and admired, with thanks, the good hand of God; and, what I considered as not less extraordinary, the captain, who was very avaricious, did not attempt to take it from me, there being only him and I on board; for the rest were all gone ashore trading. Sometimes the people did not come off for some days: this used to fret the captain, and then he would vent his fury on me by beating me, or making me feel in other cruel ways. One day especially, in his wild, wicked, and mad career, after striking me several times with different things, and once across my mouth, even with a red burning stick out of the fire, he got a barrel of gunpowder on the deck, and swore that he would blow up the vessel. I was then at my wit's end, and earnestly prayed to God to direct me. The head was out of the barrel; and the captain took a lighted stick out of the fire to blow himself and me up, because there was a vessel then in sight coming in, which he supposed was a Spaniard, and he was afraid of falling into their hands. Seeing this I got an axe, unnoticed by him, and placed myself between him and the powder, having resolved in myself as soon as he attempted to put the fire in the barrel to chop him down that instant. I was more than an hour in this situation; during which he struck me often, still keeping the fire in his hand for this wicked purpose. I really should have thought myself justifiable in any other part of the world if I had killed him, and prayed to God, who gave me a mind which rested solely on himself. I prayed for resignation, that his will might be done; and the following two portions of his holy word, which occurred to my mind, buoyed up my hope, and kept me from taking the life of this wicked man. "He hath determined the times before appointed, and set bounds to our habitations," Acts xvii. 26. And, "Who is there amongst you that feareth the Lord, that obeyeth the voice of his servant, that walketh in darkness and hath no light? let him trust in the name of the Lord, and stay upon his God," Isaiah l [50]. 10. And thus by the grace of God I was enabled to do. I found him a present help in the time of need, and the captain's fury began to subside as the night approached: but I found,

> That he who cannot stem his anger's tide
> Doth a wild horse without a bridle ride.[1]

The next morning we discovered that the vessel which had caused such a fury in the captain was an English sloop. They soon came to an anchor where we were, and, to my no small surprise, I learned that Doctor Irving was on board of her on his way from the Musquito shore to Jamaica. I was for going immediately to see this old master and friend, but the captain would not suffer me to leave the vessel. I then informed the doctor, by letter, how I was treated, and begged that he would take me out of the sloop: but he informed me that it was not in his power, as he was a passenger himself; but he sent me some rum and sugar for my own use. I now learned that after I had

---

1   From a 1696 play, *Love's Last Shift* 2.7, by Colley Cibber (1671-1757).

left the estate which I managed for this gentleman on the Musquito shore, during which the slaves were well fed and comfortable, a white overseer had supplied my place: this man, through inhumanity and ill-judged avarice, beat and cut the poor slaves most unmercifully; and the consequence was, that every one got into a large Puriogua canoe, and endeavoured to escape; but not knowing where to go, or how to manage the canoe, they were all drowned; in consequence of which the doctor's plantation was left uncultivated, and he was now returning to Jamaica to purchase more slaves and stock it again. On the 14th of October the Indian Queen arrived at Kingston in Jamaica. When we were unloaded I demanded my wages, which amounted to eight pounds and five shillings sterling; but Captain Baker refused to give me one farthing, although it was the hardest-earned money I ever worked for in my life. I found out Doctor Irving upon this, and acquainted him of the captain's knavery. He did all he could to help me to get my money; and we went to every magistrate in Kingston (and there were nine), but they all refused to do any thing for me, and said my oath could not be admitted against a white man. Nor was this all; for Baker threatened that he would beat me severely if he could catch me for attempting to demand my money; and this he would have done, but that I got, by means of Dr. Irving, under the protection of Captain Douglas of the Squirrel man of war. I thought this exceedingly hard usage; though indeed I found it to be too much the practice there to pay free men for their labour in this manner. One day I went with a free negroe taylor, named Joe Diamond, to one Mr. Cochran, who was indebted to him some trifling sum; and the man, not being able to get his money, began to murmur. The other immediately took a horse-whip to pay him with it; but, by the help of a good pair of heels, the taylor got off. Such oppressions as these made me seek for a vessel to get off the island as fast as I could; and by the mercy of God I found a ship in November bound for England, when I embarked with a convoy, after having taken a last farewell of Doctor Irving. When I left Jamaica he was employed in refining sugars; and some months after my arrival in England I learned, with much sorrow, that this my amiable friend was dead, owing to his having eaten some poisoned fish. We had many very heavy gales of wind in our passage; in the course of which no material incident occurred, except that an American privateer, falling in with the fleet, was captured and set fire to by his Majesty's ship the Squirrel. On January the seventh, 1777, we arrived at Plymouth. I was happy once more to tread upon English ground; and, after passing some little time at Plymouth and Exeter among some pious friends, whom I was happy to see, I went to London with a heart replete with thanks to God for all past mercies.

CHAP. XII.

Different transactions of the author's life till the present time — His application to the late Bishop of London to be appointed a missionary to Africa — Some account of his share in the conduct of the late expedition to Sierra Leona[1] — Petition to the Queen — Conclusion.

SUCH were the various scenes which I was a witness to, and the fortune I experienced until the year 1777. Since that period my life has been more uniform, and the incidents of it fewer, than in any other equal number of years preceding; I therefore hasten to the conclusion of a narrative, which I fear the reader may think already sufficiently tedious.

I had suffered so many impositions in my commercial transactions in different parts of the world, that I became heartily disgusted with the seafaring life, and I was determined not to return to it, at least for some time. I therefore once more engaged in service shortly after my return, and continued for the most part in this situation until 1784.

Soon after my arrival in London, I saw a remarkable circumstance relative to African complexion, which I thought so extraordinary, that I beg leave just to mention it: A white negro woman, that I had formerly seen in London and other parts, had married a white man, by whom she had three boys, and they were every one mulattoes, and yet they had fine light hair. In 1779 I served Governor Macnamara, who had been a considerable time on the coast of Africa. In the time of my service, I used to ask frequently other servants to join me in family prayers; but this only excited their mockery. However, the Governor, understanding that I was of a religious turn, wished to know of what religion I was; I told him I was a protestant of the church of England, agreeable to the thirty-nine articles of that church, and that whomsoever I found to preach according to that doctrine, those I would hear. A few days after this, we had some more discourse on the same subject: the Governor spoke to me on it again, and said that he would, if I chose, as he

---

1   The government project to outfit a ship for transporting British blacks for resettlement in the West African colony of Sierra Leone.

thought I might be of service in converting my countrymen to the Gospel faith, get me sent out as a missionary to Africa. I at first refused going, and told him how I had been served on a like occasion by some white people the last voyage I went to Jamaica, when I attempted (if it were the will of God) to be the means of converting the Indian prince; and I said I supposed they would serve me worse than Alexander the coppersmith did St. Paul, if I should attempt to go amongst them in Africa. He told me not to fear, for he would apply to the Bishop of London to get me ordained. On these terms I consented to the Governor's proposal to go to Africa, in hope of doing good if possible amongst my countrymen; so, in order to have me sent out properly, we immediately wrote the following letters to the late Bishop of London:

To the Right Reverend Father in God,
ROBERT, *Lord Bishop of London:*

The MEMORIAL of GUSTAVUS VASSA

SHEWETH,
THAT your memorialist is a native of Africa, and has a knowledge of the manners and customs of the inhabitants of that country.

That your memorialist has resided in different parts of Europe for twenty-two years last past, and embraced the Christian faith in the year 1759.

That your memorialist is desirous of returning to Africa as a missionary, if encouraged by your Lordship, in hopes of being able to prevail upon his countrymen to become Christians; and your memorialist is the more induced to undertake the same, from the success that has attended the like undertakings when encouraged by the Portuguese through their different settlements on the coast of Africa, and also by the Dutch: both governments encouraging the blacks, who, by their education are qualified to undertake the same, and are found more proper than European clergymen, unacquainted with the language and customs of the country.

Your memorialist's only motive for soliciting the office of a missionary is, that he may be a means, under God, of reforming his countrymen and persuading them to embrace the Christian religion. Therefore your memorialist humbly prays your Lordship's encouragement and support in the undertaking.

GUSTAVUS VASSA.

At Mr. Guthrie's, taylor,
No. 17, Hedge-lane.

MY LORD,

I HAVE resided near seven years on the coast of Africa, for most part of the time as commanding officer. From the knowledge I have of the country and its inhabitants, I am inclined to think that the within plan will be attended with great success, if countenanced by your Lordship. I beg leave further to represent to your Lordship, that the like attempts, when encouraged by other governments, have met with uncommon success; and at this very time I know a very respectable character a black priest at Cape Coast Castle. I know the within named Gustavus Vassa, and believe him a moral good man.

I have the honour to be,
My Lord,
Your Lordship's
Humble and obedient servant,

MATT. MACNAMARA.

Grove, 11th March 1779.

This letter was also accompanied by the following from Doctor Wallace, who had resided in Africa for many years, and whose sentiments on the subject of an African mission were the same with Governor Macnamara's.

March 13, 1779.

MY LORD,

I HAVE resided near five years on Senegambia on the coast of Africa, and have had the honour of filling very considerable employments in that province. I do approve of the within plan, and think the undertaking very laudable and proper, and that it deserves your Lordship's protection and encouragement, in which case it must be attended with the intended success.

I am,

My Lord,

Your Lordship's

Humble and obedient servant,

THOMAS WALLACE.

With these letters, I waited on the Bishop by the Governor's desire, and presented them to his Lordship. He received me with much condescension and politeness; but, from some certain scruples of delicacy, declined to ordain me.

My sole motive for thus dwelling on this transaction, or inserting these papers, is the opinion which gentlemen of sense and education, who are acquainted with Africa, entertain of the probability of converting the inhabitants of it to the faith of Jesus Christ, if the attempt were countenanced by the legislature.

Shortly after this I left the Governor, and served a nobleman in the Devonshire militia, with whom I was encamped at Coxheath for some time; but the operations there were too minute and uninteresting to make a detail of.

In the year 1783 I visited eight counties in Wales, from motives of curiosity. While I was in that part of the country I was led to go down into a coal-pit in Shropshire, but my curiosity nearly cost me my life; for while I was in the pit the coals fell in, and buried one poor man, who was not far from me: upon this I got out as fast as I could, thinking the surface of the earth the safest part of it.

In the spring 1784 I thought of visiting old ocean again. In consequence of this I embarked as steward on board a fine new ship called the London, commanded by Martin Hopkin, and sailed for New-York. I admired this city very much; it is large and well-built, and abounds with provisions of all kinds. While we lay here a circumstance happened which I thought extremely singular: – One day a malefactor was to be executed on a gallows; but with a condition that if any woman, having nothing on but her shift, married the man under the gallows, his life was to be saved. This extraordinary privilege was claimed; a woman presented herself; and the marriage ceremony was performed. Our ship having got laden we returned to London in January 1785. When she was ready again for another voyage, the captain being an agreeable man, I sailed with him from hence in the spring, March 1785, for Philadelphia. On the fifth of April we took our departure from the Land's-end, with a pleasant gale; and about nine o'clock that night the moon shone bright, and the sea was smooth, while our ship was going free by the wind, at the rate of about four or five miles an hour. At this time another ship was going nearly as fast as we on the opposite point, meeting us right in the teeth, yet none on board observed either ship until we struck each other forcibly head and head, to the astonishment and consternation of both crews. She did us much damage, but I believe we did her more; for when we passed by each other, which we did very quickly, they called to us to bring to, and hoist out our boat, but we had enough to do to mind ourselves; and in about eight minutes we saw no more of her. We refitted as well as we could the next day, and proceeded on our voyage, and in May arrived at Philadelphia. I was very glad to see this favourite old town once more; and my pleasure was much increased in seeing the worthy quakers freeing and easing the burthens of many of my oppressed African brethren. It rejoiced my heart when one of these friendly people took me to see a free-school they had erected for every denomination of black people, whose minds are cultivated here and forwarded to virtue; and thus they are made useful members of the community. Does not the success of this practice say loudly to the planters in the language of scripture – "Go ye and do likewise?"

In October 1785 I was accompanied by some of the Africans, and presented this address of thanks to the gentlemen called Friends or Quakers, in Gracechurch-Court Lombard-Street:

GENTLEMEN,

By reading your book, entitled a Caution to Great Britain and her Colonies,[1] concerning the Calamitous State of the enslaved Negroes: We the poor, oppressed, needy, and much-degraded negroes, desire to approach you with this address of thanks, with our inmost love and warmest acknowledgment; and with the deepest sense of your benevolence, unwearied labour, and kind interposition, towards breaking the yoke of slavery, and to administer a little comfort and ease to thousands and tens of thousands of very grievously afflicted, and too heavy burthened negroes.

Gentlemen, could you, by perseverance, at last be enabled, under God, to lighten in any degree the heavy burthen of the afflicted, no doubt it would, in some measure, be the possible means, under God, of saving the souls of many of the oppressors; and, if so, sure we are that the God, whose eyes are ever upon all his creatures, and always rewards every true act of virtue, and regards the prayers of the oppressed, will give to you and yours those blessings which it is not in our power to express or conceive, but which we, as a part of those captived, oppressed, and afflicted people, most earnestly wish and pray for.

These gentlemen received us very kindly, with a promise to exert themselves on behalf of the oppressed Africans, and we parted.

While in town I chanced once to be invited to a quaker's wedding. The simple and yet expressive mode used at their solemnizations is worthy of note. The following is the true form of it:

After the company have met they have seasonable exhortations by several of the members; the bride and bridegroom stand up, and, taking each other by the hand in a solemn manner, the man audibly declares to this purpose:

"Friends, in the fear of the Lord, and in the presence of this

---

1   The Quakers distributed copies of Anthony Benezet's antislavery work, *A Caution and Warning to Great Britain and her Colonies*, which had first appeared in Philadelphia in 1766.

assembly, whom I desire to be my witnesses, I take this my friend, M.N. to be my wife; promising, through divine assistance, to be unto her a loving and faithful husband till death separate us:" and the woman makes the like declaration. Then the two first sign their names to the record, and as many more witnesses as have a mind. I had the honour to subscribe mine to a register in Gracechurch-Court, Lombard-Street.

We returned to London in August; and our ship not going immediately to sea, I shipped as a steward in an American ship called the Harmony, Captain John Willet, and left London in March 1786, bound to Philadelphia. Eleven days after sailing we carried our foremast away. We had a nine weeks passage, which caused our trip not to succeed well, the market for our goods proving bad; and, to make it worse, my commander began to play me the like tricks as others too often practise on free negroes in the West Indies. But I thank God I found many friends here, who in some measure prevented him. On my return to London in August I was very agreeably surprised to find that the benevolence of government had adopted the plan of some philanthropic individuals to send the Africans from hence to their native quarter; and that some vessels were then engaged to carry them to Sierra Leone; an act which redounded to the honour of all concerned in its promotion, and filled me with prayers and much rejoicing. There was then in the city a select committee of gentlemen for the black poor, to some of whom I had the honour of being known; and, as soon as they heard of my arrival they sent for me to the committee. When I came there they informed me of the intention of government; and as they seemed to think me qualified to superintend part of the undertaking, they asked me to go with the black poor to Africa. I pointed out to them many objections to my going; and particularly I expressed some difficulties on the account of the slave dealers, as I would certainly oppose their traffic in the human species by every means in my power. However these objections were over-ruled by the gentlemen of the committee, who prevailed on me to go, and recommended me to the honourable Commissioners of his Majesty's Navy as a proper person to act as commissary for government in the intended expedition; and they accordingly appointed me in November 1786 to that office, and gave me sufficient power to act for the government in the capacity of commissary, having received my warrant and the following order.

By the principal Officers and Commissioners of his Majesty's Navy.

WHEREAS you were directed, by our warrant of the 4th of last month, to receive into your charge from Mr. Joseph Irwin the surplus provisions remaining of what was provided for the voyage, as well as the provisions for the support of the black poor, after the landing at Sierra Leone, with the cloathing, tools, and other articles provided at government's expense; and as the provisions were laid in at the rate of two months for the voyage, and for four months after the landing, but the number embarked being so much less than was expected, whereby there may be a considerable surplus of provisions, cloathing, &c. These are, in addition to former orders, to direct and require you to appropriate or dispose of such surplus to the best advantage you can for the benefit of government, keeping and rendering to us a faithful account of what you do herein. And for your guidance in preventing any white persons going, who are not intended to have the indulgence of being carried thither, we send you herewith a list of those recommended by the Committee for the black poor as proper persons to be permitted to embark, and acquaint you that you are not to suffer any others to go who do not produce a certificate from the committee for the black poor, of their having their permission for it. For which this shall be your warrant. Dated at the Navy Office, January 16, 1787.

> J. HINSLOW,
> GEO. MARSH,
> W. PALMER.

To Mr. Gustavus Vassa, Commissary of Provisions and Stores for the Black Poor going to Sierra Leone.

I proceeded immediately to the execution of my duty on board the vessels destined for the voyage, where I continued till the March following.

During my continuance in the employment of government, I was struck with the flagrant abuses committed by the agent, and endeavoured to remedy them, but without effect. One instance, among many which I could produce, may serve as a specimen. Government had ordered to be provided all necessaries (slops, as they are called, included) for 750 persons; however, not being able to muster more than 426, I was ordered to send the superfluous slops, &c. to the king's stores at Portsmouth; but, when I demanded them for that purpose from the agent, it appeared they had never been bought, though paid for by government. But that was not all, government were not the only objects of peculation; these poor people suffered infinitely more; their accommodations were most wretched; many of them wanted beds, and many more cloathing and other necessaries. For the truth of this, and much more, I do not seek credit from my own assertion. I appeal to the testimony of Capt. Thompson, of the Nautilus, who convoyed us, to whom I applied in February 1787 for a remedy, when I had remonstrated to the agent in vain, and even brought him to be a witness of the injustice and oppression I complained of. I appeal also to a letter written by these wretched people, so early as the beginning of the preceding January, and published in the Morning Herald of the 4th of that month, signed by twenty of their chiefs.

I could not silently suffer government to be thus cheated, and my countrymen plundered and oppressed, and even left destitute of the necessaries for almost their existence. I therefore informed the Commissioners of the Navy of the agent's proceeding; but my dismission was soon after procured, by means of a gentleman in the city, whom the agent, conscious of his peculation, had deceived by letter, and whom, moreover, empowered the same agent to receive on board, at the government expense, a number of persons as passengers, contrary to the orders I received. By this I suffered a considerable loss in my property: however, the commissioners were satisfied with my conduct, and wrote to Capt. Thompson expressing their approbation of it.

Thus provided, they proceeded on their voyage; and at last, worn out by treatment, perhaps not the most mild, and wasted by sickness, brought on by want of medicine, cloaths, bedding, &c. they reached Sierra Leone just at the commencement of the rains. At that season of the year it is impossible to cultivate the lands; their provisions therefore were exhausted before they could derive any benefit from agriculture; and it is not surprising that many, especially the lascars,[1] whose constitutions are very tender, and who had been cooped up in ships from October to June, and accommodated in the manner I have mentioned, should be so wasted by their confinement as not long to survive it.

Thus ended my part of the long-talked-of expedition to Sierra Leone; an expedition which, however unfortunate in the event, was humane and politic in its design, nor was its failure owing to government: every thing was done on their part; but there was evidently sufficient mismanagement attending the conduct and execution of it to defeat its success.

I should not have been so ample in my account of this transaction, had not the share I bore in it been made the subject of partial animadversion, and even my dismission from my employment thought worthy of being made by some a matter of public triumph.[2] The motives which might influence any person to descend to a petty contest with an obscure African, and to seek gratification by his depression, perhaps it is not proper here to inquire into or relate, even if its detection were necessary to my vindication; but I thank Heaven it is not. I wish to stand by my own integrity, and not to shelter myself under the impropriety of another; and I trust the behaviour of

---

1   Lascars were sailors from the East Indies. A large group of them boarded the vessel for Sierra Leone.

2   [Equiano's note] See the *Public Advertiser*, July 14, 1787. [Equiano refers to a newspaper letter he wrote to *The Public Advertiser*, in which he defended his actions and attempted to clear up misrepresentation about his conduct on the Sierra Leone project.]

the Commissioners of the Navy to me entitle me to make this assertion; for after I had been dismissed, March 24, I drew up a memorial thus:

To the Right Honourable the Lords Commissioners
of his Majesty's Treasury:

The Memorial and Petition of GUSTAVUS VASSA *a black Man, late Commissary to the black Poor going to* AFRICA.

HUMBLY SHEWETH,

THAT your Lordships' memorialist was, by the Honourable the Commissioners of his Majesty's Navy, on the 4th of December last, appointed to the above employment by warrant from that board;

That he accordingly proceeded to the execution of his duty on board of the Vernon, being one of the ships appointed to proceed to Africa with the above poor;

That your memorialist, to his great grief and astonishment, received a letter of dismission from the Honourable Commissioners of the Navy, by your Lordships' orders;

That, conscious of having acted with the most perfect fidelity and the greatest assiduity in discharging the trust reposed in him, he is altogether at a loss to conceive the reasons of your Lordships' having altered the favourable opinion you were pleased to conceive of him, sensible that your Lordships would not proceed to so severe a measure without some apparent good cause; he therefore has every reason to believe that his conduct has been grossly misrepresented to your Lordships; and he is the more confirmed in his opinion, because, by opposing measures of others concerned in the same expedition, which tended to defeat your Lordships' humane intentions, and to put the government to a very considerable additional expense, he created a number of enemies, whose misrepresentations, he has too much reason to believe, laid the foundation of his dismission. Unsupported by friends, and unaided by the advantages of a liberal education, he can only hope for redress from the justice of his cause, in addition to the mortification of having been removed from his employment, and the advantage which he reasonably might have expected to have derived therefrom. He has had the misfortune to have sunk a considerable part of his little property in fitting himself out, and in other expenses arising out of his situation, an account of which he here annexes. Your memorialist will not trouble your Lordships with a vindication of any part of his conduct, because he knows not of what crimes he is accused; he, however, earnestly entreats that you will be pleased to direct an inquiry into his behaviour during the time he acted in the public service; and, if it be found that his dismission arose from false representations, he is confident that in your Lordships' justice he shall find redress.

Your petitioner therefore humbly prays that your Lordships will take his case into consideration, and that you will be pleased to order payment of the above referred-to account, amounting to £32 4s. and also the wages intended, which is most humbly submitted.

London, May 12, 1787.

The above petition was delivered into the hands of their Lordships, who were kind enough, in the space of some few months afterwards, without hearing, to order me £50 sterling – that is, £18 wages for the time (upwards of four months) I acted a faithful part in their service. Certainly the sum is more than a free negro would have had in the western colonies!!![1]

March the 21st, 1788, I had the honour of presenting the Queen with a petition on behalf of my African brethren, which was received most graciously by her Majesty:[2]

---

1 The following short paragraph appears here in later editions:
      From that period to the present time my life has passed in an even tenor, and great part of my study and attention has been to assist in the cause of my much injured countrymen.
2 [Equiano's note] At the request of some of my most particular friends, I take the liberty of inserting it here.

To the QUEEN'S *most Excellent Majesty*.

MADAM,

Your Majesty's well known benevolence and humanity emboldens me to approach your royal presence, trusting that the obscurity of my situation will not prevent your Majesty from attending to the sufferings for which I plead.

Yet I do not solicit your royal pity for my own distress; my sufferings, although numerous, are in a measure forgotten. I supplicate your Majesty's compassion for millions of my African countrymen, who groan under the lash of tyranny in the West Indies.

The oppression and cruelty exercised to the unhappy negroes there, have at length reached the British legislature, and they are now deliberating on its redress; even several persons of property in slaves in the West Indies, have petitioned parliament against its continuance, sensible that it is as impolitic as it is unjust – and what is inhuman must ever be unwise.

Your Majesty's reign has been hitherto distinguished by private acts of benevolence and bounty; surely the more extended the misery is, the greater claim it has to your Majesty's compassion, and the greater must be your Majesty's pleasure in administering to its relief.

I presume, therefore, gracious Queen, to implore your interposition with your royal consort, in favour of the wretched Africans; that, by your Majesty's benevolent influence, a period may now be put to their misery; and that they may be raised from the condition of brutes, to which they are at present degraded, to the rights and situation of freemen, and admitted to partake of the blessings of your Majesty's happy government; so shall your Majesty enjoy the heart-felt pleasure of procuring happiness to millions, and be rewarded in the grateful prayers of themselves, and of their posterity.

And may the all-bountiful Creator shower on your Majesty, and the Royal Family, every blessing that this world can afford, and every fulness of joy which divine revelation has promised us in the next.

I am your Majesty's most dutiful and
devoted servant to command,

GUSTAVUS VASSA,
The Oppressed Ethiopian.

No. 53, Baldwin's Gardens.

The negro consolidated act, made by the assembly of Jamaica last year, and the new act of amendment now in agitation there, contain a proof of the existence of those charges that have been made against the planters relative to the treatment of their slaves.

I hope to have the satisfaction of seeing the renovation of liberty and justice resting on the British government, to vindicate the honour of our common nature. These are concerns which do not perhaps belong to any particular office: but, to speak more seriously to every man of sentiment, actions like these are the just and sure foundation of future fame; a reversion, though remote, is coveted by some noble minds as a substantial good. It is upon these grounds that I hope and expect the attention of gentlemen in power. These are designs consonant to the elevation of their rank, and the dignity of their stations: they are ends suitable to the nature of a free and generous government; and, connected with views of empire and dominion, suited to the benevolence and solid merit of the legislature. It is a pursuit of substantial greatness. – May the time come – at least the speculation to me is pleasing – when the sable people shall gratefully commemorate the auspicious aera of extensive freedom. Then shall those persons[1] particularly be named with praise and honour, who generously proposed and stood forth in the cause of humanity, liberty, and good policy; and brought to the ear of the legislature designs worthy of royal patronage and adoption. May Heaven make the British senators the dispersers of light, liberty, and science, to the uttermost parts of the earth: then will be glory to God on the highest, on earth peace, and

---

1   [Equiano's note] Granville Sharp, Esq; the Reverend Thomas Clarkson; the Reverend James Ramsay; our approved friends, men of virtue, are an honour to their country, ornamental to human nature, happy in themselves, and benefactors to mankind!

good-will to men: – Glory, honour, peace, &c. to every soul of man that worketh good, to the Britons first, (because to them the Gospel is preached) and also to the nations. "Those that honour their Maker have mercy on the poor." "It is righteousness exalteth a nation; but sin is a reproach to any people; destruction shall be to the workers of iniquity, and the wicked shall fall by their own wickedness." May the blessings of the Lord be upon the heads of all those who commiserated the cases of the oppressed negroes, and the fear of God prolong their days; and may their expectations be filled with gladness! "The liberal devise liberal things, and by liberal things shall stand," Isaiah xxxii. 8. They can say with pious Job, "Did not I weep for him that was in trouble? was not my soul grieved for the poor?" Job xxx. 25.

As the inhuman traffic of slavery is to be taken into the consideration of the British legislature, I doubt not, if a system of commerce was established in Africa, the demand for manufactures would most rapidly augment, as the native inhabitants will insensibly adopt the British fashions, manners, customs, &c. In proportion to the civilization, so will be the consumption of British manufactures.

The wear and tear of a continent, nearly twice as large as Europe, and rich in vegetable and mineral productions, is much easier conceived than calculated.

A case in point. – It cost the Aborigines of Britain little or nothing in clothing, &c. The difference between their forefathers and the present generation, in point of consumption, is literally infinite. The supposition is most obvious. It will be equally immense in Africa – The same cause, viz. civilization, will ever have the same effect.

It is trading upon safe grounds. A commercial intercourse with Africa opens an inexhaustible source of wealth to the manufacturing interests of Great Britain, and to all which the slave trade is an objection.

If I am not misinformed, the manufacturing interest is equal, if not superior, to the landed interest, as to the value, for reasons which will soon appear. The abolition of slavery, so diabolical, will give a most rapid extension of manufactures, which is totally and diametrically opposite to what some interested people assert.

The manufacturers of this country must and will, in the nature and reason of things, have a full and constant employ by supplying the African markets.

Population, the bowels and surface of Africa, abound in valuable and useful returns; the hidden treasures of centuries will be brought to light and into circulation. Industry, enterprize, and mining, will have their full scope, proportionably as they civilize. In a word, it lays open an endless field of commerce to the British manufactures and merchant adventurer. The manufacturing interest and the general interests are synonymous. The abolition of slavery would be in reality an universal good.

Tortures, murder, and every other imaginable barbarity and iniquity, are practised upon the poor slaves with impunity. I hope the slave trade will be abolished. I pray it may be an event at hand. The great body of manufacturers, uniting in the cause, will considerably facilitate and expedite it; and, as I have already stated, it is most substantially their interest and advantage, and as such the nation's at large, (except those persons concerned in the manufacturing neck-yokes, collars, chains, hand-cuffs, leg-bolts, drags, thumb-screws, iron muzzles, and coffins; cats, scourges, and other instruments of torture used in the slave trade). In a short time one sentiment alone will prevail, from motives of interest as well as justice and humanity. Europe contains one hundred and twenty millions of inhabitants. Query – How many millions doth Africa contain? Supposing the Africans, collectively and individually, to expend £5 a head in raiment and furniture yearly when civilized, &c. an immensity beyond the reach of imagination!

This I conceive to be a theory founded upon facts, and therefore an infallible one. If the blacks were permitted to remain in their own country, they would double themselves every fifteen years. In proportion to such increase will be the demand for manufactures. Cotton and indigo grow spontaneously in most parts of Africa; a consideration this of no small consequence to the manufacturing towns of Great Britain. It opens a most immense, glorious, and happy prospect – the clothing, &c. of a continent ten thousand miles in circumference, and immensely rich in productions of every denomination in return for manufactures.[1]

I have only therefore to request the reader's indulgence and conclude. I am far from the vanity of thinking there is any merit in this narrative: I hope censure will be suspended, when it is considered that it was written by one who was as unwilling as unable to adorn the plainness of truth by the colouring of imagination. My life and fortune have been extremely chequered, and my adventures various. Even those I have related are considerably abridged. If any incident in this little work should appear uninteresting and trifling to most readers, I can only say, as my excuse for mentioning it, that almost every event of my life made an impression on my mind and influenced my conduct. I early accustomed myself to look for the hand of God in the minutest occurrence, and to learn from it a lesson of morality and religion; and in this light every circumstance I have related was to me of importance. After all, what

---

1 At this point Equiano added in later editions the following paragraph and notes:
Since the first publication of my Narrative, I have been in a great variety of scenes in many parts of Great Britain, Ireland, and Scotland, an account of which might well be added here;* but this would swell the volume too much, I shall only observe in general, that in May 1791, I sailed from Liverpool to Dublin where I was very kindly received, and from thence to Cork, and then travelled over many counties in Ireland. I was every where exceedingly well treated, by persons of all ranks. I found the people extremely hospitable, particularly in Belfast, where I took my passage on board of a vessel for Clyde, on the 29th of January, and arrived at Greenock on the 30th. Soon after I returned to London, where I found persons of note from Holland and Germany, who requested me to go there; and I was glad to hear that an edition of my Narrative had been printed in both places, also in New York. I remained in London till I heard the debate in the house of Commons on the Slave Trade, April the 2d and 3d. I then went to Soham in Cambridgeshire, and was married on the 7th of April to Miss Cullen, daughter of James and Ann Cullen, late of Ely.**
* Viz. Some curious adventures beneath the earth, in a river in Manchester, – and a most astonishing one under the Peak of Derbyshire – and in Sept. 1792, I went 90 fathoms down St. Anthony's Colliery, at Newcastle, under the river Tyne, some hundreds of yards on Durham side.
**See *Gentleman's Magazine* for April 1792, *Literary and Biographical Magazine and British Review* for May 1792, and the *Edinburgh Historical Register or Monthly Intelligencer* for April 1792.

makes any event important, unless by its observation we become better and wiser, and learn "to do justly, to love mercy, and to walk humbly before God?"[1] To those who are possessed of this spirit, there is scarcely any book or incident so trifling that does not afford some profit, while to others the experience of ages seems of no use; and even to pour out to them the treasures of wisdom is throwing the jewels of instruction away.

THE END.

---

1   Micah 6.8.

Appendix A: Letters and Reviews

1. Letters and Reviews Added to Later Editions of *The Interesting Narrative*

[The following letters, testimonials, and favorable reviews comprise some of the additional materials Equiano included in later editions of his autobiography. Most of the persons who wrote in support of Equiano and his work and those mentioned in the articles of correspondence were leaders in the antislavery movement, many of whom were his personal friends and helped him to sell his autobiography.]

i. To the Reader.

AN invidious falsehood having appeared in the Oracle of the 25th, and the Star of the 27th of April 1792 [see Part Two of this Appendix], with a view to hurt my character, and to discredit and prevent the sale of my Narrative, asserting, that I was born in the Danish island of Santa Cruz [St. Croix], in the West Indies, it is necessary that, in this edition, I should take notice thereof, and it is only needful for me to appeal to those numerous and respectable persons of character who knew me when I first arrived in England, and could speak no language but that of Africa.

Under this appeal, I now offer this edition of my Narrative to the candid reader, and to the friends of humanity, hoping it may still be the means, in its measure, of showing the enormous cruelties practised on my sable brethren, and strengthening the generous emulation now prevailing in this country, to put a speedy end to a traffic both cruel and unjust.

Edinburgh, June 1792.

ii. Letter, of Alexander Tillock to John Monteith, Esq. Glasgow.

DEAR SIR,

Your note of the 30th ult. [last] I would have answered in course; but wished first to be able to inform you what paper we had taken the article from which respected GUSTAVUS VASSA. By this day's post, have sent you a copy of the Oracle of Wednesday the 25th – in the last column of the 3d page, you will find the article from which we inserted the one in the Star of the 27th ult. – If it be erroneous, you will see it had not its origin with us. As to G.V. I know nothing about him.

After examining the paragraph in the Oracle, which immediately follows the one in question, I am inclined to believe that the one respecting G. V. may have been fabricated by some of the advocates for continuing the Slave-trade, for the purpose of weakening the force of the evidence brought against that trade; for, I believe, if they could, they would stifle the evidence altogether.

Having sent you the Oracle, we have sent all that we can say about the business. I am,

DEAR SIR,
Your most humble Servant,
ALEX. TILLOCH.

Star Office, 5th May, 1792.

iii. Letter from the Rev. Dr. J. Baker, of May Fair Chapel, London, to Mr. Gustavus Vassa, at David Dale's Esq. Glasgow.

DEAR SIR,
I went after Mr. [Buchanan] Millan (the printer of the Oracle), but he was not at home. I understood that an apology would be made to you, and I desired it might be a proper one, such as would give fair satisfaction, and take off any disadvantageous impressions which the paragraph alluded to may have made. Whether the matter will bear an action or not, I do not know, and have not inquired whether you can punish by law; because I think it is not worth while to go to the expence of a law-suit, especially if a proper apology is made; for, can any man that

reads your Narrative believe that you are not a native of Africa? I see therefore no good reason for not printing a fifth edition, on account of a scandalous paragraph in a newspaper.

I remain,
DEAR SIR,
Your sincere Friend,
J. BAKER.

Grosvenor-street, May 14, 1792.

iv. To the Chairman of the Committees for the Abolition of the Slave Trade.

Magdalen College, Cambridge, May 26, 1790.

GENTLEMEN,

I TAKE the liberty, as being joined with you in the same laudable endeavours to support the cause of humanity in the abolition of the Slave Trade, to recommend to your protection the bearer of this note GUSTAVUS VASSA, an African; and to beg the favour of your assistance to him in the sale of this book.

I am, with great respect,
GENTLEMEN,
Your most obedient servant,
P. PECKARD,

v.

Manchester, July 23, 1790.

THOMAS WALKER has great pleasure in recommending the sale of the NARRATIVE of GUSTAVUS VASSA to the friends of justice and humanity, he being well entitled to their protection and support, from the united testimonies of the Rev. T. Clarkson, of London; Dr. Peckard, of Cambridge; and Sampson and Charles Lloyd, Esqrs. of Birmingham.

vi.

Sheffield, August 20, 1790.

In consequence of the recommendation to Dr. Peckard of Cambridge; Messrs. Lloyd of Birmingham; the Rev. T. Clarkson of London; Thomas Walker, Thomas Cooper, and Isaac

Moss, Esqrs. of Manchester; we beg leave also to recommend the sale of the NARRATIVE of GUSTAVUS VASSA to the friends of humanity in the town and neighbourhood of Sheffield.

Dr. Brown,   Rev. Ja. Wilkinson,
Wm. Shore, Esq.   Rev. Edw. Goodwin,
Samuel Marshall,   John Barlow.

vii. Letter to Mr. O'Brien, Carrickfergus. (*Per favour of* Mr. Gustavus Vassa.)

Belfast, December 25, 1791.

DEAR SIR,

The bearer of this, MR. GUSTAVUS VASSA, an enlightened African, of good sense, agreeable manners, and of an excellent character, and who comes well recommended to this place, and noticed by the first people here, goes to-morrow for your town, for the purpose of vending some books, written by himself, which is a Narrative of his own Life and Sufferings, with some account of his native country and its inhabitants. He was torn from his relatives and country (by the more savage white men of England) at an early period in life; and during his residence in England, at which time I have seen him, during my agency for the American prisoners, with Sir William Dolben, Mr. Granville Sharp, Mr. Wilkes, and many other distinguished characters; he supported an irreproachable character, and was a principal instrument in bringing about the motion for a repeal of the Slave-act. I beg leave to introduce him to your notice and civility; and if you can spare the time, your introduction of him personally to your neighbours nay be of essential benefit to him.

I am,
Sir,
Your obedient humble servant,
THOS. DIGGES.

[Thomas Digges was an American reformer living in Northern Ireland. During the Revolutionary War, he worked in England to help American prisoners.]

viii. Letter to Rowland Webster, Esq. Stockton. (*Per favour of* Mr. Gustavus Vassa.)

DEAR SIR,

I TAKE the liberty to introduce to your knowledge Mr. GUSTAVUS VASSA, an African of distinguished merit. He has recommendation to Stockton, and I am happy in adding to the number. To the principal supporters of the bill for the Abolition of the Slave-trade he is well known; and he has, himself, been very instrumental in promoting a plan so truly conducive to the interests of Religion and Humanity. Mr. VASSA has published a Narrative which clearly delineates the iniquity of that unnatural and destructive commerce; and I am able to assert, from my own experience, that he has not exaggerated in a single particular. This work has been mentioned in very favourable terms by the Reviewers, and fully demonstrate that genius and worth are not limited to country or complexion. – He has with him some copies for sale, and if you can conveniently assist him in the disposal thereof, you will greatly oblige,

DEAR SIR,
Your friend and servant,
William Eddis.

Durham, October 25, 1792.

ix. Letter to William Hughes, Esq. *Devizes.*

DEAR SIR,

WHETHER you will consider my introducing to your acquaintance the bearer of this letter, OLAUDAH EQUIANO, the enlightened African, (or GUSTAVUS VASSA) as a liberty or a favour, I shall not anticipate.

He came recommended to me by men of distinguished talents and exemplary virtue, as an honest and benevolent man;

and his conversation and manners as well as his book do more than justice to the recommendation.

The active part he took in bringing about the motion for a repeal of the Slave act, has given him much celebrity as a public man; and, in all the varied scenes of chequered life, through which he has passed, his private character and conduct have been irreproachable.

His *business* in your part of the world is to promote the sale of his book, and it is a part of *my business*, as a friend to the cause of humanity, to do all the little service that is in my poor power to a man who is engaged in so noble a cause as the freedom and salvation of his enslaved and unenlightened countrymen.

The simplicity that runs through his Narrative is singularly beautiful, and that beauty is heightened by the idea that it is *true*; this is all I shall say about this book, save only that I am sure those who buy it will not regret that they have laid out the price of it in the purchase.

Your notice, civility, and personal introduction of this fair-minded black man, to your friends in Devizes, will be gratifying to your own feelings, and laying a considerable weight of obligation on

Dear Sir,
Your most obedient and obliged servant,
William Langworthy.

Bath, October 10th, 1793.

x. Monthly Review for June 1789. Page 551.

We entertain no doubt of the general authenticity of this very intelligent African's story; though it is not improbable that some English writer has assisted him in the compilement, or, at least, the correction of his book; for it is sufficiently well-written. The Narrative wears an honest face; and we have conceived a good opinion of the man, from the artless manner in which he has detailed the variety of adventures and vicissitudes which have fallen to his lot. His publication appears very seasonable, at a time when negroe-slavery is the subject of public investigation; and it seems calculated to increase the odium that has been excited against the West-India planters, on account of the cruelties that some are said to have exercised on their slaves, many instances of which are here detailed.

The sable author of this volume appears to be a very sensible man; and he is, surely, not the less worthy of credit from being a convert to Christianity. He is a Methodist, and has filled many pages towards the end of this work, with accounts of his dreams, visions, and divine influences; but all this, supposing him to have been under any delusive influence, only serves to convince us that he is guided by principle, and that he is not one of those poor converts, who, having undergone the ceremony of baptism, have remained content with that portion only of the Christian religion; instances of which are said to be almost innumerable in America and the West Indies.

GUSTAVUS VASSA appears to possess a very different character; and, therefore, we heartily wish success to his publication, which we are glad to see has been encouraged by a very respectable subscription.

xi. The General Magazine and Impartial Review for July 1789, characterizes this Work in the following Terms:

"This is 'a round unvarnished tale' [see Shakespeare's *Othello* 1.3.89] of the chequered adventures of an African, who early in life, was torn from his native country, by those savage dealers in a traffic disgraceful to humanity, and which has fixed a stain on the legislature of Britain. The Narrative appears to be written with much truth and simplicity. The author's account of the manners of the natives of his own province (Eboe) is interesting and pleasing; and the reader, unless perchance he is either a West-India planter, or Liverpool merchant, will find his humanity often severely wounded by the shameless barbarity practised towards the author's hapless countrymen in all our colonies; if he feel, as he ought, the oppressed and the oppressors will equally excite his pity and indignation. That so unjust, so iniquitous a commerce may be abolished, is our ardent wish; and we heartily join in our author's prayer, 'That the God of Heaven may inspire the hearts of our Representatives in Parliament, with peculiar benevolence on that important day when so interesting a question is to be discussed; when thousands, in consequence of their determination, are to look for happiness or misery!' "

xii. N.B. These letters, and the Reviewers' remarks, would not have appeared in the Narrative, were it not on the account of the false assertions of my enemies.

xiii. THE kind reception which this Work has met with from many hundred persons, of all denominations, demands the Author's most sincere thanks to his numerous friends; and he most respectfully solicits the favour and encouragement of the candid and unprejudiced friends of the Africans.

2. Reviews of *The Interesting Narrative* Not Included in Equiano's Editions

i. *The Analytical Review*, May 1789.

[This article was written by well-known women's rights advocate Mary Wollstonecraft (1759-1797).]

The life of an African, written by himself, is certainly a curiosity, as it has been a favourite philosophic whim to degrade the numerous nations, on whom the sun-beams more directly dart, below the common level of humanity, and hastily to conclude that nature, by making them inferior to the rest of the human race, designed to stamp them with a mark of slavery. How they were shaded down, from the fresh colour of northern rustics, to the sable hue seen on the African sands, is not our task to inquire, nor do we intend to draw a parallel between the abilities of a negro and European mechanic; we shall only observe, that if these volumes do not exhibit extraordinary intellectual powers, sufficient to wipe off the stigma, yet the activity and ingenuity, which conspicuously appear in the character of Gustavus, place him on a par with the general mass of men, who fill the subordinate stations in a more civilized society than that which he was thrown into at his birth.

The first volume contains, with a variety of other matter, a short description of the manners of his native country, an account of his family, his being kidnapped with his sister, his journey to the sea coast, and terror when carried on shipboard. Many anecdotes are simply told, relative to the treatment of male and female slaves, on the voyage, and in the West Indies, which make the blood turn its course; and the whole account of his unwearied endeavours to obtain his freedom, is very interesting. The narrative should have closed when he once more became his own master. The latter part of the second volume appears flat; and he is entangled in many, comparatively speaking, insignificant cares, which almost efface the lively impression made by the miseries of the slave. The long account of his religious sentiments and conversion to methodism, is rather tiresome.

Throughout, a kind of contradiction is apparent: many childish stories and puerile remarks, do not agree with some more solid reflections, which occur in the first pages. In the style also we observed a striking contrast: a few well written periods do not smoothly unite with the general tenor of the language.

An extract from the part descriptive of the national manners, we think will not be unacceptable to our readers.

[Two paragraphs (beginning with the sentence, "We are almost a nation of dancers , musicians, and poets.") are printed here from Equiano's narrative (1.10-12).]

ii. *The Gentleman's Magazine*, June 1789.

AMONG other contrivances (and perhaps one of the most innocent) to interest the national humanity in favour of the Negro slaves, one of them here writes his own history, as formerly another of them published his correspondence (see our vol. LII. p. 437) [refers to the 1782 publication of *The Letters of the Late Ignatius Sancho*]. – These memoirs, written in a very unequal style, place the writer on a par with the general mass of men in the subordinate stations of civilized society, and prove that there is no general rule without an exception. The first volume treats of the manners of his countrymen, and his own adventures till he obtained his freedom; the second, from that period to the present, is uninteresting; and his conversion to methodism oversets the whole.

iii. *The Oracle*, 25 April, 1792.

[The author mentions William Wilberforce (1759-1833), who led the Parliamentary efforts to abolish the slave trade, and the Thorntons – Henry (1760-1815) and William (1761-1828) – who were involved in the Sierra Leone resettlement of black Britons. The accusation that Wilberforce and the Thorntons attempted to set up sugar plantations in Africa is not true.]

It was well observed by Chubb [might refer to Thomas Chubb (1679-1747), who wrote on self-delusion], that there is no absurdity, however gross, but popular credulity has a throat wide enough to swallow it. It is a fact that the Public may depend on, that *Gustavus Vasa*, who has publicly asserted that he was kidnapped in Africa, never was upon that Continent, but was born and bred up in the Danish Island of Santa Cruz, in the West Indies. *Ex hoc uno disce omnes* [this one fact tells all]. What, we will ask any man of plain understanding, must that cause be, which can lean for support on falsehoods as audaciously propagated as they are easily detected?

Modern Patriotism, which wantons so much in sentiment, is *really* founded rather in private interested views, than in a regard for the Public Weal. The conduct of the friends to the Abolition is a proof of the justice of this remark. It is a fact, of which, perhaps, the People are not apprized, but which it well becomes them to know, that WILBERFORCE and the THORNTONS are concerned in settling the Island of Bulam in Sugar Plantations; of course their interests clash with those of the present Planters and hence their clamour against the Slave Trade.

"Old Cato is as great a Rogue as You." [Alexander Pope, *The Epistle to Bathurst* (London, 1733), 68.]

iv. *The Star*, 27 April, 1792.

The Negro, called GUSTAVUS VASSA, who has published an history of his life, and gives so admirable an account of the laws, religion, and natural productions of the interior parts of Africa; and in which he relates his having been kidnapped in his infancy, is neither more nor less, than a native of the Danish island of Santa Cruz.

Appendix B: *Writings of the First Abolitionist Movement*

[Many of Equiano's contemporaries who worked with him in the eighteenth century responded to the principles of the Enlightenment Movement. They acted in accord with humanistic ideas related to equality, freedom, and universal reason. At the same time, a spiritual revival led by evangelical Methodists, Baptists, and Unitarians questioned the morality involved in enslaving men and women. Thus, in the battle to end slavery, many diverse individuals joined in the endeavors to transmit accurate information and to impart truth that would change the opinions and perceptions on human bondage held by the majority populations.

Convincing and authentic (often based on firsthand experience) though many antislavery works were, they did not go unchallenged by those who supported slavery. Moreover, proponents on both sides of the battle were sometimes ambivalent about their position, refusing to commit themselves wholeheartedly to either abolition or unqualified support.

Several of the authors represented here, including Edmund Burke, Benjamin Franklin, Thomas Jefferson, and Mary Wollstonecraft, are familiar to us because of their achievements in other areas of life. However, lesser-known writers such as Quobna Ottobah Cugoano, Granville Sharp, and James Ramsay also contributed greatly to the slavery debate.

Some of the works chosen for inclusion in this edition are those that Equiano himself knew and often alluded to in his narrative. From these writings, he borrowed concepts and opinions required for building up his arguments against slavery, and this meant that at times he included proslavery ideas for the sole purpose of refuting them. One example of this latter usage can be seen in *The Interesting Narrative* when Equiano mentions and rejects the arguments put forward by slavery advocate James Tobin, an opponent to the abolitionist work of James Ramsay.]

1. Anthony Benezet

A Caution to Great Britain and her Colonies. Philadelphia, 1766.
London: James Phillips, 1785.

[Benezet was an influential Quaker living in Philadelphia when he wrote a series of antislavery texts published throughout British America. His works had an enormous impact on the abolitionist writers of his day, including Equiano who refers to him in *The Interesting Narrative* (see note 1: pp. 47, 53, 241; note 3, p. 122). Benezet especially had a strong effect on the work of Thomas Clarkson, who composed his prize dissertation at Cambridge University (see p. 272) on the information in Benezet's books. During the fight to end the slave trade, Benezet corresponded with the leading English abolitionists.]

From these Accounts, both of the good Disposition of the Natives, and the Fruitfulness of most parts of *Guinea*, which are confirmed by many other Authors, it may well be concluded, that their acquaintance with the *Europeans* would have been a happiness to them, had those last not only borne the name, but indeed been influenced by the Spirit of *Christianity*; but, alas! how hath the Conduct of the Whites contradicted the Precepts and Example of Christ? Instead of promoting the End of his Coming, by preaching the Gospel of Peace and Good-will to Man, they have, by their practices, contributed to enflame every noxious passion of corrupt nature in the Negroes; they have incited them to make war one upon another, and for this purpose have furnished them with prodigious quantities of ammunition and arms, whereby they have been hurried into confusion, bloodshed, and all the extremities of temporal misery, which must necessarily beget in their minds such a general detestation and scorn of the *Christian* name, as may deeply affect, if not wholly preclude, their belief of the great Truths of our holy Religion. Thus an insatiable desire of gain hath become the principal and moving cause of the most abominable and dreadful scene, that was perhaps ever acted upon the face of the earth; even the power of their Kings hath been made subservient to answer this wicked purpose; instead of being Protectors of their people, these Rulers, allured by the tempting bait laid before them by the *European* Factors, &c. have invaded the Liberties of their unhappy subjects, and are become their Oppressors....

Those who are acquainted with the Trade agree, that many Negroes on the sea-coast, who have been corrupted by their intercourse and converse with the *European* Factors, have learnt to stick at no act of cruelty for gain. These make it a practice to steal abundance of little Blacks of both sexes; when found on the roads or in the fields, where their parents keep them all day to watch the corn, &c. Some authors say, the Negroe Factors go six or seven hundred miles up the country with goods, bought from the *Europeans*, where markets of men are kept in the same manner as those of beasts with us. When the poor slaves, whether brought from far or near, come to the sea-shore, they are stripped naked, and strictly examined by the *European* Surgeons, both men and women, without the least distinction or modesty; those which are approved as good, are marked with a red-hot iron with the ship's mark; after which they are put on board the vessels, the men being shackled with irons two and two together. Reader, bring the matter home, and consider whether any situation in life can be more completely miserable than that of those distressed captives. When we reflect that each individual of this number had some tender attachment which was broken by this cruel separation; some parent or wife, who had not an opportunity of mingling tears in a parting embrace; perhaps some infant or aged parent whom his labour was to feed and vigilance protect; themselves under the dreadful apprehension of an unknown perpetual slavery; pent up within the narrow confines of a vessel, sometimes six or seven hundred together, where they lie as close as possible. Under these complicated distresses they are often reduced to a state of desperation, wherein many have leaped into the sea, and have kept themselves under water till they were drowned; others have starved themselves to death, for the prevention whereof some masters of vessels have cut off the legs and arms of a number of those poor desperate creatures, to terrify the rest. Great numbers have also frequently been killed, and some deliberately put to death under the greatest torture, when they have attempted to rise, in order to free themselves from their present misery, and the slavery designed them. An instance of the last kind appears particularly in an account give by the master of a vessel, who brought a cargo of slaves to *Barbadoes*; indeed it appears so irreconcileable to the common dictates of humanity, that one would doubt the truth of it, had it not been related by a serious person of undoubted credit, who had it from the captain's own mouth. Upon an enquiry, What had been the success of his voyage? he answered, "That he had found it a difficult matter to set the negroes a fighting with each other, in order to procure the number he wanted; but that when he had obtained this end, and had got his vessel filled with slaves, a new difficulty arose from their refusal to take food; those desperate creatures chusing rather to die with hunger, than to be carried from their native country." Upon a farther inquiry, by what means he had prevailed upon them to forego this desperate resolution? he answered, "That he obliged all the negroes to come upon deck, where they persisted in their resolution of not taking food, he caused his sailors to lay hold upon one of the most obstinate, and chopt the poor creature into small pieces, forcing some of the others to eat a part of the mangled body; withal swearing to the survivors that he would use them all, one after the other, in the same manner, if they did not consent to eat." This horrid execution he applauded as a good act, it having had the desired effect, in bringing them to take food.

2.Anthony Benezet

Some Historical Account of Guinea. Philadelphia: Joseph Crukshank, 1771.

[In the first volume of *The Interesting Narrative*, Equiano acknowledges using information from *Some Historical Account of Guinea*, which went through many editions in the 1770s and 1780s. The following passage describes the corrupting effects of slavery on both slave and master, which became a common theme in much abolitionist writing. It also reveals the great degree of influence exerted on Enlightenment thought by the French political philosopher Montesquieu (1689-1755), whose 1748 work *De l'esprit des loix* appeared in English as *The Spirit of Laws* in 1750.]

That celebrated civillian Montesquieu, in his treatise *on the spirit of laws*, on the article of slavery says, "*It is neither useful to the master nor slave; to the slave, because he can do nothing through principle (or virtue,) to the master because he contracts with his slave all sorts of bad habits, insensibly accustoms himself to want all moral virtues, becomes, haughty, hasty, hard hearted, passionate, voluptuous and cruel.*" The lamentable truth of this assertion was quickly verified in the English plantations. When the practice of slave keeping was introduced, it soon produced its natural effects; it reconciled men of otherwise good dispositions to the most hard and cruel measures. It quickly proved what under the law of Moses was apprehended would be the consequence of unmerciful chastisements. Deut. xxv. 2. "*And it shall be if the wicked man be worthy to be beaten, that the judge shall cause him to lie down, and to be beaten before his face, according to his fault, by a certain number; forty stripes he may give him and not exceed.*" And the reason rendered is out of respect to human nature, viz. "*Lest if he should exceed and beat him above these with many stripes, then thy brother should seem vile unto thee.*" As this effect soon followed the cause, the cruelest measures were adopted, in order to make the most of the poor *wretches* labour; and in the minds of the masters such an idea was excited of inferiority in the nature of these their unhappy fellow creatures, that they soon esteemed and treated them as beasts of burden: pretending to doubt, and some of them, even presuming to deny, the efficacy of the death of Christ extended to them....

3. Edmund Burke

An Account of the European Settlements in America. London: R. and J. Dodsley, 1758.

[In addition to his philosophical work, Burke also produced a two-volume geographical and historical work on the American colonies and territories, including the prevalence of slavery. He did not, however, advocate abolition, suggesting only that living conditions and religious instructions for the slaves should be improved because this would result in cheaper prices for buying slaves, greater productivity from their labors, and calmer behavior. Burke also hoped that civil strife could be avoided by encouraging more white men and women to settle in those places where blacks outnumbered the white population.]

... I am far from contending in favour of an effeminate indulgence to these people [the slaves]. I know that they are stubborn and intractable for the most part, and that they must be ruled with a rod of iron. I would have them ruled, but not crushed with it....

... But surely, one cannot hear without horror of a trade which must depend for its support upon the annual murder of several thousands of innocent men; and indeed nothing could excuse the slave trade at all, but the necessity we are under of peopling our colonies, and the consideration that the slaves we buy were in the same condition in Africa, either hereditary, or taken in war.

... The principal time I would have reserved for the indulgence I propose to be granted to the slaves, is Sunday, or the Lord's day; a day which is profaned in a manner altogether scandalous in our colonies. On this day, I would have them regularly attend at church. I would have them, particularly the children, carefully ... instructed in the principles of religion and virtue, and especially in the humility, submission and honesty which become their condition.... Such methods would by degrees habituate their masters, not to think them a sort of beasts, and without souls, as some of them do at present, who treat them accordingly; and the slaves would of course grow more honest, tractable, and less of eye-servants....

4. Thomas Clarkson

An Essay on the Slavery and Commerce of the Human Species, Particularly the African. London: J. Phillips, 1788.

[In 1785 Clarkson submitted for prize consideration to the University of Cambridge his Latin dissertation on the slavery issue. The topic assigned by the prize committee at the university had been practically unknown to Clarkson until one day he chanced to read a newspaper advertisement for Anthony Benezet's *Historical Account of Guinea.* Clarkson hurried to London to purchase Benezet's book, in which he found all that he required to write his essay. More importantly, Benezet's revelations about human bondage in the West shook Clarkson's heart and mind so forcefully that the young scholar decided to devote the rest of his life to the abolitionist crusade.]

With respect to the liberal arts, their [the African slaves] proficiency is certainly less; but not less in proportion to their time and opportunity of study; not less, because they are less capable of attaining them, but because they have seldom or ever an opportunity of learning them at all. It is yet extraordinary that their talents appear, even in some of these sciences, in which they are totally uninstructed. Their abilities in musick are such, as to have been generally noticed. They play frequently upon a variety of instruments, without any other assistance than their own ingenuity. They have also tunes of their own composition. Some of these have been imported among us, are now in use, and are admired for their sprightliness and ease, though the ungenerous and prejudiced importer has concealed their original.

Neither are their talents in poetry less conspicuous. Every occurrence, if their spirits are not too greatly depressed, is turned into a song. These songs are said to be incoherent and nonsensical. But this proceeds principally from two causes, an improper conjunction of words, arising from an ignorance of the language in which they compose; and a wildness of thought, arising from the different manner, in which the organs of rude and civilized people will be struck by the same object. And as to their want of harmony and rhyme, which is the last objection, the difference of pronounciation is the cause. Upon the whole, as they are perfectly consistent with their own ideas, and are strictly musical as pronounced by themselves, they afford us as high a proof of their poetical powers, as the works of the most acknowledged poets.

But where these impediments have been removed, where they have received an education, and have known and pronounced the language with propriety, these defects have vanished, and their productions have been less objectionable. For a proof of this, I appeal to the writings of an African girl [Clarkson's note: Phillis Wheatley, negroe slave to Mr. John Wheatley, of Boston, in New-England], who made no contemptible appearance in this species of composition. She was kidnapped when only eight years old, and, in the year 1761, was transported to America, where she was sold with other slaves. She had no school education there, but receiving some little instruction from the family, with whom she was so fortunate as to live, she obtained such a knowledge of the English language within sixteen months from the time of her arrival, as to be able to speak it and read it to the astonishment of those who heard her. She soon afterwards learned to write, and, having a great inclination to learn the Latin tongue, she was indulged by her master, and made a progress. Her poetical works were published with his permission, in the year 1773. They contain thirty-eight pieces on different subjects. I shall beg leave to make a short extract from two or three of them, for the observation of the reader.

From an Hymn to the Evening.

Fill'd with the praise of him who gives the light,
And draws the sable curtains of the night,

Let placid slumbers sooth each weary mind,
At morn to wake more heav'nly and refin'd;
So shall the labours of the day begin,
More pure and guarded from the snares of sin.
——— &c. &c.

From an Hymn to the Morning.

Aurora hail! and all the thousand dyes,
That deck thy progress through the vaulted skies!
The morn awakes, and wide extends her rays,
On ev'ry leaf the gentle zephyr plays.
Harmonious lays the feather'd race resume,
Dart the bright eye, and shake the painted plume.
——— &c. &c.

From Thoughts on Imagination.

Now here, now there, the roving *fancy* flies,
Till some lov'd object strikes her wand'ring eyes,
Whose silken fetters all the senses bind,
And soft captivity involves the mind.
Imagination! who can sing thy force,
Or who describe the swiftness of thy course?
Soaring through air to find the bright abode,
Th'empyreal palace of the thund'ring God,
We on thy pinions can surpass the wind,
And leave the rolling universe behind:
From star to star the mental opticks rove,
Measure the skies, and range the realms above.
There in one view we grasp the mighty whole,
Or with new worlds amaze th'unbounded soul.
——— &c. &c....

To this poetry I shall add, as a farther proof of their abilities,
the Prose compositions of Ignatius Sancho [*The Letters of the
Late Ignatius Sancho*, 1782], who received some little education.
His letters are too well known, to make any extract, or indeed

any farther mention of him, necessary. If other examples of African genius should be required, suffice it to say, that they can be produced in abundance; and that if I were allowed to enumerate instances of African gratitude, patience, fidelity, honour, as so many instances of good sense, and a sound understanding, I fear that thousands of the enlightened Europeans would have occasion to blush....

But I shall now mention a circumstance, which, in the present case, will have more weight than all the arguments which have hitherto been advanced. It is an opinion, which the *Africans* universally entertain, that, as soon as death shall release them from the hands of their oppressors, they shall immediately be wafted back to their native plains, there to exist again, to enjoy the sight of their beloved countrymen, and to spend the whole of their new existence in scenes of tranquility and delight: and so powerfully does this notion operate upon them, as to drive them frequently to the horrid extremity of putting a period to their lives. Now if these suicides are frequent, (which no person can deny) what are they but a proof, that the situation of those who destroy themselves must have been insupportably wretched: and if the thought of returning to their country after death, *when they have experienced the colonial joys,* constitutes their supreme felicity, what are they but a proof, that they think there is as much difference between the two situations, as there is between misery and delight?

5. William Cowper

"The Negro's Complaint." London, 1788.

[The Society for Effecting the Abolition of the Slave Trade circulated thousands of copies of Cowper's antislavery ballad, "The Negro's Complaint." At times distributed under the title of "A Subject for Conversation at the Tea-table," the poem was set to music and sung in the streets of London and in other English cities. Cowper knew John Newton, the former and repentant slave captain, and collaborated with him in writing a book of religious verse called *Olney Hymns* (1779). Other poems Cowper wrote against slavery include "Pity for Poor Africans" and "Sweet Meat has Sour Sauce."]

Forc'd from home, and all its pleasures,
   Afric's coast I left forlorn;
To increase a stranger's treasures,
   O'er the ranging billows borne.
Men from England bought and sold me,
   Paid my price in paltry gold;
But, though theirs they have enroll'd me,
   Minds are never to be sold.

Still in thought as free as ever,
   What are England's rights, I ask,
Me, from my delights to sever,
   Me to torture, me to task?
Fleecy locks, and black complexion
   Cannot forfeit nature's claim;
Skins may differ, but affection
   Dwells in white and black the same....
Deem our nation brutes no longer
   Till some reason ye shall find
Worthier of regard and stronger
   Than the colour of our kind.
Slaves of gold, whose sordid dealings
   Tarnish all your boasted pow'rs,
Prove that you have human feelings,
   Ere you proudly question ours!

6. J. Hector St. John de Crèvecoeur

Letters from an American Farmer. London: T. Davies, 1782.

[Born in France, Crèvecoeur also lived in England, Canada, and the American colonies. His perceptive observation of American society in his philosophical travel work *Letters* was widely discussed in Europe and America. Although he viewed the new country as an egalitarian land of opportunity and an escape from Europe's corrupt institutions, Crèvecoeur candidly described its flaws, the primary one being slavery. In the following excerpt from his "Letter IX," he writes about the prosperous settlement of what later became Charleston, South Carolina, but notes its evil underpinning.]

While all is joy, festivity, and happiness in Charles Town, would you imagine that scenes of misery overspread in the country? Their ears by habit are become deaf, their hearts are hardened; they neither see, hear, nor feel for the woes of their poor slaves, from whose painful labours all their wealth proceeds. Here the horrors of slavery, the hardship of incessant toils, are unseen; and no one thinks with compassion of those showers of sweat and tears which from the bodies of Africans daily drop and moisten the ground they till. The cracks of the whip urging these miserable beings to excessive labour are far too distant from the gay capital to be heard. The chosen race eat, drink, and live happy, while the unfortunate one grubs up the ground, raises indigo, or husks the rice, exposed to a sun full as scorching as their native one, without the support of good food, without the cordials of any cheering liquor....

The following scene will, I hope, account for these melancholy reflections and apologize for the gloomy thoughts with which I have filled this letter: my mind is, and always has been, oppressed since I became a witness to it. I was not long since invited to dine with a planter who lived three miles from ——, where he then resided. In order to avoid the heat of the sun, I resolved to go on foot, sheltered in a small path leading through a pleasant wood. I was leisurely travelling along, attentively examining some peculiar plants which I had collected, when all at once I felt the air strongly agitated, though the day was perfectly calm and sultry. I immediately cast my eyes toward the cleared ground, from which I was but a small distance, in order to see whether it was not occasioned by a sudden shower, when at that instant a sound resembling a deep rough voice, uttered, as I thought, a few inarticulate monosyllables. Alarmed and surprised, I precipitately looked all round, when I perceived at about six rods distance something resembling a cage, suspended to the limbs of a tree, all the branches of which appeared covered with large birds of prey, fluttering about and anxiously endeavouring to perch on the cage. Actuated by an involuntary motion of my hands more than by any design of my mind, I fired at them; they all flew to a short distance, with a most hideous noise, when, horrid to think and painful to repeat, I perceived a Negro, suspended in the cage and left there to expire! I shudder when I recollect that the birds had already picked out his eyes; his cheek-bones were bare; his arms had been attacked in several places; and his body seemed covered with a multitude of wounds. From the edge of the hollow sockets and from the lacerations with which he was disfigured, the blood slowly dropped and tinged the ground beneath. No sooner were the birds flown than swarms of insects covered the whole body of this unfortunate wretch, eager to feed on his mangled flesh and to drink his blood. I found myself suddenly arrested by the power of affright and terror; my nerves were convulsed; I trembled; I stood motionless, involuntarily contemplating the fate of this Negro in all its dismal latitude. The living spectre, though deprived of his eyes, could still distinctly hear, and in his uncouth dialect begged me to give him some water to allay his thirst. Humanity herself would have recoiled back with horror; she would have balanced whether to lessen such reliefless distress or mercifully with one blow to end this dreadful scene of agonizing torture! Had I had a ball in my gun, I certainly should have dispatched him, but finding myself unable to perform so kind an office, I sought, though trembling, to relieve him as well as I could. A shell ready fixed to a pole, which had been used by some Negroes, presented itself to me; I filled it with water, and with trembling hands I guided it to the quivering lips of the wretched sufferer. Urged by the irresistible power of thirst, he endeavoured to meet it, as he instinctively guessed its approach by the noise it made in passing through the bars of the cage. "Tanky you, white man; tanky you; puta some poison and give me." "How long have you been hanging there?" I asked him. "Two days, and me no die; the birds, the birds; aaah me!" Oppressed with the reflections which this shocking spectacle afforded me, I mustered strength enough to walk away and soon reached the house at which I intended to dine. There I heard that the reason for this slave's being thus punished was on account of his having killed the overseer of the plantation. They told me that the laws of self-preservation rendered such executions necessary, and supported the doctrine of slavery with the arguments generally made use of to justify the practice, with the repetition of which I shall not trouble you at present. Adieu.

7. Quobna Ottobah Cugoano

Thoughts and Sentiments on the Evil and Wicked Traffic of the Slavery and Commerce of the Human Species. London, 1787.

[Cugoano, like Equiano before him, had been kidnapped on the western coast of Africa, transported to the West Indies, and sold into slavery. In 1772, at the time of the famous Mansfield decision,[1] Cugoano's master took him to England where the young slave somehow declared himself free. *Thoughts and Sentiments* is the first direct antislavery work by a black writer. There is no doubt that Cugoano was encouraged to write his polemic after the appearances in 1784 and 1786 of powerful antislavery essays by white abolitionists James Ramsay and Thomas Clarkson.[2] Cugoano based his closely reasoned and deeply emotional appeal on Christian values, morals, and ethics. He used a pulpit style of writing that incorporated the sermonic elements of stating and explaining God's biblical laws, applying them to actions in the world, and, lastly, exhorting those who did not follow the laws to reform or suffer the dreadful consequences from a vengeful God. However, as many other antislavery fighters understood, Cugoano recognized the profit motive supporting slavery and also tried to handle this troublesome issue.]

---

1   Lord Mansfield in the famous Somerset court case in 1772 decided that a black person in England could not forcibly be returned to slavery (see page 315, note 1).
2   James Ramsay was the author of the much-debated *An Essay on the Treatment and conversion of Slaves in the British Sugar Colonies* (1784). Thomas Clarkson's prize-winning work, *An Essay on the Slavery and Commerce of the Human Species* (1786), had an enormous effect on the leaders of the abolitionist movement.

But why should total abolition, and an universal emancipation of slaves, and the enfranchisement of all the Black People employed in the culture of the Colonies, taking place as it ought to do, and without any hesitation, or delay for a moment, even though it might have some seeming appearance of loss either to government or to individuals, be feared at all? Their labour, as freemen, would be as useful in the sugar colonies as any other class of men that could be found; and should it even take place in such a manner that some individuals, at first, would suffer loss as a just reward for their wickedness in slave-dealing, what is that to the happiness and good of doing justice to others; and, I must say, to the great danger, otherwise, that must eventually hang over the whole community? It is certain, that the produce of the labour of slaves, together with all the advantages of the West-India traffic, bring in an immense revenue to government; but let that amount be what it will, there might be as much or more expected from the labour of an equal increase of free people, and without the implication of any guilt attending it, and which, otherwise, must be a greater burden to bear, and more ruinous consequences to be feared from it, than if the whole national debt was to sink at once, and to rest upon the heads of all that might suffer by it. Whereas, if a generous encouragement were to be given to a free people, peaceable among themselves, intelligent and industrious, who by art and labour would improve the most barren situations, and make the most of that which is fruitful; the free and voluntary labour of many, would soon yield to any government, many greater advantages than any thing that slavery can produce. And this should be expected, wherever a Christian government is extended, and the true religion is embraced, that the blessings of liberty should be extended likewise, and that it should diffuse its influences first to fertilize the mind, and then the effects of its benignity would extend, and arise with exuberant blessings and advantages from all its operations. Was this to be the case, every thing would increase and prosper at home and abroad, and ten thousand times greater and greater advantages would arise to the state, and more permanent and solid benefit to individuals from the service of freemen, than ever they can reap, or in any possible way enjoy, by the labour of slaves....

And let me now hope that you will pardon me in all that I have been thus telling you, O ye inhabitants of Great-Britain! to whom I owe the greatest respect; to your king! to yourselves! and to your government! And tho' many things which I have written may seem harsh, it cannot be otherwise evaded when such horrible iniquity is transacted: and tho' to some what I have said may appear as the rattling leaves of autumn, that may soon be blown away and whirled in a vortex where few can hear and know: I must yet say, although it is not for me to determine the manner, that the voice of our complaint implies a vengeance, because of the great iniquity that you have done, and because of the cruel injustice done unto us Africans; and it ought to sound in your ears as the rolling waves around your circum-ambient shores; and if it is not hearkened unto, it may yet arise with a louder voice, as the rolling thunder, and it may encrease in the force of its volubility, not only to shake the leaves of the most stout in heart, but to rend the mountains before them, and to cleave in pieces the rocks under them, and to go on with fury to smite the stoutest oaks in the forest; and even to make that which is strong, and wherein you think that your strength lieth, to become as stubble, and as the fibres of rotten wood, that will do you no good, and your trust in it will become a snare of infatuation to you!

8. Alexander Falconbridge

An Account of the Slave Trade on the Coast of Africa. London: J. Phillips, 1788.

[Falconbridge (d. 1792) had served as a surgeon aboard slave ships. He provided valuable testimony to the Parliamentary committee examining the slave trade in the late 1780s. Falconbridge's *Account* was sponsored and widely distributed by the Society for Effecting the Abolition of the Slave Trade. The following excerpt recalls the conditions aboard the slave ship that transported Equiano to the Americas.]

... The men negroes, on being brought aboard the ship, are immediately fastened together, two and two, by hand-cuffs on their wrists, and by irons rivetted on their legs. They are then sent down between the decks, and placed in an apartment partitioned off for that purpose. The women likewise are placed in a separate apartment between decks, but without being ironed. And an adjoining room, on the same deck, is besides appointed for the boys. Thus are they all placed in different apartments.

But at the same time, they are frequently stowed so close, as to admit of no other posture than lying on their sides. Neither will the height between decks, unless directly under the grating, permit them the indulgence of an erect posture; especially where there are platforms, which is generally the case. These platforms are a kind of shelf, about eight or nine feet in breadth, extending from the side of the ship towards the centre. They are placed nearly midway between the decks, at the distance of two or three feet from each deck. Upon these the negroes are stowed in the same manner as they are on the deck underneath.

In each of the apartments are placed three or four large buckets, of a conical form, being near two feet in diameter at the bottom, and only one foot at the top, and in depth about twenty-eight inches; to which, when necessary, the negroes have recourse. It often happens, that those who are placed at a distance from the buckets, in endeavouring to get to them, tumble over their companions, in consequence of their being shackled. These accidents, although unavoidable, are productive of continual quarrels, in which some of them are always bruised. In this distressed situation, unable to proceed, and prevented from getting to the tubs, they desist from the attempt; and, as the necessities of nature are not to be repelled, ease themselves as they lie. This becomes a fresh source of broils and disturbances, and tends to render the condition of the poor captive wretches still more uncomfortable. The nuisance arising from these circumstances, is not unfrequently increased by the tubs being much too small for the purpose intended, and their being usually emptied but once every day. The rule for doing this, however, varies in different ships, according to the attention paid to the health and convenience of the slaves by the captain....

The diet of the negroes, while on board, consists chiefly of horse-beans, boiled to the consistence of a pulp; of boiled yams and rice, and sometimes of a small quantity of beef or pork. The latter are frequently taken from the provisions laid in for the sailors. They sometimes make use of a sauce, composed of palm-oil, mixed with flour, water, and pepper, which the sailors call *slabber-sauce*. Yams are the favourite food of the Eboe, or Bight negroes, and rice or corn, of those from the Gold and Windward Coasts; each preferring the produce of their native soil....

They are commonly fed twice a day, about eight o'clock in the morning and four in the afternoon. In most ships they are only fed with their *own food* once a day. Their food is served up to them in tubs, about the size of a small water bucket. They are placed round these tubs in companies of ten to each tub, out of which they feed themselves with wooden spoons. These they soon lose, and when they are not allowed others, they feed themselves with their hands. In favourable weather they are fed upon deck, but in bad weather their food is given them below. Numberless quarrels take place among them during their meals; more especially when they are put upon short allowance.... Their allowance of water is about half a pint each at every meal. It is handed round in a bucket, and given to each negroe in a pannekin; a small utensil with a strait handle, somewhat similar to a sauce-boat....

Upon the negroes refusing to take sustenance, I have seen coals of fire, glowing hot, put on a shovel, and placed so near their lips, as to scorch and burn them. And this has been accompanied with threats, of forcing them to swallow the coals, if they any longer persisted in refusing to eat. These means have generally had the desired effect. I have also been credibly informed, that a certain captain in the slave trade, poured melted lead on such of the negroes as obstinately refused their food.

Exercise being deemed necessary for the preservation of their health, they are sometimes obliged to dance, when the weather will permit their coming on deck. If they go about it reluctantly, or do not move with agility, they are flogged; a person standing by them all the time with a cat-o'-nine-tails in his hand for that purpose. Their musick, upon these occasions, consists of a drum, sometimes with only one head; and when that is worn out, they do not scruple to make use of the bottom of one of the tubs before described. The poor wretches are frequently compelled to sing also; but when they do so, their songs are generally, as may naturally be expected, melancholy lamentations of their exile from their native country....

On board some ships, the common sailors are allowed to have intercourse with such of the black women whose consent they can procure. And some of them have been known to take the inconstancy of their paramours so much to heart, as to leap overboard and drown themselves. The officers are permitted to indulge their passions among them at pleasure, and sometimes are guilty of such brutal excesses, as disgrace human nature.

... Some wet and blowing weather having occasioned the port-holes to be shut, and the grating to be covered, fluxes and fevers among the negroes ensued. While they were in this situation, my profession requiring it, I frequently went down among them, till at length their apartments became so extremely hot, as to be only sufferable for a very short time. But the excessive heat was not the only thing that rendered their situation intolerable. The deck, that is, the floor of their rooms, was so covered with the blood and mucus which had proceeded from them in consequence of the flux, that it resembled a slaughter-house. It is not in the power of the human imagination, to picture to itself a situation more dreadful or disgusting. Numbers of the slaves having fainted, they were carried upon deck, where several of them died, and the rest were, with great difficulty, restored. It had nearly proved fatal to me also. The climate was too warm to admit the wearing of any clothing but a shirt, and that I had pulled off before I went down; notwithstanding which, by only continuing among them for about a quarter of an hour, I was so overcome with the heat, stench, and foul air, that I had nearly fainted; and it was not without assistance, that I could get upon deck. The consequence was, that I soon after fell sick of the same disorder, from which I did not recover for several months.

... And, to conclude on this subject, I could not help being sensibly affected, on a former voyage, at observing with what apparent eagerness a black woman seized some dirt from off an African yam, and put it into her mouth; seeming to rejoice at the opportunity of possessing some of her native earth.

9. Gilbert Francklyn

An Answer to the Rev. Mr. Clarkson's Essay on the Slavery and Commerce of the Human Species, particularly the African; in a Series of Letters from a Gentleman in Jamaica, to His Friend in London. London: Logographic Press, 1789.

[Francklyn's lengthy letters in defense of slavery were written primarily to attack the credibility of Thomas Clarkson's antislavery research and to bring into doubt the motives of the educators at Cambridge University who in 1785 had awarded the dissertation prize to Clarkson for his essay opposing slavery and the slave trade.]

Dear Sir, ...
In calling upon me to give you [Francklyn's friend in London] my opinion upon this subject, you put me upon a service of danger. The abuse so liberally bestowed on the West Indians, has been now so long and so often repeated, that many persons, in Britain, believe it to be well founded. He who is hardy enough to oppose a popular and prevailing opinion, has little chance of obtaining a favourable hearing, especially if such opinion should be entertained by men of worth and virtue. I shall not, however, shrink from the talk you have imposed on me, but endeavour to give you, and all good and unprejudiced men, such reasonable satisfaction, with respect to the subject under consideration, as my long and intimate knowledge of, and acquaintance with, the Sugar Colonies, may, in some measure, enable me to do....
Silent contempt has too long been considered, by the

Planters, as the only treatment merited by the authors of the paragraphs, hand-bills, newspapers, and pamphlets, in which they have of late been abused. They conceived, and they thought, with reason, that the terms of reproach and obloquy, which bigotry alone could furnish, and which, with an equal degree of illiberality and ignorance, have been employed in describing the treatment of the Negroes in the West Indies, would have been disregarded or despised by every man of discernment; and that the inventors and propagators of such idle and malicious stories, would have been confounded and abashed, and have sunk into oblivion....

Mr. Tobin [author of *Cursory Remarks* (1785), an attack on antislavery writer James Ramsay's *An Essay on the Treatment and Conversion of African Slaves* (1784)], a gentleman resident in England, but a native of the island of Nevis, appears to have been the first person who judged it proper to employ his pen in defence of his countrymen and friends, whom he conceived to be injured by the misrepresentations of the Reverend Mr. Ramsay: this he did most effectually, by plain and faithful narrative of the general treatment which slaves receive in Nevis, St. Kitt's , and the neighbouring British Islands. This account, conceived in language equally manly, moderate, and decent, (the truth of which, I am sure, will be attested by every gentleman conversant with those islands,) has, it seems, raised the sympathetic anger of Mr. Clarkson....

Among the causes of this outcry against the colonists becoming so general, may be reckoned as not the slightest, that the University of Cambridge having thought fit to offer a prize for the best Dissertation on Slavery, as a subject wherein to exercise the ingenuity and imagination of the junior members of that society – a young man of a fertile fancy obtained the prize: – A matter, surely, of triumph and exultation to him. – The topic was popular; and, in pursuit of his object, he thought proper to exclaim against the commerce carried on in Africa from the remotest antiquity, and to paint the condition of the slaves, obtained by that medium, as miserable in their own country, from the manner in which that commerce is carried on; and as still more insupportable, from the manner of their treatment after they have been transplanted to the British Sugar Colonies in the West Indies. The Author of the Dissertation which gained the plaudit of the University, runs no hazard of having the judgment of that learned tribunal appealed from by me. It is not to be doubted, but the decision was just, and this merit, upon this occasion, was superior to that of his competitors. But in what are we to suppose *this merit* consisted? Surely, in the classic purity of his language, the happy turn of his periods, his choice of epithets, and the conduct of his *fable.* These his judges were competent to decide upon. Whether Mr. Clarkson's pen was guided by truth or fiction, did not necessarily enter into their consideration.... The artist, indeed, who painted a bunch of grapes so well that the birds came and pecked at it, received the most unequivocal testimony of his excellence, because the birds had seen grapes in their natural state upon the vines: but as the members of the University of Cambridge possessed no such occular evidence of African or West Indian slavery, the applause Mr. Clarkson received from them, could only regard his composition as a piece of fine writing....

10. Benjamin Franklin

"On the Slave Trade." *Federal Gazette.* March 23, 1790.

[Franklin, the extraordinary Pennsylvania businessman, inventor, civic leader, American statesman, and writer, firmly positioned himself against slavery. He was active in the first antislavery society founded in Philadelphia in 1775, and in 1790 he led an abolitionist group in petitioning the United States Congress to end the slave trade. An accomplished satirical essayist, Franklin wrote the following parody of a proslavery proposal shortly before his death.]

Sir,
Reading last night in your excellent Paper the speech of Mr. Jackson in Congress against their meddling with the Affair of Slavery, or attempting to mend the Condition of Slaves, it put

me in mind of a similar One made about 100 Years since by Sidi Mehemet Ibrahim, a member of the Divan of Algiers, which may be seen in Martin's account of his Consulship, anno 1687. It was against granting the Petition of the Sect called *Erika*, or Purists, who pray'd for the Abolition of Piracy and Slavery as being unjust. Mr. Jackson does not quote it; perhaps he has not seen it. If, therefore, some of its Reasonings are to be found in his eloquent Speech, it may only show that men's Interests and Intellects operate and are operated on with surprising similarity in all Countries and Climates, when under similar Circumstances. The African's Speech, as translated, is as follows.

"*Allah Bismillah, &c. God is great, and Mahomet is his Prophet.*"

"Have these *Erika* considered the Consequences of granting their Petition? If we cease our Cruises against the Christians, how shall we be furnished with the Commodities their Countries produce, and which are so necessary for us? If we forbear to make Slaves of their People, who in this hot climate are to cultivate our Lands? Who are to perform the common Labours of our City, and in our Families? Must we not then be our own slaves? And is there not more Compassion and more Favour due to us as Mussulmen, than to these Christian Dogs? We have now above 50,000 Slaves in and near Algiers. This Number, if not kept up by fresh Supplies, will soon diminish, and be gradually annihilated. If we then cease taking and plundering the Infidel Ships, and making Slaves of the Seamen and Passengers, our Lands will become of no Value for want of Cultivation; the Rents of Houses in the City will sink one half; and the Revenues of Government arising from its Share of Prizes be totally destroy'd! And for what? To gratify the whims of a whimsical Sect, who would have us, not only forbear making more Slaves, but even to manumit those we have...."

"How grossly are they mistaken in imagining Slavery to be disallow'd by the Alcoran! Are not the two Precepts, to quote no more, '*Masters, treat your Slaves with kindness; Slaves, serve your Masters with Cheerfulness and Fidelity,*' clear Proofs to the contrary? Nor can the Plundering of Infidels be in that sacred Book forbidden, since it is well known from it, that God has

given the World, and all that it contains, to his faithful Mussulmen, who are to enjoy it of Right as fast as they conquer it. Let
us then hear no more of this detestable Proposition, the Manumission of Christian Slaves, the Adoption of which would, be
depreciating our Lands and Houses, and thereby depriving so
many good citizens of their Properties, create universal Discontent, and provoke Insurrections, to the endangering of Government and producing general Confusion. I have therefore no
doubts, but this wise Council will prefer the Comfort and
Happiness of a whole Nation of true Believers to the Whim of
a few *Erika*, and dismiss their Petition."

The Result was, as Martin tells us, that the Divan came to
this Resolution; "The Doctrine, that Plundering and Enslaving
the Christians is unjust, is at best *problematical*; but that it is the
Interest of this State to continue the Practice, is clear; therefore
let the Petition be rejected."

And it was rejected accordingly.

And since like Motives are apt to produce in the Minds of
Men like Opinions and Resolutions, may we not, Mr. Brown,
venture to predict, from this Account, that the Petitions to the
Parliament of England for abolishing the Slave-Trade, to say
nothing of other Legislatures, and the Debates upon them, will
have a similar Conclusion? I am, Sir, your constant Reader and
humble Servant,

Historicus.

11. James Albert Ukawsaw Gronniosaw

*A Narrative of the Most Remarkable Particulars in the Life of James
Albert Ukawsaw Gronniosaw, an African Prince, as Related by
Himself,* Bath, 1772.

[Before Equiano wrote about his early life in Africa, Gronniosaw related the events of his youth and kidnapping on the
African continent. Brought to America, Gronniosaw worked
in New York for a Dutch master, who on his deathbed freed
the young slave. Like Equiano, Gronniosaw spent several years
aboard ships sailing the Caribbean and engaging in naval war-

fare. Eventually, he migrated to England where for a long time he had wanted to be close to the Methodist communities he had heard about. Like many other blacks in Britain, Gronniosaw was befriended by the Countess of Huntingdon. Because of her kindness, he later dedicated to her his spiritual autobiography that he had written to support his poverty-stricken family. The work proved very popular with the abolitionists, going through several editions in both England and America. Cugoano and Equiano were familiar with Gronniosaw's story, and they referred to his intensely religious life in their narratives. The following excerpt describes one of the first instances of the "talking book" episode that acts as a trope or recurring event in several slave narrative accounts. Its significance reveals the awakening desire for learning, which the young slave believes will combat white prejudice and hate. The story also appears in the works of Marrant, Cugoano, and Equiano.]

... My master [aboard the slave ship] grew very fond of me, and I loved him exceedingly; I watched every look, was always ready when he wanted me, and endeavoured to convince him, by every action, that my only pleasure was to serve him well. I have since thought that he must have been a serious man. His actions corresponded very well with such a character. – He used to read prayers in public to the ship's crew every Sabbath day; and when first I saw him read, I was never so surprized in my life, as when I saw the book talk to my master, for I thought it did, as I observed him to look upon it; and move his lips. – I wished it would do so to me. As soon as my master had done reading, I followed him to the place where he put the book, being mightily delighted with it, and when nobody saw me, I opened it and put my ear down close upon it, in great hopes that it would say something to me; but was very sorry, and greatly disappointed when I found it would not speak, this thought immediately presented itself to me, that every body and every thing despised me because I was black....

I was one day in a most delightful frame of mind, my heart so overflowed with love and gratitude to the author of all my comforts. – I was so drawn out of myself, and so filled and awed by the presence of GOD, that I saw (or thought I saw) light inexpressible dart down from heaven upon me, and shone around me for the space of a minute. I continued on my knees, and joy unspeakable took possession of my soul. The peace and serenity which filled my mind after this, was wonderful, and cannot be told. I would not have changed situations, or been any one but myself for the world. I blessed GOD for my poverty, that I had no worldly riches or grandeur to draw my heart from Him. I wished at that time if it had been possible for me, to have continued on that spot for ever. I felt an unwillingness in myself to have any thing more to do with the world, or to mix with society again. I seemed to possess a full assurance that my sins were forgiven me. I went home all my way rejoicing....

12. Raymund Harris

Scriptural Researches on the Licitness of the Slave-Trade, Shewing Its Conformity with the Principles of Natural and Revealed Religion, Delineated in the Sacred Writings of the Word of God. Liverpool: M. Hodgson, 1788.

[Harris was a Jesuit priest who attempted to justify slavery in a tract he dedicated to the political officials of Liverpool, a busy British port that occupied an important slave-trading position in the eighteenth century. Equiano attacked Harris's work in a letter published in *The Public Advertiser* on April 28, 1788. In the letter addressed to Harris, Equiano wrote, "I could not have believed any man in your office would have dared to come forth in public in these our days to vindicate the accursed Slave Trade on any ground; but least of all by the law of Moses, and by that of Christ in the Gospel."]

... The farther I proceed in my Scriptural Researches, the stronger the evidences appear to me in favour of the SLAVE-TRADE. Indeed, I have every encouragement given me in this Sacred Book of Leviticus to advance a step farther, and maintain, that the SLAVE-TRADE, has not only the sanction of Divine

Authority in its support, but was also positively encouraged (I had almost said, *commanded*) by that Authority, under the Dispensation of the Mosaic Law. The following plain and explicit words of one of the laws respecting that Trade, and registered in this Book, can admit of no other construction.

"Both thy bond-men and bond-maids, *says the Supreme Lawgiver*, which thou shalt have, shall be of the heathen that are round about you; of them shall ye buy bond-men and bond-maids. Moreover, of the Children of the Strangers that do sojourn among you; of them shall ye buy; and of their families that are with you, which they begat in your land: and they shall be your possession. And ye shall take them as an inheritance for your children after you to inherit them for a possession; they shall be your bond-men for ever" (Leviticus, c. 25. v. 44-46)....

... From this most decisive, most explicit, and irrefragable authority of the Written Word of God, visibly encouraging the prosecution of the SLAVE-TRADE, and declaring in the most categorical language that words can devise, that a Slave is the real, indisputable, and lawful property of the purchaser and his heirs for ever, it necessarily follows by force of consequence, that either the SLAVE-TRADE must be in its own intrinsic nature a just and an honest Trade, and by no means deserving those harsh epithets and names with which it is so frequently branded and degraded; or, that, if it does still deserve those odious names and epithets in consequence of its intrinsic turpitude and immorality, the Almighty did so far forget himself, when he made the above Law, as to patronize a manifest injustice, encourage a most criminal violation of his other laws, and give his sacred sanction to what humanity itself must for ever abhor and detest. – As there can be no medium betwixt these two unavoidable inferences, and the latter is one of the most daring blasphemies that the human heart can conceive, I leave the religious Reader to judge for himself, which side of the Question is the safest to embrace....

... several of my Readers will be apt to imagine, that, by the establishment of the Christian Religion, the Law of Moses was wholly abolished and annulled in every part of it, and to every intent and purpose, both typical and moral, of its original institution; and that, of course, the arguments drawn in vindication of the SLAVE-TRADE from the Writings of the Old Testament, can have no weight of conviction or authority with persons, who are subject to no other Laws and Ordinances, but those of a Dispensation, by which that was entirely laid aside....

... If the Writings of the New Testament mention nothing, as it is *falsely supposed* in vindication of the SLAVE-TRADE, neither do they *in reality* and *truth* mention any thing in condemnation of it; if then the *supposed* silence of the Inspired Writers respecting the licitness of that Trade, that is, their not mentioning that Trade at all, as it is *supposed,* can be brought as an argument of its moral inconsistency with the principles of true Christianity; the *real* silence of the same respecting the pretended illicitness of it, that is, their not condemning the Trade at all, though publickly practised in their time, and by the very persons whom they were deputed to teach the principles and duties of Christianity, must be a stronger argument by far of the inherent moral conformity of the SLAVE-TRADE with the principles and tenets of the Religion of Christ: for it shews in the strongest light, that the first Teachers of Christianity, who were also the Inspired Writers of the New Testament, never considered the SLAVE-TRADE, or had been taught by their Master to consider it, as an infraction of any of the principles or moral precepts of his Gospel.

13. David Hume

"Of National Characters." *Essays and Treatises on Several Subjects*. Edinburgh and London, 1753-54.

[Hume was a Scottish philosophical essayist, one of the great thinkers of the Enlightenment period. Like Locke before him, Hume studied the intricate ways by which humans achieve understanding, mainly through experience and inductive reasoning. The first part of the following excerpt is from a footnote Hume added in subsequent editions to his 1748 work, *Three Essays: Moral and Political*. Hume's thoughts here reveal that he believed black men and women were naturally inferior to whites. Later, however, he came to oppose slavery as detrimental to the good of society. In *Thoughts and Sentiments* Cugoano makes an adverse reference to Hume, but many of Hume's ideas influenced those white abolitionists in the late eighteenth century who worked against slavery but held misgivings about black equality.]

I am apt to suspect the negroes to be naturally inferior to the whites. There scarcely ever was a civilized nation of that complexion, nor ever any individual eminent either in action or speculation. No ingenious manufactures amongst them, no arts, no sciences. On the other hand, the most rude and barbarous of the whites, such as the ancient GERMANS, the present TARTARS, have still something eminent about them, in their valour, form of government, or some other particular. Such a uniform and constant difference could not happen, in so many countries and ages, if nature had not made an original distinction between these breeds of men. Not to mention our colonies, there are NEGROE slaves dispersed all over EUROPE, of whom none ever discovered any symptoms of ingenuity; though low people, without education, will start up amongst us, and distinguish themselves in every profession. In JAMAICA, indeed, they talk of one negroe [poet Francis Williams (c. 1700–c. 1770)] as a man of parts and learning; but it is likely he is admired for slender accomplishments, like a parrot, who speaks a few words plainly....

... You may obtain any thing of the NEGROES by offering them strong drink; and may easily prevail with them to sell, not only their children, but their wives and mistresses, for a cask of brandy....

14. Thomas Jefferson

Notes on the State of Virginia. London: John Stockdale, 1787.

[Much of Jefferson's work expresses the ideas of the Enlightenment. When he wrote the American Declaration of Independence, he included a section on the abolition of the slave trade;

however, he later was forced to omit it for political reasons. Jefferson owned slaves, and the long-standing rumor that he had fathered a child by his slave mistress Sally Hemings was proven true in 1998 by means of scientific DNA testing. Furthermore, in January 2000, the Thomas Jefferson Memorial Foundation reported that DNA evidence indicates that Jefferson fathered all six of Hemings's children. Although Jefferson viewed bondage as an evil institution and desired its end, he was unconvinced that blacks were equal to whites. In a few of his letters he praised the accomplishments of talented blacks, including the poet Phillis Wheatley (1753-1784) and the surveyor Benjamin Banneker (1731-1806), who contributed to the design of Washington, D.C. But at times, especially in his early statements, Jefferson regarded black achievers as being exceptions to the rule of black inferiority. However, he subsequently changed his mind. The letters he wrote then reveal that he came to believe that black persons were just as capable of mental and artistic accomplishment as whites. The following passage is Jefferson's chapter on "Manners."]

It is difficult to determine on the standard by which the manners of a nation may be tried, whether *catholic*, or *particular*. It is more difficult for a native to bring to that standard the manners of his own nation, familiarized to him by habit. There must doubtless be an unhappy influence on the manners of our people produced by the existence of slavery among us. The whole commerce between master and slave is a perpetual exercise of the most boisterous passions, the most unremitting despotism on the one part, and degrading submissions on the other. Our children see this, and learn to imitate it; for man is an imitative animal. This quality is the germ of all education in him. From his cradle to his grave he is learning to do what he sees others do. If a parent could find no motive either in his philanthropy or his self-love, for restraining the intemperance of passion towards his slave, it should always be a sufficient one that his child is present. But generally it is not sufficient. The parent storms, the child looks on, catches the lineaments of wrath, puts on the same airs in the circle of smaller slaves, gives a loose to his worst of passions, and thus nursed, educated, and daily exercised in tyranny, cannot but be stamped by it with odious peculiarities. The man must be a prodigy who can retain his manners and morals undepraved by such circumstances. And with what execration should the statesman be loaded, who permitting one half the citizens thus to trample on the rights of the other, transforms those into despots, and these into enemies, destroys the morals of the one part, and the amor patriae of the other. For if a slave can have a country in this world, it must be any other in preference to that in which he is born to live and labour for another: in which he must lock up the faculties of his nature, contribute as far as depends on his individual endeavours to the evanishment of the human race, or entail his own miserable condition on the endless generations proceeding from him. With the morals of the people, their industry also is destroyed. For in a warm climate, no man will labour for himself who can make another labour for him. This is so true, that of the proprietors of slaves a very small proportion indeed are ever seen to labour. And can the liberties of a nation be thought secure when we have removed their only firm basis, a conviction in the minds of the people that these liberties are of the gift of God? That they are not to be violated but with his wrath? Indeed I tremble for my country when I reflect that God is just: that his justice cannot sleep for ever: that considering numbers, nature and natural means only, a revolution of the wheel of fortune, an exchange of situation, is among possible events: that it may become probable by supernatural interference! The Almighty has no attribute which can take side with us in such a contest. – But it is impossible to be temperate and to pursue this subject through the various considerations of policy, of morals, of history natural and civil. We must be contented to hope they will force their way into every one's mind. I think a change already perceptible, since the origin of the present revolution. The spirit of the master is abating, that of the slave rising from the dust, his condition mollifying, the way I hope preparing, under the auspices of heaven, for a total emancipation, and that this is disposed, in the order of events, to be with the consent of the masters, rather than by their extirpation.

15. John Marrant

A Narrative of the Lord's Wonderful Dealings with John Marrant, a Black. London: 2nd ed., 1785.

[Marrant's Indian captivity and spiritual conversion account became a popular work on both sides of the Atlantic. Born a free person in America, Marrant in his youth was introduced to Christianity after his abortive attempt to disrupt a sermon preached by the great George Whitefield, who then helped the miscreant mend his ways. Marrant's pious life was praised by both Cugoano and Equiano in their narratives.]

About this time I went with my brother, who was a house-carpenter, to repair a plantation belonging to Mr. Jenkins, of Cumbee, about seventy miles from Charles-Town, where after I had done work in the evening, I used to spend my time in reading God's Word, singing Watt's hymns and in Prayer, the little negro children would often come round the door with their pretty wishful looks, and finding my heart much drawn out in Love to their souls, I one evening called several of them in, and asked them if they could say the Lord's Prayer, &c. finding they were very ignorant, I told them, if they would come every evening I would teach them, which they did, and learned very fast, some of them in about four weeks could say the Lord's Prayer, ... one of the negro boys made a very great proficiency in that time, and could exercise in extemporary prayer much to my satisfaction. We are well advised in Ecclesiasticus, chap. ii. v. 1. *My Son, if thou come to serve the Lord, prepare thy heart for temptation:* Nor was it long before they were made to pledge our dear Lord in the bitter cup of suffering; for now the old Lion began to roar, their mistress became acquainted with our proceedings, and was full of rage at it, and determined to put a stop to it. She had two of the children brought before her to examine, and made them say the Lord's prayer to her, she then asked who taught them? and they told her the free Carpenter. She also enquired, how many he has instructed, and at what time he taught them; and they told her, it was in the Evening after they had done work. She then stirred up her husband against us, who before had several times come in while I was instructing the children, and did not appear displeased with it: she told him it was the ready way to have all his negroes ruin'd, and made him promise to examine further into the matter, and break up our meeting; which he then very soon did, for a short space; for he, together with his overseer and negro-driver, and some of his neighbours, beset the place wherein we met, while we were at prayers; and as the poor creatures came out they caught them, and tied them together with cords, till the next morning, when all they caught, men, women, and children were strip'd naked and tied, their feet to a stake, their hands to the arm of a tree, and so savagely flogg'd that the blood ran from their backs and sides to the floor, to make them promise they would leave off praying, &c. though several of them fainted away with the pain and loss of blood, and lay upon the ground as dead for a considerable time after they were untied. I did not hear that she obtained her end of any of them. She endeavoured to perswade her husband to flog me also, but he told her he did not dare to do it because I was free, and would take the law of him, and make him pay for it; which she told him, she had rather he should run the hazard of, than let me go without the benefit of a good flogging, and was afterwards very angry with him because he was afraid to gratify her....

16. John Newton

Thoughts upon the African Slave Trade. London: Buckland & Johnson, 1788.

[A successful captain of a slave ship in the early 1750s, Newton later regretted his involvement in the slave trade. He turned to religion and came under the influence of the Methodist leaders George Whitefield and John Wesley. Newton was ordained and appointed curate at Olney, Buckinghamshire, in the English countryside, where he met the poet William Cowper and collaborated with him on a book of religious poems published in 1779 as *Olney Hymns*. In 1780, Newton became rector of St.

Mary Woolnoth in the City of London. Here he achieved recognition and praise preaching to large crowds. When William Wilberforce went to him for spiritual counseling, the emerging political leader was persuaded by Newton to join the abolitionist cause. In 1789 and 1790, Newton testified against the slave trade to members of Parliament. Today, he is mostly remembered worldwide for his moving and deeply spiritual hymn, "Amazing Grace."]

When we hear of a town taken by storm, and given up to the ravages of an enraged and licentious army, of wild and unprincipled Cossacks, perhaps no part of the distress affects a feeling mind more, than the treatment to which women are exposed. But the enormities frequently committed in an African ship, though equally flagrant, are little known *here*, and are considered *there*, only as matters of course. When the women and girls are taken on board a ship, naked, trembling, terrified, perhaps almost exhausted with cold, fatigue, and hunger, they are often exposed to the wanton rudeness of white savages. The poor creatures cannot understand the language they hear, but the looks and manner of the speakers are sufficiently intelligible. In imagination, the prey is divided, upon the spot, and only reserved till opportunity offers. Where resistance or refusal, would be utterly in vain, even the solicitation of consent is seldom thought of. But I forebear. – This is not a subject for declamation. Facts like these, so certain and so numerous, speak for themselves. Surely, if the advocates for the Slave Trade attempt to plead for it, before the wives and daughters of our happy land, or before those who have wives or daughters of their own, they must lose their cause.

Perhaps some hard-hearted pleader may suggest, that such treatment would indeed be cruel, in Europe: but the African women are negroes, savages, who have no idea of the nicer sensations which obtain among civilized people. I dare to contradict them in the strongest terms. I have lived long, and conversed much, amongst these supposed savages. I have often slept in their towns, in a house filled with goods for trade, with no person in the house but myself, and with no other door than a mat; in that security, which no man in his senses would expect in this civilized nation, especially in this metropolis, without the precaution of having strong doors, strongly locked and bolted. And with regard to the women, in Sherbro [on the Windward coast of Africa], where I was most acquainted, I have seen many instances of modesty, and even delicacy, which would not disgrace an English woman. Yet, such is the treatment which I have known permitted, if not encouraged, in many of our ships – they have been abandoned, without restraint, to the lawless will of the first comer....

17. Malachy Postlethwayt

Britain's Commercial Interest Explained and Improved. London: D. Browne, et. al., 1757.

[The proposal to replace the slave trade with a commerce in manufactured goods was urged by many abolitionists after Postlethwayt made his suggestion in 1757. Anthony Benezet and Thomas Clarkson used this economic argument in their writings, and Equiano discussed it in his letters, petitions, and narrative. The abolitionists believed the commercial proposal would allay the fears of those who depended on and prospered from slavery. After his two-volume publication, Postlethwayt became an active participant in the antislavery movement; the following extract is from the second volume of his work.]

Have we not all reason to believe, that Africa will admit of a very extensive and lucrative commerce, if we can propagate the same into the very heart and center of these extensive territories? We know little of that infinite variety of vegetable, mineral, and animal production, that we may presume abound in this part of the world, and which might afford an infinite variety of trafficable objects. But do we not know, from our little coasting traffic, that these countries abound with commodities of inestimable value, though we have participated of but a small share of them? Do we not know that their vegetables afford us fine woods, as well for dying as workmanship; and may we not suppose that here are as fine drugs as any in other parts of the world, if we took proper measures to obtain a knowledge of them? We know with what a valuable commodity their elephants furnish us; and what numberless other animals this country may abound, that would afford matter for traffic, we are but very little acquainted with. Certain we are also, that this country does no less abound in gold than in delicate vegetables, gums and ivory; and why not in diamonds and other precious stones, as well as innumerable fossils and minerals of inestimable worth? Certain likewise it is, that there are scarce any productions in all our British American islands but might be cultivated on the continent of Africa, and that perhaps within few miles of the sea-coast: and if ever we should be unhappy enough to be dispossessed of our sugar-colonies, our trade in this part of the world might contribute to make us compensation: at all events, however, it is wise and prudent to make every advantage in our power that this trade will admit of; for we know not what occasion we may have to make the most of every thing we have the least claim to.

In tracing mankind as near as we can to their origin, we find them in the general to have been no better civilized, than the Africans. What has so much tended to civilize the human species as commerce? This being the parent of treasure, splendor, and magnificence, have not these prevailing motives been conducive to the general propagation of all the commercial arts? And wherever they have been duly introduced, they have scarce ever failed to polish and humanize the most brutish savages. And why not the Africans? However some countries may abound with what we Europeans are pleased to denominate humane barbarians; yet, we well know, that nature is one and the same in all parts of the world, suitable to it's climate and it's situation; and the colour, and stature in men is as little to be despised as the soil where they inhabit, and the productions of the earth: and soils of all kinds, and in all climes are improveable; and why not the human nature? Are not the rational faculties of the negroe people in the general equal to those of any other of the human species? And experience has shewn that they are no less capable of the mechanical and manufactural arts and trades, than the bulk of the Europeans. I shall enter no further into the philosophy of human nature.

For my own part, I cannot help expressing my dislike to the slave-trade, and wish an end could be put to it; and I am inclined to believe that practicable without injury to our plantations. At present, however, we shall take things as they are, and reason from them in their present state, and not from that wherein we could hope them to be. Certain it is that wherever the commercial Europeans have humanely cultivated a trade with the most savage people, they have always reaped advantages sufficient to induce to pursue the practice. The Dutch afford us an eminent example of this in their East India settlements. Have they not by dint of trade civilized innumerable of the natives, and thereby brought them to the European way of cloathing, and imbibed most of their peculiar customs and habits? Why then may not numberless of the Africans be brought to do the same? If their country affords productions valuable enough to pay for our manufactures, why should we neglect to induce them to a general wear of them? If they posses wherewith to give an advantageous barter for any of our productions of arts, why should not effectual policy be used with them to induce them to a general liking thereof? That they have estimable commodities that will turn to profit to give in exchange for ours, is certain; and that it is practicable to bring them to a general use of multitudes of our commodities, is not less so, from what little we have experienced of their disposition. If we could so exert our commercial policy amongst these people, as to bring a few hundred thousands of them to cloath with our commodities, and to erect buildings to deck with our furniture, and to live something in the European way, would not such traffic prove far more lucrative than the slave-trade only, or the dealing with them only for those small quantities of gold, and other commodities which we do?

If once we could propagate and establish our fashions amongst them; if they could be brought to pride themselves in living in our manner, and that it was thought disgraceful not to cloathe and live in such certain manner; would not this naturally rouse their passion to obtain those productions of their country, to give in return for our commodities? Would not this animate and inspire them to search their countries for every thing valuable both above ground, and below, to maintain a traffic, that once became generally fashionable amongst them? And as they have innumerable things in the several kingdoms of nature, whose uses, and whose virtues they cannot be so well acquainted with, they would lay in time all nature's work at our feet; they would clear their lands; take to the cultivation of those things, we have found valuable amongst them, breed those animals we esteemed, and search, at our instigation, to the very center of the earth for all her invaluable treasures. May we not very reasonably judge that this would prove the natural consequence of cultivating such a commercial correspondence with these people? And when our people came to obtain a free and friendly trading intercourse with the natives, may we not presage that great must be the consequence? For our customs and fashions would spread from nation to nation; from country to country; till by travel and commerce, we became as familiarly acquainted with this rich and extensive country as with any in Europe.

And what infinite advantages might arise to these kingdoms, if we should prove the first who cut out such new tracts of commerce? For the first establishers will always obtain the greatest advantages; and may so fix ourselves in the favour and friendship of those savage nations, as not easily to be supplanted by any rival traders.

By such like measures, have not all branches of traffic with foreign countries been obtained? And what reason have we to despair of extending the commerce of this part of the world to a degree equal to that of any other belonging to the whole British empire? With a commerce that must prove of such a nature and extent; and so beneficial to these kingdoms, what comparison will the mere slave-trade bear, and that small quantity of African commodities wherein we, at present, deal?

18. James Ramsay

An Essay on the Treatment and Conversion of African Slaves in the British Sugar Colonies. London: Phillips, 1784.

[As a former West Indian planter and slave owner, Ramsay could offer detailed personal observations on slave conditions in British America. When he had returned to England, he had entered the ministry, and this no doubt accounted for the religious thesis of his proposals. Ramsay's *Essay* is credited with being the first provocative work of the abolitionist movement. It caused a stir of controversy that was played out in newspapers, pamphlets, and other publications. Both Equiano and Cugoano praised Ramsay in their narratives and defended his testimony when it came under attack by proslavery critic James Tobin, who in *Cursory Remarks upon the Reverend Mr. Ramsay's Essay* (1785), wrote on the mental inferiority and disreputable traits of black men and women. In raising the issue of freedom for the slaves, Ramsay emphasized the economic, religious, and social benefits that would occur for society.]

A state of absolute freedom is indeed a revolution that we may rather wish for, than expect for some time to see, though doubtless it is within the plan of providence, and of man's progressive advancement in society. It supposes a regard for religion, a looking beyond immediate profit, and a soundness of policy, foreign to the estimation, and opinion of the present age. To make the plan effectual, it should prevail in every European settlement; an event so little to be expected from the manners which now prevail, that a man would not venture the imputation of such extravagance, as the bare suggestion of it would be deemed. For could so many opposing interests be reconciled; and should a partial innovation take place, that present bugbear of European policy, the balance of trade, would be supposed to be in danger.

But were slaves instructed in the simple precepts of religion; were they taught to distinguish right from wrong; did the law secure to them a more plentiful subsistence, more humane usage; were they permitted to acquire and enjoy property; were the rights of a family made sacred; could they look forward to freedom, as the reward of merit, or the purchace of industry; in short, were they considered as having some rights, some claims, as intitled to some of the unalienable, some of the reserved rights of human nature; their condition would in consequence be advanced, they would become more useful, more profitable subjects, and, might even be trusted with arms, in defence of the colony in which they have an interest. Indeed it is not their want of arms, but their good sense and moderation, in most colonies, that are a present security to the inhabitants. I forbear to say more on so dangerous a topic....

I HAVE now gone through the several preliminary articles that respect slaves in our sugar colonies. I have described their condition at present. I have shewn that there would be good policy and much profit, both to the state and the master, in advancing it; that this advancement must go hand in hand with their instruction in religion; and, again, that instruction is necessary to make them good and useful subjects. I have vindicated for them the natural equality and common origin of mankind. I have claimed, as their due, the attention of government. I have endeavoured to interest humanity, policy, and religion in their favour. It only remains to point out the method in which these should cooperate for their advantage. That which I am now to offer, I propose not as the best possible, but as the most practicable method, having respect to the selfishness and prejudices of the age. Were government and people once well awakened to their own interest, and heartily inclined, something much more promising might be struck out. The chief advantages of the following plan is, that it would be set on foot by government, without depending on the caprice of individuals, or affecting their interest; that it will be gradual in its operation, and therefore more likely to accommodate itself to the ordinary course of human affairs. At the worst, it adds only one more to the many Utopian schemes that volunteer reformers produce for the benefit of the heedless public. Should it ever be found as impracticable in itself, as it is in respect of me, it may lead some more happy man to a scheme both practicable and successful. In the mean time it may contribute to soften their present treatment; and it will be a testimony of the author's affection to the cause of humanity, religion, and his country. The event must be left to Providence....

On the other hand, till the minds of our slaves be more enlightened, till their situation be made more easy, till they have a refuge against the effects of the caprice, ignorance, cruelty, poverty of their masters, till they think themselves intitled to the protection of society, we cannot expect them to take their proper rank in the state, nor to make any considerable progress in religious knowledge. At present they know and feel nothing of society, but the hardships and punishments that it cruelly and capriciously inflicts; they lie far beyond its care, and out of the circle of its comforts. And I believe it will be found, that Christianity has seldom made any great progress, except where society was in an advanced state. Nor has it supported itself, but in the polished parts of Europe and America....

19. Benjamin Rush

A Vindication of the Address, to the Inhabitants of the British Settlements, on the Slavery of the Negroes in America. Philadelphia: John Dunlap, 1773.

[A prominent Philadelphia physician and signer of the American Declaration of Independence, Rush became involved in the antislavery cause at the urging of fellow Philadelphian Anthony Benezet. Rush anonymously published two widely circulated and controversial pamphlets, *An Address to the Inhabitants of the British Settlements in America, upon Slave-Keeping. By a Pennsylvanian* and *A Vindication of the Address.* The latter was in response to a vicious attack on his *Address* by Richard Nesbit, a proslavery West Indian planter from Philadelphia, in his "Slavery not Forbidden by Scripture; or a Defence of the West-India Planters from the Aspersions thrown out against them by the Author of the *Address.*" When it became known that Rush was the author of both antislavery essays, a cry of vilification arose against him that briefly damaged his well-established medical practice. However, his name became known among the abolitionists in Britain, and he received letters of praise from James Ramsay and Granville Sharp.]

IMPROVEMENTS of all kinds in Society are progressive. It is impossible to review the Constitution and Laws of Great Britain, without admiring the gradual Improvements which have been made in both: Many of which at their first Proposal were no Doubt treated as visionary and impracticable. The abolition of domestic Slavery is not an Utopian Scheme. It was abolished by Constantine the first Christian Emperor throughout the Roman Empire. It ceased in many parts of Europe after the Reformation. It is unknown in Britain. It's Foundations are now shaking in Spain and Portugal. It begins to loose Ground in America. The Assembly of Virginia have petitioned for a Law to prevent the future importation of Negroes amongst them. The Assembly of Pennsylvania have imposed a Duty of twenty Pounds Currency upon every Negro, imported into the Province. The inhabitants of the Province of Massachusetts Bay have instructed their Representatives to enact Laws to restrain it. Reason and Humanity with respect to Negro slavery, have at last awakened in the West-Indies, and many respectable Planters now wish to extricate themselves from it. With such Success, and Prospects, I venture once more to take up my Pen in behalf of the poor Africans. Great Events have often been brought about by slender Means. Permanent changes in Government are seldom produced suddenly. It shall be our Business to collect Materials: — The next Generation we hope, will behold and admire the finished TEMPLE OF AFRICAN LIBERTY IN AMERICA....

The Amusements, Songs &c. of the Negroes, are urged as signs of their Happiness, or Contentment in Slavery. Every one knows how often the Mind flies to these, to relieve itself from Melancholy. Although some of their Songs, like those of *civilized* Nations, are Obscene and Warlike, yet I have been informed that many of them, as well as their Tunes, are of a most plaintive Nature, and very expressive of their Misery.

To a Mind divested of those Prejudices with which Custom

leads us to view objects, the same Follies and Vices will appear under different forms in every state of Society, not only in the Individuals of the different Ranks and Characters of Mankind, but amongst different Nations likewise.

Where is the difference between an African Prince, with his face daubed with Grease, and his Head adorned with a Feather; and a modern Macaroni with his artificial Club of Hair daubed with Powder and Pomatum? Where is the difference between the British Senator who attempts to enslave his fellow subjects in America, by imposing Taxes upon them contrary to Law and Justice; and the American Patriot who reduces his African Brethren to Slavery, contrary to Justice and Humanity? Where is the difference between the sceptical Philosopher who will not allow those Men to be his equals in Genius or Manners, who differ from him in a few trifling Customs; and the bigotted Christian who will not allow those Christians to partake of the merits of his Saviour who mix with their worship a few trifling Ceremonies? Where is the difference between the Mahometan Negro who maintains three or four Wives agreeable to the Religion of his Country; and the European Christian who keeps three or four Mistresses contrary to the Religion of his Country? Where is the difference between the Pagan Negro who worships an evil Spirit, and uses a few ceremonies at a Funeral; and the superstitious Christian who worships God from a fear of the Devil, and connects his future Happiness with a Sacrament before, and a Funeral right after, his Death? Where is the difference between the African Savage, whose scanty wants are supplied by Nature; and the European Nobleman, whose numerous wants are supplied by Art? They are both alike free from the Obligations of Friendship and Gratitude.... – Lastly; where is the difference between that civilized Nation that yearly destroys 50,000 souls by her Trade under the sanction of Laws; and that barbarous Nation which destroys the same number with the Sword, without the sanction of Laws? The proportion of Vice is the same in both Nations....

20. Ignatius Sancho

The Letters of the Late Ignatius Sancho, an African. London, 1782.

[Born aboard a slave ship, Sancho eventually was taken to England where after a few years he found employment as a family retainer in the Duchess of Montagu's household. Here he was encouraged to learn to read and write and to develop his talents for poetry and music. Sancho became an art critic and a lover of stage performance, and he especially enjoyed carrying on frequent correspondence with his many notable friends. In later life, he became a London grocer known for his extremely overweight figure. After his death, Sancho's book of letters was widely publicized by the abolitionists who proclaimed his accomplishments as proof of black intellectual ability. The following letter was sent in 1766 to the famous English author Laurence Sterne (1713-1768), who had included a moving description of a "negro girl" in his popular book *Tristram Shandy* (published in nine volumes between 1759 and 1767). The "humane author of Sir George Ellison" referred to by Sancho was Sarah Robinson Scott. Her novel, *The History of Sir George Ellison* (1766), depicted the protagonist as a kind and paternalistic slave owner.]

Reverend Sir,

It would be an insult on your humanity (or perhaps look like it) to apologize for the liberty I am taking. – I am one of those people whom the vulgar and illiberal call "*Negurs*." – The first part of my life was rather unlucky, as I was placed in a family who judged ignorance the best and only security for obedience. – A little reading and writing I got by unwearied application. – The latter part of my life has been – thro' God's blessing, truly fortunate, having spent it in the service of one of the best families in the kingdom. – My chief pleasure has been books. – Philanthropy I adore. – How very much, good Sir, am I (amongst millions) indebted to you for the character of your amiable uncle Toby! – I declare, I would walk ten miles in the dog-days, to shake hands with the honest corporal. – Your Sermons have touch'd me to the heart, and I hope have amended it, which brings me to the point. – In your tenth discourse, page seventy-eight, in the second volume – is this very affecting passage – "Consider how great a part of our species – in all ages down to this – have been trod under the feet of cruel and capricious tyrants, who would neither hear their cries, nor pity their distresses. – Consider slavery – what it is – how bitter a draught – and how many millions are made to drink it! – Of all my favorite authors, not one has drawn a tear in favor of my miserable black brethren – excepting yourself, and the humane author of Sir George Ellison. – I think you will forgive me; – I am sure you will applaud me for beseeching you to give one half-hour's attention to slavery, as it is at this day practised in our West Indies. – That subject, handled in your striking manner, would ease the yoke (perhaps) of many – but if only of one – Gracious God! – what a feast to a benevolent heart! – and , sure I am, you are an epicurean in acts of charity. – You, who are universally read, and as universally admired – you could not fail – Dear Sir, think in me you behold the uplifted hands of thousands of my brother Moors. – Grief (you pathetically observe) is eloquent; – figure to yourself their attitudes; – hear their supplicating addresses! – alas! – you cannot refuse. – Humanity must comply – in which hope I beg permission to subscribe myself,

Reverend Sir, &c.
IGN SANCHO.

21. Granville Sharp

A Representation of the Injustice and Dangerous Tendency of Tolerating Slavery; or of Admitting the Least Claim of Private Property in the Persons of Men, in England. London: Benjamin White, 1769.

[This essay represents one of Sharp's earliest efforts to plead the cause of the abolition of slavery. His work in seeking justice for black men and women encouraged Equiano to ask for his assistance in attempting to free the ex-slave John Annis, who had been kidnapped in England. However, before any efforts could prove successful, Annis was secretly transported to the West Indies where he was tortured to death. Equiano also sought Sharp's help in bringing to public attention the crimes committed in 1781 aboard the slave ship Zong, on which over 132 gravely-ill blacks were thrown overboard for insurance purposes. Sharp was much influenced by the antislavery ideas of Anthony Benezet, and at times the works of both writers were published together.]

At present the inhumanity of *constrained labour in excess* extends no farther in England, than to our beasts, as post and hackney horses, land asses, &c.

But thanks to our laws, and not to the general good disposition of masters, that it is so; for the wretch, who is bad enough to maltreat a helpless beast, would not spare his fellow man, if he had him as much in his power.

The maintenance of civil liberty is therefore absolutely necessary to prevent an increase of our national guilt, by the addition of the horrid crime of tyranny.

It is not my business at present to examine, how far a toleration of Slavery may be necessary or justifiable in the West-Indies. 'Tis sufficient for my purpose, that it is not so here. But notwithstanding, that the plea of necessity cannot here be urged, yet this is no reason, why an increase of the practice is not to be feared.

Our North America colonies afford us a melancholy instance to the contrary – for tho' the climate in general is so wholesome and temperate, that it will not authorize this plea of necessity for the employment of Slaves, any more than our own, yet the pernicious practice of Slave-holding is become almost general in those parts.

At New York, for instance, this infringement on civil or domestic liberty is become notorious and scandalous, notwithstanding that the political controversies of the inhabitants are stuffed with theatrical bombast and ranting expressions in praise of liberty.

But no panegyrick on this subject (howsoever elegant in

itself) can be graceful or edifying from the mouth or pen of one of those Provincials; because men, who do not scruple to detain others in Slavery, have but a very partial and unjust claim to the protection of the laws of liberty: and indeed it too plainly appears, that they have no real regard for liberty, farther than their own private interests are concerned; and (consequently) that they have so little detestation for despotism and tyranny, that they do not scruple to exercise them with the most unbounded rigour, whenever their caprice excites them, or their private interest, seems to require an exertion of their power over their miserable Slaves....

The *boasted liberty* of our American colonies, therefore, has so little right to that sacred name, that it seems to differ from the arbitrary power of despotic monarchies only in one circumstance; viz. that it is a *many-headed monster of tyranny*, which entirely subverts our most excellent constitution; because liberty and slavery are so opposite to each other, that they cannot subsist in the same community....

Every inhabitant of the British colonies, black as well as white, bond as well as free, are undoubtedly *the King's subjects*, during their residence within the limits of the *King's dominions*, and as such, are entitled to personal protection, howsoever bound in service to their respective masters. Therefore, when any of these are put to death, "WITHOUT THE SOLEMNITY OF A JURY," I fear that there is too much reason to attribute the GUILT OF MURDER, to every person concerned in ordering the same, or in consenting thereto; and all such persons are certainly responsible TO THE KING AND HIS LAWS, *for the loss of a subject.* The horrid iniquity, injustice, and dangerous tendency of the several plantation laws, which I have quoted, are so apparent, that it is unnecessary for me to apologize for the freedom with which I have treated them. If such laws are not absolutely necessary for the government of Slaves, the law-makers must unavoidably allow themselves to be the most cruel and abandoned tyrants upon earth, or perhaps, that ever were on earth. On the other hand, if it be said, that it is impossible to govern Slaves without such inhuman severity and detestable injustice, the same will certainly be an invincible argument against the least toleration of Slavery amongst Christians; because the temporal profits of the planter or master, howsoever lucrative, cannot compensate the forfeiture of his everlasting welfare, or (at least I may be allowed to say) the apparent danger of such a forfeiture.

Oppression is a most grievous crime; and the cries of these much injured people (though they are only poor ignorant heathens) will certainly reach Heaven! The Scriptures (*which are the only true foundation of all laws*) denounce a tremendous judgment against the man who should *offend* even ONE *little one....* May it not be said with like justice – It were better for the English nation, that these American dominions had never existed, or even that they should have been sunk into the sea, than that the kingdom of Great Britain, should be loaded with the horrid guilt of tolerating such abominable wickedness! In short, if THE KING'S PREROGATIVE is not speedily exerted for *the relief* of his Majesty's oppressed and much injured subjects in the British colonies ... and for the extension of the British constitution to the most distant colonies, whether in the East or West Indies, it must inevitably be allowed, that great share of this *enormous guilt* will certainly rest on this side of the water!

22. James Tobin

Cursory Remarks upon the Reverend Mr. Ramsay's Essay on the Treatment and Conversion of African Slaves in the Sugar Colonies. London: G. and T. Wilkie, 1785.

[Both Cugoano and Equiano in their narratives made a point of opposing several of Tobin's proslavery arguments. In addition, Equiano's long letter to Tobin defending intermarriage appeared in *The Public Advertiser* on January 28, 1788. Tobin's pamphlet delivered a sarcastic attack in a page by page refutation of the ideas in James Ramsay's antislavery work. At the beginning of his essay, Tobin claims he is on Ramsay's side in hoping that slavery will be abolished; however, he argues that freeing the slaves now would wreak havoc upon the economy and security of the British Empire.]

... Since this essay [James Ramsay's *An Essay on the Treatment and Conversion of African Slaves in the British Sugar Colonies*] first fell into my hands, I have been waiting with impatience, in hopes of seeing some much abler pen than my own, employed in detecting its fallacies, answering its injurious and ill-founded aspersions, and exposing its palpable, and numerous contradictions. Nothing, however, adequate to my wishes, having yet appeared, I am induced to offer the following remarks upon this specious and plausible performance, many parts of which call aloud for some kind of reply, and ought not longer to circulate unnoticed.... conscious, however, of the rectitude of my own intentions, I shall freely venture to deliver my sentiments, regardless of such censure as is founded only in the prejudices of the misinformed multitude; and in firm reliance, that while I am defending the characters of so valuable, respectable, and useful a set of men, as the British West India planters, against the acrimonious misrepresentations of intemperate zeal, or offended self-sufficiency, I shall not be so far misunderstood by the candid, and judicious part of mankind, as to be ranked among the advocates for slavery; as I most sincerely join Mr. Ramsay, and every other man of sensibility, in hoping, the blessings of freedom will in due time, be equally diffused over the face of the whole globe. I cannot, however help expressing my doubts, as to any additional support the cause of general liberty is likely to receive, from his present attempt; as most of his arguments seem to be produced in a very "questionable shape." – It may, perhaps, be shrewdly demanded, how it has happened, that neither Mr. Ramsay, or any other of his professed brother reformers, have, by way of experiment, set the benevolent example, of manumitting such slaves, as they have been possessed of, after they had no further call for their services, instead of dispersing them by sale, among such a set of illiberal tyrants, as the inhabitants of the West India islands are represented to be. If such a question should actually be asked, I leave it to Mr. Ramsay....

... The collected scope of everything the author introduces in this section [p. 58 of Ramsay's work], is to prove, that the negroes (although, in several places, he describes them as already oppressed and overpowered with labour) would do much more work, if they were free, than they perform in their present situation. I have been in most of the English and French islands; in every one of which there are large numbers of free negroes, as well as mulattoes, &c. yet I never saw a single instance of a free negro's working for hire in the field of any plantation, either of sugar, coffee, indigo, &c. nor did I ever hear that such a circumstance had once occurred. Indeed, so far from its being ever likely to happen, it is universally known, that there are very few even of the mechanics, who do not get disgusted with the light labour of their trades, soon after they acquire their freedom; they therefore generally turn hucksters, pedlers, fishermen, or domestic servants; or, which is worse, they keep little, low dram-shops, or set up destructive negro gaming-houses; and not a few, becoming arrant vagabonds, maintain themselves entirely by cheating and pilfering. For the truth of this observation, I may safely venture to appeal to Mr. Ramsay himself. In the year 1773, when the case of Somerset[1] gave occasion for the subject of slavery to be much agitated, it was pretty accurately determined, that there were at that time in England at least fifteen thousand negroes; and that they have greatly increased since is beyond a doubt. A very small proportion of this number are females; it may, therefore, be fairly presumed, that there are ten or twelve thousand able negro men now in England. Out of all this number, I will ask Mr. Ramsay whether he ever saw a single one employed in any laborious task? Did he ever meet with a black ploughman, hedger, ditcher, mower, or reaper, in the country; or a black porter, or chairman, in London? On the contrary, I will be free to affirm, that out of the whole of this number, those who are not in livery are in rags; and such as are not servants, are thieves or mendicants. Even the sentimental Ignatius Sancho himself, the humble friend and imitator of Sterne, continued to prefer the station of a menial servant, till the infirmities of obesity disqualified him.

---

1 James Somerset was a slave from Massachusets who had been brought to England by his master. When Somerset refused to return to America with his master, the abolitionists took Somerset's case to court. In a landmark decision in 1772, Lord Chief Justice Mansfield ruled in favour of Somerset. The decision was widely interpreted as outlawing slavery throughout the British Isles.

If it is objected that their aversion to labour in Europe may be owing to the rigour of the climate, it may be asked in reply, how do they bear the rains, the snows, and the frosts of our worst winter nights, stuck up for hours behind the carriages of their masters, or posted, for a still longer time, in the chill avenues of our places of public entertainment.

[At this point Tobin includes the following note:] The great number of negroes at present in England, the strange partiality shewn for them by the lower orders of women, and the rapid increase of a dark and contaminated breed, are evils which have long been complained of, and call every day more loudly for enquiry and redress. – The lower ranks in Spain are avowedly debased, by their long intercourse with the Moors; and the Portuguese still much more so, from the importation of negroes among them. – In France proper regulations are made to prevent this evil; the French even deem it humanity to send them back to the plantations. And if we may judge from the numbers of this complexion who perish in our jails, or expire on our gibbets, they are not mistaken. – It is not more than six weeks ago, that three negroes died in Newgate on the same day; two of them under sentence of death, and the third committed for a capital offence.

23. Gordon Turnbull

An Apology for Negro Slavery: or, the West-India Planters Vindicated from the Charge of Inhumanity. London: Stuart and Stevenson, 1786.

[In defending the established institution of slavery in the British West Indies, Turnbull claimed that Europeans were rescuing the kidnapped Africans from the brutal conditions existing in their native lands. He depicted the slaves in the English colonies as living in a well-provided and happy state. Turnbull's work was attacked in a long letter from Equiano in *The Public Advertiser,* February 5, 1788.]

As a contrast to the horrid and fictitious picture, which has been drawn of the state of the negroes in the West-Indies, I shall here exhibit a true and more pleasing representation, taken from the life.

To begin then with the period of the Guinea negroe's arrival in one of the islands. – As soon as the ship that brings them is at anchor, the master or surgeon goes on shore to procure fresh provisions, fruit, and vegetables of all kinds, which are immediately sent on board for the slaves. Parties of them are sent on shore at different times, and conducted a little way into the country, where they frequently meet with many natives of their own country, who speak the same language, and sometimes with near and dear relations, who all appear very cheerful and happy. These agreeable and unexpected meetings are truly affecting, and excite the most tender and pleasing sensations in the breasts of the by-standers. It is not uncommon for these newly arrived guests, to mingle in the dance, or to join in the song, with their country people. If any of them appear dull or desponding, the old negroes endeavour to enliven them, by the most soothing and endearing expressions, telling them, in their own tongue, not to be afraid of the white men; that the white men are very good; that they will get plenty of *yam, yam,* (their general name for victuals) and that their work will be of the easiest kind. By these means, they are perfectly reconciled to the white men, and to a change of country, and of situation, which many of them declare, to be far superior to that which they had quitted. When the day of sale arrives, they not only meet the planter's looks, and answer his enquiries, by means of an interpreter, with great firmness, but they try, by offering their stout limbs to his inspection, jumping to shew their activity, and other allurements, to induce those, whose appearance pleases them, to buy them, and to engage, if possible, a preference in their favour....

As soon as the new negroes are brought home to the plantation, if a planter has purchased them they are properly clothed. – A sufficient quantity of wholesome food is prepared, and served to them three times a day. They are comfortably lodged in some room of the manager's own house, or in some other convenient place, where they can be immediately under his eye for a few days. During this time they are not put to any kind of labour whatever, but are regularly conducted to bathe in the river, or in the sea, if it is nigh, twice a day. In the evenings they sing and dance, after the manner of their own nation, together with the old negroes who happen to be from the same country, one or two of whom are commonly instrumental performers, in these very noisy, but very joyous assemblies. In a very short time, they are taken into the houses of the principal and best disposed negroes, who adopt one of two of these new subjects into each family, to assist them in all the little domestic offices of cookery, carrying water, wood, &c. This is almost the only work they are employed in for the first two or three months, at the expiration of which, they are put to the easiest kind of labour for some months more....

24. John Wesley

Thoughts upon Slavery. London, 1774. *Views of American Slavery*. Philadelphia: Assoc. of Friends, 1858:

[Wesley founded the Methodist faith and preached to congregations in England and America about actively pursuing social and humanitarian goals. When the Englishman James Oglethorpe (1696-1785) established the American colony of Georgia for the benefit of orphans, Wesley visited Georgia, which had originally outlawed slavery, and supported Oglethorpe in his work. Equiano listed Wesley as a subscriber to *The Interesting Narrative* – the book Wesley read on his deathbed in 1792. In his work on slavery, Wesley presents a numbered list of proslavery arguments in order to refute them one by one.]

5. ... "The whole method now used by the original purchasers of negroes is necessary to the furnishing our colonies yearly with a hundred thousand slaves." I grant this is necessary to that end. But how is that end necessary? How will you prove it necessary that one hundred, that one, of those slaves should be procured? "Why, it is necessary to my gaining a hundred thousand pounds." Perhaps so; but how is this necessary? It is very possible you might be both a better and a happier man if you had

not a quarter of it. I deny that your gaining one thousand is necessary either to your present or eternal happiness. "But, however, you must allow these slaves are necessary for the cultivation of our islands, inasmuch as white men are not able to labor in hot climates." I answer, first, it were better that all those islands should remain uncultivated forever, yea, it were more desirable that they were altogether sunk in the depth of the sea, than that they should be cultivated at so high a price as the violation of justice, mercy, and truth. But, secondly, the supposition on which you ground your argument is false; for white men, even Englishmen, are well able to labor in hot climates, provided they are temperate both in meat and drink, and that they inure themselves to it by degrees. I speak no more than I know by experience. It appears from the thermometer that the summer heat in Georgia is frequently equal to that in Barbadoes, yea, to that under the line; and yet I and my family, eight in number, did employ all our spare time there in felling of trees and clearing of ground, – as hard labor as any negro need be employed in. The German family, likewise, forty in number, were employed in all manner of labor; and this was so far from impairing our health, that we all continued perfectly well, while the idle ones all round about us were swept away as with a pestilence. It is not true, therefore, that white men are not able to labor, even in hot climates, full as well as black. But, if they were not, it would be better that none should labor there, that the work should be left undone, than that myriads of innocent men should be murdered, and myriads more dragged into the basest slavery.

6. "But the furnishing us with slaves is necessary for the trade, and wealth, and glory of our nation." Here are several mistakes; for, first, wealth is not necessary to the glory of any nation, but wisdom, virtue, justice, mercy, generosity, public spirit, love of our country: these are necessary to the real glory of a nation, but abundance of wealth is not. Men of understanding allow that the glory of England was full as high in Queen Elizabeth's time as it is now, although our riches and trade were then as much smaller as our virtue was greater. But, secondly, it is now clear that we should have either less money

or trade (only less of that detestable trade of manstealing) if there was not a negro in all our islands, or in all English America. It is demonstrable white men, inured to it by degrees, can work as well as them, and they would do it were negroes out of the way, and proper encouragement given them. However, thirdly, I come back to the same point: better no trade than trade procured by villany; it is far better to have no wealth than to gain wealth at the expense of virtue. Better is honest poverty than all the riches bought by the tears, and sweat, and blood of our fellow-creatures.

7. "However this be, it is necessary when we have slaves to use them with severity." I pray, to what end is this usage necessary? "Why, to prevent their running away, and to keep them constantly to their labor, that they may not idle away their time, so miserably stupid is this race of men, yea, so stubborn and so wicked." Allowing them to be as stupid as you say, to whom is that stupidity owing? Without question it lies altogether at the door of their inhuman masters, who give them no means, no opportunity of improving their understanding, and, indeed, leave them no motive, either from hope or fear, to attempt any such thing. They were noway remarkable for stupidity while they remained in their own country. The inhabitants of Africa, where they have equal motives and equal means of improvement, are not inferior to the inhabitants of Europe; to some of them they are greatly superior. Impartially survey, in their own country, the natives of Benin and the natives of Lapland. Compare (setting prejudice aside) the Samoeids and the Angolans; and on which side does the advantage lie in point of understanding? Certainly the African is in no respect inferior to the European. Their stupidity, therefore, in our plantations is not natural, otherwise than it is the natural effect of their condition: consequently, it is not their fault, but yours; you must answer for it before God and man.

25. William Wilberforce

The Speech of William Wilberforce ... on Wednesday the 13th of May 1789 on the Question of the Abolition of the Slave Trade. London: Topographic Press, 1789.

[The leader of the abolitionists in the House of Commons, Wilberforce sparked the heated discussion on the slave trade that would be debated in Parliament for many years. Just two months prior to Wilberforce's 1789 speech, Equiano had published *The Interesting Narrative,* dedicated "To the Lords Spiritual and Temporal, and the Commons of the Parliament of Great Britain." Two years later, on April 19, 1791, the motion made by Wilberforce to abolish the slave trade was rejected by a vote of 163 to 88. Wilberforce formally addressed the following speech to Parliamentary Committee Chairman Sir William Dolben.]

When I consider the magnitude of the subject which I am to bring before the House – a subject, in which the interests, not of this country, nor of Europe alone, but of the whole world, and of posterity, are involved; and when I think, at the same time, on the weakness of the advocate who has undertaken this great cause – when these reflections press upon my mind, it is impossible for me not to feel both terrified and concerned at my own inadequacy to such a task. But when I reflect, however, on the encouragement which I have had, through the whole course of a long and laborious examination of this question, how much candour I have experienced, and how conviction has increased within my own mind, in proportion as I have advanced in my labours; – when I reflect, especially, that, however adverse any Gentlemen may now be, yet we shall all, most assuredly, be of one opinion in the end. When I turn myself to these thoughts, I take courage – I determine to forget all my other fears, and I march forward with a firmer step, in the full assurance that my cause will bear me out, and that I shall be able to justify, upon the clearest principles, every resolution in

my hand – the avowed end of which, Sir, is, – the total Abolition of the Slave Trade.

I wish exceedingly, in the outset, to guard both myself and
the House from entering into the subject with any sort of passion. It is not their passions I shall appeal to – I ask only for
their cool and impartial reason; and I wish not to take them by
surprize, but to deliberate, point by point, upon every part of
this question. I mean not to accuse any one, but to take the
shame upon myself, in common, indeed, with the whole Parliament of Great Britain, for having suffered this horrid trade to
be carried on, under their authority. We are all guilty – we
ought all to plead guilty, and not to exculpate ourselves, by
throwing the blame on others; and I therefore deprecate every
kind of reflection, against the various descriptions of people
who are more immediately involved in this wretched business.

In opening the nature of the Slave trade, I need only
observe, that it is found, by experience, to be just such as every
man, who uses his reason, would infallibly conclude it to be.
For my own part, so clearly am I convinced of the mischiefs
inseparable from it, that I should hardly want any further evidence than my own mind would furnish, by the most simple
deductions. Facts, however, are now laid before the House. A
report has been made by his Majesty's Privy Council, which, I
trust, every Gentleman has read, and which ascertains the Slave
Trade to be just such in practice as we know, from theory, that
it must be. What should we suppose must naturally be the consequence of our carrying on a Slave Trade with Africa? With a
country, vast in its extent, not utterly barbarous, but civilized in
a very small degree? Does any one suppose a Slave Trade would
help their civilization? That Africa would *profit* by such an
intercourse? Is it not plain, that she must *suffer* from it? That
civilization must be checked; that her barbarous manners must
be made more barbarous; and that the happiness of her millions
of inhabitants must be prejudiced by her intercourse with
Britain? Does not every one see, that a Slave Trade, carried on
around her coasts, must carry violence and desolation to her
very centre? That, in a Continent, just emerging from barbarism, if a Trade in Men is established – if her men are all converted into goods, and become commodities that can be

bartered, it follows, they must be subject to ravage just as goods are; and this too, at a period of civilization, when there is no protecting Legislature to defend this their only sort of property, in the same manner as the rights of property are maintained by the legislature of every civilized country.

We see then, in the nature of things, how easily all the practices of Africa are to be accounted for. Her kings are never compelled to war, that we can hear of, by public principles, – by national glory – still less by the love of their people. In Europe it is the extension of commerce, the maintenance of national honor, or some great public object, that is ever the motive to war with every monarch; but, in Africa, it is the personal *avarice* and *sensuality* of their kings: these two vices of avarice and sensuality, (the most powerful and predominant in natures thus corrupt) we tempt, we stimulate in all these African Princes, and we depend upon these vices for the very maintenance of the Slave Trade....

Sir, the nature and all the circumstances of this trade are now laid open to us; we can no longer plead ignorance, – we cannot evade it, – it is now an object placed before us, – we cannot pass it; we may spurn it, we may kick it out of our way, but we cannot turn aside so as to avoid seeing it; for it is brought now so directly before our eyes, that this House must decide, and must justify to all the world, and to their own consciences, the rectitude of the grounds and principles of their decision.

A Society [the Society for Effecting the Abolition of the Slave Trade in 1787] has been established for the abolition of this trade, in which Dissenters, Quakers, Churchmen – in which the most conscientious of all persuasions have all united, and made a common cause in this great question. Let not Parliament be the only body that is insensible to the principles of national justice. Let us make reparation to Africa, so far as we can, by establishing a trade upon true commercial principles, and we shall soon find the rectitude of our conduct rewarded, by the benefits of a regular and a growing commerce.

I shall now move the several Resolutions, upon which I do not ask the House to decide to-night, but shall consider the debate as adjourned to any day next week that may be thought most convenient.

26. Helen Maria Williams

"A Poem on the Bill Lately Passed for Regulating the Slave Trade." London: T. Cadell, 1788.

[When Sir William Dolben introduced his bill for alleviating the overcrowded conditions aboard slave ships, Williams, who was considered a radical poet, published a moving account of the suffering endured by captive slaves.]

> When borne at length to Western Lands,
> Chain'd on the beach the Captive stands,
> Where Man, dire merchandize! is sold,
> And barter'd life is paid for gold;
> In mute affliction, see him try
> To read his new possessor's eye;
> If one blest glance of mercy there,
> One half-form'd tear may check despair! –
> Ah, if that eye with sorrow sees
> His languid look, his quiv'ring knees,
> Those limbs, which scarce their load sustain,
> That form, consum'd in wasting pain;
> *Such* sorrow melts his ruthless eye
> Who sees the lamb, he doom'd to die,
> In pining sickness yield his life,
> And thus elude the sharpen'd knife. –
> Or, if where savage habit steels
> The vulgar mind, one bosom feels
> The sacred claim of helpless woe –
> If Pity in that soil can grow;
> Pity! Whose tender impulse darts
> With keenest force on nobler hearts;
> As flames that purest essence boast,
> Rise highest when they tremble most. –
> Yet *why* on one poor chance must rest
> The int'rests of a kindred breast?
> Humanity's devoted cause
> Recline on Humour's wayward laws?

To Passion's rules must Justice bend,
And life upon Caprice depend? – ...
Lov'd Britain! whose protecting hand
Stretch'd o'er the Globe, on Afric's strand
The honour'd base of Freedom lays,
Soon, soon the finish'd fabric raise!
And when surrounding realms would frame,
Touch'd with a spark of gen'rous flame,
Some pure, ennobling, great design,
Some lofty act, almost divine;
Which Earth may hail with rapture high,
And Heav'n may view with fav'ring eye;
Teach them to make all nature free,
And shine by emulating Thee! –

27. Mary Wollstonecraft

A Vindication of the Rights of Men. London: J. Johnson, 1790.

[Wollstonecraft became famous for her 1792 work *A Vindication of the Rights of Women*. However, two years before, by way of responding to Edmund Burke's overly conservative ideas on human freedom that she believed would perpetuate slavery, Wollstonecraft had published a more general vindication of human rights, in which she had touched upon the question of slavery. Wollstonecraft was an ardent supporter of the abolitionist cause who read and reviewed Equiano's book in 1789 (see Appendix A, Part Two).]

Is it necessary to repeat, that there are rights which we received, at our birth, as men, when we were raised above the brute creation by the power of improving ourselves – and that we receive these not from our forefathers, but from God?

My father may dissipate his property, yet I have no right to complain; – but if he should attempt to sell me for a slave, or fetter me with laws contrary to reason; nature, in enabling me to discern good from evil, teaches me to break the ignoble chain, and not to believe that bread becomes flesh, and wine blood, because my parents swallowed the Eucharist with this blind persuasion.

There is no end to this submission to authority – some where it must stop, or we return to barbarism; and the capacity of improvement is a cheat, an ignis-fatuus, that leads us from the inviting meadow into bogs and dunghills. If it be allowed that many of the precautions, with which any alteration was made, in our government, were prudent, it rather proves its weakness than substantiates an opinion of the soundness of the stamina, or the excellence of the constitution.

But on what principle Mr. Burke could defend American independence, I cannot conceive; for the whole tenor of his plausible arguments settles slavery on an everlasting foundation. Allowing his servile reverence for antiquity, and prudent attention to self-interest, to have the force which he insists on, it ought never to be abolished; and, because our ignorant forefathers, not understanding the native dignity of man, sanctioned a traffic that outrages every suggestion of reason and religion, we are to submit to the inhuman custom, and term an atrocious insult to humanity the love of our country and a proper submission to those laws which secure our property. – Security of property! Behold, in a few words, the definition of English liberty. And to this selfish principle every nobler one is sacrificed. – The Briton takes place of the man, and the image of God is lost in the citizen!

28. John Woolman

Some Considerations on the Keeping of Negroes (1754). *The Works of John Woolman.* 1800.

[A devout American Quaker and journal writer, Woolman (1720-1772) detested slavery nearly all of his life. In his youth, he had been asked to draw up a b'll of sale for a slave; an act which greatly troubled his conscience for many years. For a time, he lived and worked in the South, where he witnessed firsthand the effects of slavery on both black and white persons. Most of his life, however, was spent in business enterprises and farming in New Jersey. He refused to use sugar and other products produced by slave labor.]

There are various circumstances amongst them that keep negroes, and different ways by which they fall under their care; and, I doubt not, there are many well-disposed persons amongst them who desire rather to manage wisely and justly in this difficult matter, than to make gain of it.

But the general disadvantage which these poor Africans lie under in an enlightened christian country, having often filled me with real sadness, and been like undigested matter on my mind, I now think it my duty, through divine aid, to offer some thoughts thereon to the consideration of others....

To consider mankind otherwise than brethren, to think favours are peculiar to one nation, and exclude others, plainly supposes a darkness in the understanding: for as God's love is universal, so where the mind is sufficiently influenced by it, it begets a likeness of itself, and the heart is enlarged towards all men. Again, to conclude a people froward, perverse, and worse by nature than others, (who ungratefully receive favours, and apply them to bad ends) this will excite a behavior toward them unbecoming the excellence of true religion.

To prevent such error, let us calmly consider their circumstance; and, the better to do it, make their case ours. Suppose, then, that our ancestors and we had been exposed to constant servitude, in the more servile and inferior employments of life; that we had been destitute of the help of reading and good company; that amongst ourselves we had had few wise and pious instructors; that the religious amongst our superiors seldom took notice of us; that while others, in ease, have plentifully heaped up the fruit of our labour, we had received barely enough to relieve nature; and being wholly at the command of others, had generally been treated as a contemptible, ignorant part of mankind: should we, in that case, be less abject than they now are? Again, if oppression be so hard to bear, that a wise man is made mad by it, Eccl. vii. 7. then a series of those things altering the behaviour and manners of a people, is what may reasonably be expected....

It may be objected there is cost of purchase, and risk of their lives to them who possess them, and therefore needful that they make the best use of their time; in a practice just and reasonable, such objections may have weight; but if the work be wrong from the beginning, there is little or no force in them. If I purchase a man who hath never forfeited his liberty, the natural right of freedom is in him; and shall I keep him and his posterity in servitude and ignorance? "How should I approve of this conduct, were I in his circumstances, and he in mine?" It may be thought, that to treat them as we would willingly be treated, our gain by them would be inconsiderable: and it were, in diverse respects, better that there were none in our country.

We may further consider, that they are now amongst us, and those of our nation the cause of their being here; that whatsoever difficulty accrues thereon, we are justly chargeable with, and to bear all inconveniences attending it, with a serious and weighty concern of mind, to do our duty by them, is the best we can do. To seek a remedy by continuing the oppression, because we have power to do it, and see others do it, will, I apprehend, not be doing as we would be done by.

Select Bibliography

Acholonu, Catherine Obianju. "The Home of Olaudah Equiano—A Linguistic and Anthropological Search." *The Journal of Commonwealth Literature* 22:1 (1987): 5-16.

Allison, Robert J., ed. *The Interesting Narrative of the Life of Olaudah Equiano. Written by Himself.* Boston & New York: Bedford Books, 1995.

Andrews, William L. *To Tell a Free Story: The First Century of Afro-American Autobiography.* Bloomington: U of Illinois Press, 1986.

Bolster, W. Jeffrey. *Black Jacks: African American Seaman in the Age of Sail.* Cambridge, MA, & London: Harvard UP, 1997.

Carretta, Vincent. "Olaudah Equiano or Gustavus Vassa? New Light on an Eighteenth-Century Question of Identity." *Slavery and Abolition* 20:3 (December 1999): 96-105.

——. ed. *Olaudah Equiano: The Interesting Narrative and other Writings.* New York: Penguin Books, 1995.

——. *Quobna Ottobah Cugoano: Thoughts and Sentiments on the Evil of Slavery and Other Writings.* New York: Penguin Books, 1999.

——. *Unchained Voices: An Anthology of Black Authors in the English-Speaking World of the Eighteenth Century.* Lexington: UP of Kentucky, 1996.

Costanzo, Angelo. *Surprizing Narrative: Olaudah Equiano and the Beginnings of Black Autobiography.* New York & Westport, CT: Greenwood Press, 1987.

Drescher, Seymour. *Capitalism and Antislavery: British Mobilization in Comparative Perspective.* New York: Oxford UP, 1987.

Edwards, Paul, and James Walvin. *Black Personalities in the Era of the Slave Trade.* Baton Rouge: Louisiana State UP, 1983.

Edwards, Paul, and David Dabydeen, eds. *Black Writers in Britain, 1760-1890.* Edinburgh: Edinburgh UP, 1991.

Edwards, Paul, ed. *The Interesting Narrative of the Life of Olaudah Equiano, or Gustavus Vassa, the African. Written by Himself.* 2 vols. London, 1789. Facsimile edition in two volumes with a new introduction. London: Dawsons of Pall Mall, 1969.

———. *The Life of Olaudah Equiano, or Gustavus Vassa the African. Written by Himself.* London: Longman, 1988.

Ferguson, Moira. *Subject to Others: British Women Writers and Colonial Slavery, 1670-1834.* New York and London: Routledge, 1992.

Gates, Jr., Henry Louis, and William L. Andrews, eds. *Pioneers of the Black Atlantic: Five Slave Narratives from the Enlightenment, 1772-1815.* Washington, DC: Counterpoint Press, 1998.

Gates, Jr., Henry Louis. *The Signifying Monkey: A Theory of African-American Literary Criticism.* New York: Oxford UP, 1988.

Hofkosh, Sonia. "Tradition and *The Interesting Narrative*: Capitalism, Abolition, and the Romantic Individual." *Romanticism, Race, and Imperial Culture, 1780-1834.* Ed. Alan Richardson and Sonia Hofkosh. Bloomington and Indianapolis: Indiana UP, 1996.

Ito, Akiyo. "Olaudah Equiano and the New York Artisans: The First American Edition of *The Interesting Narrative of the Life of Olaudah Equiano, or Gustavus Vassa, the African.*" *Early American Literature* 32.1 (1997): 82-101.

Jennings, Judith. *The Business of Abolishing the British Slave Trade, 1783-1807.* London and Portland, Oregon: Frank Cass, 1997.

Mellor, Anne K. " 'Am I Not a Woman, and a Sister?': Slavery, Romanticism, and Gender." *Romanticism, Race, and Imperial Culture, 1780-1834.* Ed. Alan Richardson and Sonia Hofkosh. Bloomington and Indianapolis: Indiana UP, 1996.

Midgley, Clare. *Women Against Slavery: The British Campaigns, 1780-1870.* London and New York: Routledge, 1992.

Ogude, S.E. "Facts into Fiction: Equiano's Narrative Reconsidered." *Research in African Literatures* 13:1 (Spring 1982): 31–43.

Sandiford, Keith. *Measuring the Moment: Strategies of Protest in Eighteenth-Century Afro-English Writing.* London: Associated Universities Press, 1988.

Shyllon, Folarin Olawale. *Black People in Britain, 1555-1833.* London: Oxford University Press, 1977.

Sollors, Werner, ed. *The Interesting Narrative of the Life of Olaudah Equiano, or Gustavus Vassa, the African, Written by Himself.* New York and London: Norton Critical Editions, 2001.

Walvin, James. *An African's Life: The Life and Times of Olaudah Equiano, 1745-1797.* London: Cassell, 1998.